WELL FED
WEEKNIGHTS

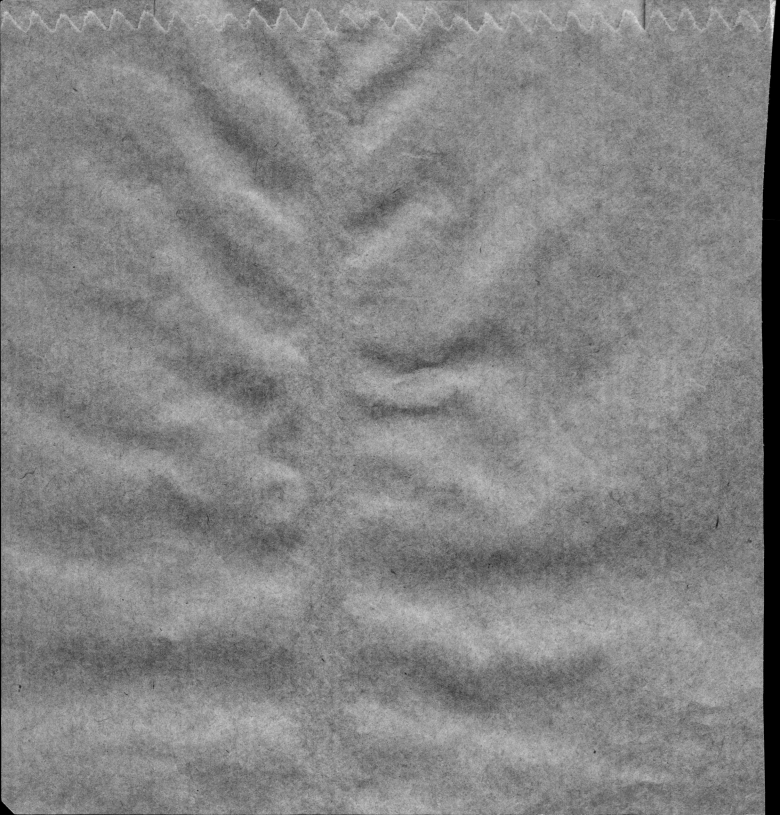

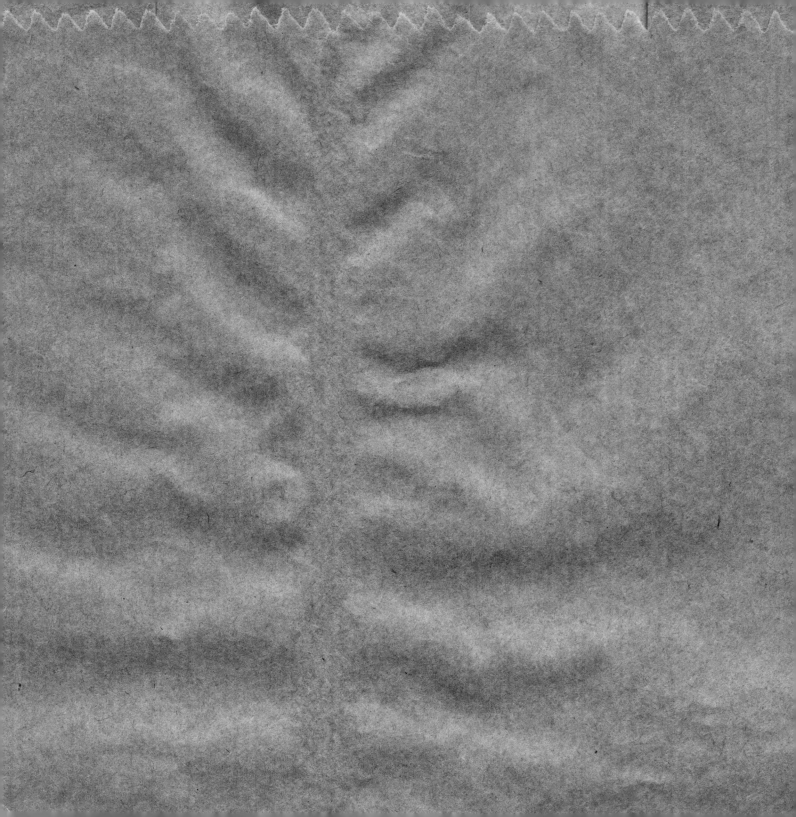

WELL FED

COMPLETE PALEO MEALS IN 45 MINUTES OR LESS!

CERTIFIED DELICIOUS · GRAIN SUGAR LEGUME DAIRY FREE FREE

FED

WEEKNIGHTS

by MELISSA JOULWAN

GREENLEAF
BOOK GROUP PRESS
www.gbgpress.com

Published by Greenleaf Book Group Press
Austin, Texas
www.gbgpress.com

Distributed by Greenleaf Book Group

For ordering information or special discounts for bulk purchases, please contact Greenleaf Book Group at PO Box 91869, Austin, TX 78709, 512.891.6100.

Well Fed Weeknights: Complete Paleo Meals in 45 Minutes or Less
Author: Melissa Joulwan
Copy Editing & Proofreading: Peggy Paul Casella, Walker Fenz Palacek
Photography & Illustration: David Humphreys, istockphoto.com, vectorstock.com
Design and Composition: Michel Vrana
Cover Design: Michel Vrana

Cataloging-in-Publication data is available.

Print ISBN: 978-1-62634-342-9

Printed in the United States of America

16 17 18 19 20 21   10 9 8 7 6 5 4 3 2 1

First Edition

TO MY
HUSBAND DAVE,
WHO MAKES
MY LIFE MORE
DELICIOUS AND
ALWAYS GIVES
ME THE LAST
FRENCH FRY

ACKNOWLEDGMENTS

To Mom and Dad,
for your unwavering support, keeping me company on the phone during my walk breaks, and all the meals we've shared.

To Tillie Walden and Kelly Swann,
for making our weekly family dinners the highlight of my week. You are two of my favorite taste-testers ever!

To Steph Gaudreau,
for the text messages that kept my spirits up, for setting the bar for humanship so very high, and the tortillas. Ah, tortillas.

To Melissa Hartwig,
for introducing me to the Whole30 and championing the program that's changed so many lives.

To Cameron Siewart,
for helping me wrestle this thing into shape and for delivering the perfect encouragement, just when I needed it.

To Michelle Tam and Henry Fong,
for the Skype visits that buoyed my spirits and your unwavering encouragement of our work.

To Eileen Laird,
for making sure my AIP-friendly recipe adaptations are compliant as well as delicious.

To Michel Vrana,
for making the book so beautiful and far exceeding how great we imagined it could be. You're the tops.

To Walker Palacek,
for never missing a detail and for swooping in with grace and good humor at the eleventh hour to save the day.

To Salakjit Getbamrungrat, a.k.a. Sandy
for refusing to let me wash dishes and for being there with what I needed before I knew I needed it. Cheers to you with pineapple juice!

To Peggy Paul Casella,
for polishing my manuscript and sustaining the illusion that I have perfect spelling.

To Andrew Zimmern,
for enriching our travel and food lives with your recommendations and evocative stories.

To Mark Sisson,
for always being so kind to me and for continuing to represent the heart and soul of the primal/paleo movement.

To Heather Cocks,
for the daily joy of *Go Fug Yourself* and for sharing your brilliant, funny, engaging writing.

To Jennifer Thomas,
for the noble Chinese Kitchen God who kept watch over our cookbook production.

To Dianne Jacob,
for being the angel on my shoulder while I write and edit. *Will Write For Food* is an essential tool for all food writers.

To the Brooks Group PR,
for always having the time to listen to my silly ideas and encourage me when my spirits are flagging. You're the best combo of supportive team and killer tigers.

To Bang Printing and Greenleaf Book Group,
for helping produce our books and ensuring they travel from our warehouse to bookstores around the world. You're first-rate partners.

To the readers of my blog,
for your enthusiasm for this book, keeping me company online, and inspiring me to keep trying to find new ways to delight you in the kitchen.

FOREWORD BY HEATHER COCKS

Let me begin with a confession: I'm not Paleo. What I am is a creature of habits. Bad ones. No, let's say ... sub-optimally healthy. I get stuck in eating ruts, and they're usually tied to foods that only involve the word "vegetable" if it's followed with "oil."

I used to blame this on working from home. Every day I would park at my computer and type until I was too hungry to breathe, then grab some peanut butter and chips to wolf down at my desk, insisting I had no time for anything better. *Right*. Let's be real: My job didn't cause that. I did.

My permissive laziness made me a prisoner of my own cravings. (But… *peanut butter!* So sweet, so glorious, so simple, with just enough protein—read: more than zero—to pretend it's good for me.) After years of making the quick and easy choice, I'd created a culinary monster. I could rationalize any snack. I put my comfort foods on pedestals, which gave them a dysfunctional power over me, like a song that won't get out of your head until you give in and listen. I'd tell myself, "Not today," and my cravings responded, "You're fine! Do better tomorrow." Lather, rinse, repeat. My stomach is a jerk, and it always won. I woke up one day undeniably heavier and sluggish, and in need of a jolt.

But I'm lousy at elimination diets; besides having two picky kids, a person with habits like I've described rarely does well going cold turkey. That's how you end up weeping into a pile of actual cold turkey, which you are only devouring because you already mowed through everything in the house that's dusted with artificial cheese powder. Instead, I wanted something I could execute incrementally, one lasting better choice at a time. No big drama; just no more excuses.

Well Fed and *Well Fed 2* were my answers. Melissa's conversational, empathetic style was the partner I needed, and her cookbooks treat food like the treasure and pleasure it is. Her recipes aren't about self-denial or sacrifice. They're about flavor. They *teem* with it. They're meals I *want* to cook, not as homework, but as hedonism. The *Well Fed* pad thai is so flavorful that I won't eat the original anymore; the plantain nachos, a snacker's and taco lover's paradise. And what are noodles, really, but handy delivery systems for mouth-watering sauces? It's not the starch, but what you plonk on it. Zucchini spirals can totally hang with a rich Bolognese, without the pants-popping consequences. My stomach still wins; the victory is just sweeter.

Well Fed Weeknights makes those battles even easier to fight. When life gets in the way and I have to whip up dinner fast, it's too easy to revert to Sandwich Hour. I need healthy, tempting variety that I can still make even if I only went to the store 15 minutes ago. Melissa to the rescue. Again.

If you're already Paleo, I admire you. I haven't gotten there. But if you're not, these books are still your best weapon. Paleo can be a fantastic lifestyle, but that doesn't mean it's *your* lifestyle, and Mel gets that. Instead, start slowly. Pick a *Well Fed* recipe that makes you salivate—good luck choosing; they all will—and put it in your rotation. Then try one more. And another. Use her protein swaps, her spice blends, her flavor alternatives. It's all there. Because you want choices that will stick, not fads that will fade. This slow-burn approach taught me I don't need—or need to crave—my old culinary crutches. I don't dwell on what *isn't* in my dinner because I'm too busy savoring what is. I pick spaghetti squash over actual spaghetti, reach for *Well Fed* leftovers instead of the Jif jar, and bought a squeeze-bottle for my Kickass Ketchup (*Well Fed 2*) because I can't go back to the hard stuff. Do I still eat sandwiches? Yeah, but fewer every month. *Every* change counts, even the small ones, because life is a long game. I'm learning to play it smarter, because I have Mel on my team. Now you do, too.

So go forth and chow down with glee. Your insides will thank you, and hey, maybe your pants will follow.

Heather Cocks is the co-author of the best-selling novel The Royal We, *and the popular celebrity-fashion website Go Fug Yourself.*

TABLE OF CONTENTS

THE FOOD COURT

inspired by takeout!

WELCOME TO WELL FED WEEKNIGHTS

In case you're new to the Well Fed cookbooks, here are a few things you should know about me, my recipes, and what this book can do for you. (And if you're already part of the family ... welcome back!)

Food, words, and travel are my favorite things.

My dad owned a roadside diner when I was a kid, and my mom won just about every cooking contest she ever entered. I'm Lebanese on my Dad's side, Italian and Slovak on Mom's. All of which means that food was not "a thing" in our house, it was "*the* thing." I clamored for cumin when most kids were pleading for pancakes. By the time I was in elementary school, I spent a lot of free time with a book in my hands, and I started to write stories and poems. I once wrote a poem about popcorn. I also started cooking my favorite "on my own" meal: Chef Boyardee ravioli fancied up with garlic salt, dried oregano, and Italian herb blend. I would narrate what I was doing to an imaginary audience, like a cooking show, while I crushed herbs between my palms and sprinkled them into the pot.

My favorite family meal was lamb shish kebabs with salad, rice, and zucchini in tomato sauce. My dad always manned the grill on the porch for the kebabs while mom tossed the salad in the kitchen. (She makes the best salads.) I was the designated rice maker. While that meal is a cherished memory, it was also a special treat when Mom cooked what we called sporty suppers: casual food like tacos and burgers that we could eat with our hands. That's why you'll find **Tuna Salad Night** (p. 229), **Taco Night** (p. 93), **Hot Dog Night** (p. 141), **The Ultimate Salad Bar** (p. 61), and **Burger Night** (p. 79) in this book. The food is healthy, but has the playful sheen of food for kids. It requires a lot of napkins.

My parents also taught me to appreciate authentic restaurants, so many of my recipes are inspired by dishes I've eaten on my travels, like **Yucatan Green Chile Sauté** (p. 101), **Mango Chicken** (p. 161), and **Street Fries** (p.

43). I've also been influenced by stories about what chefs eat in their restaurant kitchens after hours. When their shift is over and they're ready to nourish themselves and the crew, they make simple food like **Korean Beef** (p. 71) and **Sexy Scrambled Eggs** (p. 211). They're meals that deliver big flavors composed of simple ingredients.

I WANT YOUR WEEKNIGHT MEALS TO BE SPECIAL –AND FAST.

In my cookbooks *Well Fed* and *Well Fed 2*, I explain how Weekly Cookups save time in the kitchen. By batch cooking protein, steaming lots of veggies, and using lazy weekend hours to simmer stews, dinner hits the table quickly during the week. I've heard from thousands of readers who said that the Weekly Cookup has simplified their time in the kitchen.

But I also received requests for recipes in my style– multicultural flavors, plenty of spices, savory sauces—that could be prepared on the fly without a bunch of planning. So I gave myself a challenge: Go to the grocery store, buy the ingredients for a meal, then come home and cook it in under 45 minutes. I completed that exercise about 175 times, and the result is this cookbook.

I outlined rules for myself—if a recipe didn't meet these criteria, it was out:

IF YOU FOLLOW MY INSTRUCTIONS IN THE RECIPES, YOU SHOULD BE ABLE TO GET A FULL MEAL—PROTEIN, VEGGIES, AND FAT—ONTO THE TABLE (AND INTO YOUR MOUTH) IN UNDER 45 MINUTES, AND IN SOME CASES, AS LITTLE AS 25.

1. The end result had to make my husband Dave and I mumble "Oooohhmmmm ... this is so good" while we still had food in our mouths.

2. The whole meal had to come together in 45 minutes or less.

3. The recipe had to use easy-to-find and reasonably affordable ingredients. Except for coconut aminos, every ingredient in this book can be found at a regular, neighborhood grocery store.

4. The recipe had to be dead-easy to make. Who wants to deal with anything complicated at dinner time?!

Following these rules meant that I had to eliminate some recipes that tasted great, but took too long or were too fussy to prepare. Now I can say with certainty that every meal in this book should easily, comfortably fit into your lifestyle.

If you follow my instructions in the recipes, you should be able to get a full meal—protein, veggies, and fat—onto the table (and into your mouth) in under 45 minutes, and in some cases, as little as 25. If you prefer to do a Weekly Cookup, every recipe includes tips to prep components in advance, store them, and bring it together at meal time. I also included tips for how to reheat leftovers. With these meals, you and your dining companions will never be bored. The flavors are bold. The colors are vibrant. The textures are satisfying. And the recipes are easy. I want you to relax in the kitchen.

I explain a lot of details in my recipes so you always know what to do and how long to do it—but none of these recipes is complicated. I use basic techniques and equipment; in many cases, all you need is a good sharp knife, your favorite skillet, and a stick blender.

I want you to remember this (in fact, write this in Sharpie on a sticky note and hang it in your kitchen): You really can't mess up these recipes. Really. You can't. Ultimately, if you like the way your dinner tastes, you've done it right. And if you're not happy with it, you can always learn from kitchen missteps. The meat was a little overdone? Go easy on the heat next time. The veggies weren't tender enough? Cook them a little longer on the next go-round.

I hope my recipes will give you confidence in the kitchen and bring together your favorite people to share food that nourishes body and spirit. After all, preparing quality food is among the most caring things we can do for ourselves and the people we love.

You really can't mess up these recipes. Really.

WHAT IS PALEO?

You've probably heard the paleo diet called a lot of things. Just eat real food (#JERF). The caveman diet. Going primal. Living the paleo lifestyle. Around our house we sometimes call it "dino-chow."

All of these terms refer to roughly the same way of eating. They're based on the idea that we are healthier—both mentally and physically—when we remove inflammatory foods from our diet.

What's an inflammatory food? The inflamers are foods that were not part of our hunter-gatherer ancestors' daily meals but appeared later in history, after agriculture took root. Edibles like grains, dairy, added sugars, and processed foods are the big bullies of the food world, and they're linked to the "diseases of civilization," nasty stuff including heart disease, diabetes, and cancers.

When we stop eating those problematic ingredients, we not only fight disease, we also improve everything in our lives. I know that's a bold claim, but it's true!

What we put in our bodies forms the foundation for our moods, our energy, our creativity, and our vitality. When we nourish our bodies with paleo-approved foods, our energy levels are better, we look years younger, and we enjoy life more.

PALEO EXPERTS

If all you remember about paleo eating is the "Yes" and "No" lists, you'll know pretty much all you need to eat well for the rest of your life. But if you want to dig deeper and understand the science behind these nutritional guidelines, I recommend you turn to the experts who educated me.

MELISSA HARTWIG
www.whole30.com
To learn both the theoretical and practical information you need to develop healthy, happy eating habits, my number one recommendation is the Whole30 program. Begin with *The Whole30: The 30-Day Guide to Total Health and Food Freedom*, or commit to the life-changing Whole30 program by visiting the web site. Thanks to what I learned from the Whole30 program, I can enjoy my food without measuring every meal or recording every bite in a food journal. The Whole30 site is an excellent resource for knowledge and community support. If you've never experienced a full 30 days without a "cheat or treat," I recommend that you participate in a complete Whole30 at least once to see how your body and attitudes respond.

ROBB WOLF
www.robbwolf.com
The author of *The Paleo Solution* goes deep into the geeky science with a sense of humor that makes the information easy to understand and relevant to daily life. Wolf's book broadened my understanding of the "why" behind a paleo lifestyle, so it's easier to make the best food choices on a daily basis. His podcast addresses reader questions with charm and solid information.

MARK SISSON
www.marksdailyapple.com
The author of *The Primal Blueprint* presents the case for more primal living in every aspect of life: nutrition, exercise, sleep, socializing, and sex (!). I like what he has to say about making time to play. His eating guidelines allow some foods on my "No" list, but he is worth reading for new ideas. His other important book, *The Primal Connection: Follow Your Genetic Blueprint to Health and Happiness*, goes beyond food to examine other lifestyle factors that affect our well-being.

CHRIS KRESSER
www.chriskresser.com
As an acupuncturist and practitioner of integrative medicine, Chris Kresser's perspective is very helpful for anyone who follows the paleo diet to manage serious health issues like hypothyroidism, heart disease, diabetes, and depression. His web site and book *The Paleo Cure* give you a deep dive into those subjects and educate you for conversations with your own doctor.

The Resources section (p. 249) includes additional sources I turn to for inspiration, information, and paleo products.

THE "NO" LIST

Let's get the bad news out of the way immediately: Eating paleo is probably going to mean eliminating many foods that may top your list of favorites. Different paleo practitioners promote varying foods within the paleo framework. I follow the standards outlined in Melissa Hartwig's Whole30 program, as detailed in the books *The Whole30* and *It Starts With Food*. These guidelines are fairly stringent but extremely practical, and they're based on the idea that we should eat the foods that make us the healthiest.

Each of the "No" foods has its own unique properties that ensure its place on this infamous list. Generally, these foods are excluded because they either negatively affect your metabolism, cause systemic inflammation, or both. Some are so bad that they wreak havoc on your metabolism and fire up your immune system at the same time. We eschew them. *We're looking at you, grains. We eschew you!*

GRAINS

Despite conventional wisdom, even whole grains are not a good idea. Grains include wheat, rye, bulgur, buckwheat, amaranth, sprouted grains, corn, oats, rice, quinoa, barley, and millet. Avoid them in all their devilish forms: bread, tortillas, pasta, breading on fried foods, and "healthy" cereals, including oatmeal and granola.

DAIRY

The source doesn't matter—cow, sheep, or goat—milk and the creamy things made from it are off our plates, including cream, butter, cheese, yogurt, and sour cream. Some primal people eat grass-fed, full-fat dairy; for me, the negatives, like bloating and blood sugar spikes, outweigh the pleasure. One exception is organic, grass-fed ghee, also known as clarified butter.

LEGUMES

Beans—including black, kidney, pinto, white, and chickpeas—fall into this category, along with lentils, peas, and peanuts, including peanut butter. Good news! Legumes like green beans, snap peas, and snow peas get a green light because they're more pod than bean.

SOY

Soy is a legume, but I've called it out separately because it's insidious and can be found in unexpected places, like cans of tuna. Avoid soy in all its forms: edamame, soy milk, tofu, meat substitutes, and food additives like soy lecithin. Read labels!

PROCESSED FOODS

As a former Doritos diehard, I know it can be hard to give up junk food and convenience foods like salad dressings and pasta sauces. But anything found in the middle of the grocery store and sold to you inside brightly colored plastic or cardboard is not a healthy choice. Be on the lookout for carrageenan, MSG, and added sulfites in packaged foods. (Natural sulfites are OK.)

VEGETABLE OILS

Basic vegetable oil isn't made from vegetables at all! It's off the eating list, along with peanut, canola, sunflower, safflower, soybean, and corn oils. These oils are thugs that beat up on your immune system and promote inflammation.

ADDED SUGAR

All forms of added sugar—even "natural" sugars, like brown sugar, maple syrup, agave nectar, stevia, evaporated cane juice, and honey—are generally excluded. Also out are artificial sweeteners like Splenda, Equal, NutraSweet, and Aspartame. A few of the recipes in this book include a small amount of honey, maple syrup, or coconut sugar to create a balanced flavor; you can always omit the sweetener without destroying the recipe, if you prefer to be completely sugar-free.

ALCOHOL

Alcohol has no redeeming nutritional qualities. It's essentially sugar with a flirtatious attitude. Plus, you have a drink, then your drink has a drink, and soon, you're face first in a pile of chili-cheese french fries.

THE "YES" LIST

When I tell people I don't eat grains, sugar, dairy, or alcohol, they invariably look at me like I've just slapped their ice cream cone into the dirt. Then they ask The Question: "What do you eat?!" The answer: animals and plants.

Generally speaking, the paleo diet is made up of nutrient-dense foods that began with dirt, rain, and sunshine. They come from the earth, and a person from any time in history would recognize them as food.

It's just real food: animal-based protein, vegetables, fruits, and natural fat sources. Eating these foods promotes a healthy psychological and hormonal response to food, supports a healthy gut, and strengthens your immune system.

ANIMAL PROTEIN

Veal Elk Beef Bison Venison Goat Rabbit Boar Lamb Pork Chicken Eggs Duck Goose Turkey Emu Ostrich Salmon Halibut Tuna Shrimp Lobster Clams Mussels Tilapia Sole Bass Trout Flounder Snapper Mackerel Sardines Anchovies Cod

FATS

Almonds Cashews Pecans Hazelnuts Walnuts Macadamias Chestnuts Filberts Olives Pine Nuts Coconuts Avocados Pistachios Grass-fed Ghee

FRUITS

Apples Apricots Bananas Blackberries Blueberries Cantaloupe Cherries Cranberries Dates Kiwis Pears Lemons Figs Papayas Plums Honeydew Grapes Grapefruits Limes Melons Mangoes Nectarines Oranges Pomegranates Peaches Raspberries Pineapples Tangerines Strawberries Watermelons

VEGETABLES

Acorn Squash Artichokes Arugula Asparagus Beets Bell Peppers Bok Choy Broccoli Brussels Sprouts Butternut Squash Cabbage Carrots Fennel Cauliflower Chard Celery Cucumbers Kale Collard Greens Garlic Jicama Eggplant Leeks Lettuce Parsnips Mushrooms Okra Green Beans Mustard Greens Plantains Red Onions Onions Spinach Onions Scallions Pumpkin Radishes Shallots Spaghetti Snap Peas Snow Peas Sweet Potatoes Summer Squash Squash Yams Turnip Greens Turnips Tomatoes Zucchini

MY PALEO STORY

Way back in 2009, I was one of the first people to try the Whole30, long before it had that catchy name and had helped hundreds of thousands of people change their lives. I've been committed to this way of eating ever since. And while my story isn't a success story in the traditional sense—there's no "after" photo of me with six-pack abs or a tale of massive, overnight weight loss—it is a success story. Eating Whole30-style has kept me fit, mostly happy, and fighting the good fight while wrestling with I-have-no-thyroid complications.

I have excellent habits 95 percent of the time. I sleep eight to nine hours per night to recover from and prepare for heavy lifting at the gym, occasional sprints, and plenty of yoga and walking. I keep the house stocked with paleo ingredients and cook nutrient-dense meals so my husband Dave and I can eat real food every day.

Then on rare occasions, I indulge. I become a temporary slug and give in to the temptation of corn-based chip products, buttered popcorn, an icy cold glass of Prosecco, or a shot of Ouzo. I have a known whipped cream problem.

These minor transgressions are possible because I make regular deposits in the good health bank the rest of the time.

Every workout, every good night's sleep, every paleo meal is a deposit, so that every once in a while, I can make withdrawals for a food treat.

This way of living started in 2009 when I made the switch to the paleo diet. Before then, I didn't have such excellent habits.

From grade school to the day I graduated from college, I was a chubby nerd. My parents are both exceptionally good cooks—my dad brought his restaurant training home and my mom won almost every cooking contest that she entered. By the time I was about eight, I was wearing Sears "Pretty Plus" jeans, mostly because I really liked food, but also because I really didn't like to sweat. After a broken ankle and vicious playground taunts, I stuck with reading, practicing the piano, and

roller-skating to the library. I don't know how many gym classes I missed because I was "sick" or "forgot" my gym clothes. I do know that my P.E. attendance put my otherwise stellar grade point average in jeopardy.

Even though I avoided sports, I secretly admired the athletic kids; they walked taller than the rest of us. When I was in tenth grade, my dad took me to Annapolis to see the Navy band play a concert, and for about three weeks I was determined to get in shape so that I could apply to the Naval Academy. I abandoned that dream because I was incapable of doing push-ups and sit-ups—and I was too embarrassed and overwhelmed to ask for help.

For most of my life, I was haunted by a deep desire to be different than I was. To be thin. To feel confident. To break the cycle of thinking of food—and my behavior—as "good" and "bad."

I joined Weight Watchers and eventually became a Lifetime Member with a weight loss of more than 50 pounds. I joined a CrossFit gym and learned to love being intimidated by my workouts. I developed a deep affection for lifting barbells. But despite my successes, it was still my habit to celebrate, grieve, stress out, and relax with food. Although I worked out regularly, I didn't feel as strong—inside or out—as I wanted to. I had insomnia, allergies, and stomach aches. My body didn't feel like it belonged to me.

ABOUT THIS BOOK

THIS IS NOT A DIET BOOK.

Yes, the recipes are healthy and the paleo framework is one of the best ways to lose fat and manage body weight. I truly believe that this is the healthiest way to eat.

But I'm not going to clobber you with the nutrition facts of every recipe or boss you around with rules for calorie restriction. My mission is to inspire you with tasty stories and to tempt you with recipes that motivate you to willingly, happily eat this food every day.

All of these recipes are free of gluten, grains, legumes, dairy, and alcohol. They rely on protein, vegetables, fruits, fats, and spices to make everyday meals feel like special occasions. When I've used calorie-dense foods like nuts, dried fruit, or optional sweeteners, they're condiments rather than primary ingredients.

JUST EAT

There's no nutritional information included with the recipes. My approach to the paleo framework is to eat protein, fat, and carbohydrates in fairly equal proportions. I'm not high fat, high protein, or low carb; I'm moderate. My recipes reflect this balance and don't require over-analysis of macronutrients to keep you healthy. If you have specific fitness, sports, or macronutrient goals, you can easily adapt the recipes to fit into your personal paleo template by adjusting the fat, carb, and protein amounts.

AUTOIMMUNE PROTOCOL (AIP) AND WHOLE30® COMPLIANCE.

Some of my recipes are compliant with the Autoimmune Protocol of paleo, and most of them can be adapted to be AIP-friendly. Visit www.meljoulwan.com/wellfedweeknights to download a free PDF with detailed AIP modifications for all of the recipes.

I kept the Whole30 guidelines in mind while I developed these recipes. If a recipe includes a non-compliant ingredient, it's clearly marked, with suggestions to make the recipe fit within the Whole30 template.

HOW TO USE THIS BOOK

If you're not familiar with my recipes and style of cooking, start with The Recipe Pages (p. 13), Cooking & Storage Tips (p. 18), and Your Paleo Kitchen (p. 29). These sections explain the philosophy of fast cooking and how my recipes are constructed, as well as the ingredients and tools you need to make these meals.

When you're ready to start cooking, you'll find the recipes are organized by their primary ingredient: protein. I like to build meals around a protein source, then supplement the plate, and bolster nutrients, with veggies, fruit, and fat. Each protein section of the book —Beef, Pork & Lamb, Chicken, Eggs, and Fish & Seafood—includes recipes for meatballs, salads, sautés, and oven-roasted meals.

THE MINI COOKUP

You'll want to dog ear the Mini Cookup (p. 39). It's complete, step-by-step instructions for preparing six paleo kitchen staples in under an hour. Cook once and supplement your meals all week long with potatoes, zucchini noodles, cauliflower rice, mayo, and more.

THE FOOD COURT.

Distributed throughout the book are The Food Court recipes: takeout and food truck–inspired meals that teach you a basic preparation technique, then empower you with multiple adaptations you can customize according to your cravings. It's like a restaurant chalkboard in your kitchen!

Chicken Paillard: A quick-cooking, still-juicy chicken breast that can be dressed up with seven different vibrant sauces.

Burger Night: A celebration of the bunless burger that goes beyond basics with eight creative topping combos.

Meat & Potatoes: Your choice of stuffed baked potato, oven fries, or home fries topped with eleven concepts for meat, veggies, and sauces from around the world.

Hot Dog Night: The ultimate finger food with eight unexpected (and shockingly delicious) topping ideas.

Taco Night: Step-by-step instructions and recipes for a weeknight fiesta!

Tuna Salad Platters: Fresh crudité and unusual mix-ins make these eight tuna salad recipes something special.

The Ultimate Salad Bar: Six fresh salad dressing recipes and dozens of salad schemes will make you a pro with a bowl of greens.

PORK MEDALLIONS WITH BLACKBERRY COMPOTE AND CAULIFLOWER PURÉE

ramble in a bramble

Pork and apples are a classic combination, so I wanted to diverge from the familiar path for something spicier, moodier, and a little syrupy. Blackberries are sweet enough and bring a hint of rose, cedar, and clove mixed with the berriness. When you apply a touch of heat and acid, they acquiesce to become a luxe liquid that's somewhere between a sauce and a glaze. Make a perfect bite—cauliflower mash, pork, and berry compote on the fork all at once—and let the contrasting and complementary textures roll around your tongue.

Serves 2–4
Total time: 30–35 minutes
Tools: stick blender

YOU KNOW HOW YOU COULD DO THAT?

Replace the black... ries with raspberries, blueberries, or a mix. You might also toss in a diced fresh peach or apricot!

COOKUP TIPS

Prepare the cauliflower purée and berry compote in advance; store both in separate airtight containers in the fridge. When it's time to eat, reheat the purée and compote while you cook the pork.

CAULIFLOWER PURÉE:
- 1–2 cups water
- 1 large head cauliflower
- 2 tablespoons ghee
- ½ teaspoon salt
- ¼ teaspoon ground black pepper

COMPOTE:
- 1 tablespoon ghee
- 2 cups blackberries
- 1 teaspoon arrowroot powder
- 1 teaspoon lemon juice
- ¼ teaspoon powdered ginger
- pinch salt

PORK MEDALLIONS:
- 1 teaspoon extra-virgin olive oil
- 1½ pounds pork tenderloin
- 1 teaspoon salt
- ½ teaspoon ground black pepper

Preheat the oven to 250F.

Steam the cauliflower. Place 1 cup water in a medium saucepan and bring it to a boil. While it heats, coarsely chop the cauliflower. Add the cauliflower to the pan, bring it back to a boil, cover with a lid, and steam it until it's very tender, 10–15 minutes. Check the pan occasionally and add more water, if necessary. Meanwhile…

Make the compote. In a small saucepan, warm the ghee over medium heat, 2 minutes. In a medium bowl, toss the berries with the arrowroot powd... then add the berries, lemon juice, ginger, and ... to the pan. Cook over low heat until the some o... the berries have collapsed and the liquid is syrupy, about 10 minutes. While the compote cooks…

Cook the pork. Warm the oil in a large, nonstick skillet over medium-high heat, 2 minutes. While it heats, cut the tenderloin into ½-inch-thick medallions. Season them on both sides with the salt and pepper. Add half the pork to the pan and cook undisturbed 3 minutes, flip and cook the other side, 3 minutes. Transfer the cooked pork to a plate and cover with foil to keep it warm while you cook ... remaining pork.

Finish the purée. Add the ghee, salt, and pepper to the steamed cauliflower and purée with a stick blender until very smooth.

To serve, place pork medallions on a bed of cauliflower purée and top with berry compote.

THE RECIPE PAGES

The recipe pages are brimming with details and descriptions to help you recreate these meals in your kitchen. I want you to feel like we're at your stove, cooking and dishing together, with plenty of dance breaks. (I recommend Jennifer Lopez or The Clash for just this purpose.) To make things as easy as possible, I've included the following information in each recipe.

1. SERVES / MAKES

Almost all of the recipes in this book serve 2–4 people. Serving size is based on an estimate of 4–6 ounces of protein per person and at least 1 cup of vegetables per person. Keep this in mind if you need to feed hard-charging athletes or tiny/growing offspring, and adjust quantities accordingly.

2. TOTAL TIME / HANDS-OFF TIME

The total time for each recipe is based on how long it takes me to prepare the dish, with some padding added because I'm pretty fast in the kitchen. For these recipes, I did not include instructions for creating a *mise en place* before cooking (see page 19 to learn why), and I didn't clean up as I cooked. The times listed are a representation of how long it takes me follow the instructions described in the recipe. The hands-off time indicates that you can walk away from the kitchen for a bit, usually while a dish is finishing in the oven.

The times specified apply only to the recipe as written; if you double the recipe, it will take a bit longer to prepare. For example, when I cooked a double batch of Fried Chicken Meatballs (p. 163), it took 50 minutes, rather than the 30–35 minutes listed on the recipe.

3. TOOLS

To speed up the process, I've listed the non-standard cooking tools you need for the recipe: a gadget that might be hiding in the back of a drawer or an appliance that needs to be hauled out of a cabinet. Tools that are needed for just about every recipe—knife, cutting board, skillets, wooden spoons, spatula, measuring spoons, measuring cup, aluminum foil or parchment, etc.—are not listed. You know you need a sharp knife, right?!

4. INGREDIENTS

The ingredients are listed in the order they're used in the recipe. When substitutions can be made, they're usually listed at the end of the recipe.

5. DIRECTIONS

The directions are very detailed so that you can recreate the recipes in roughly the same amount of time it takes me to cook them. If you follow my recommended steps, you should be a smashing success. I've cooked all of the recipes in this book at least a half dozen times, so the directions I recommend are based on plenty of trial and error. Where I used tricks my parents taught me, I erred on the side of over-explanation so you can learn from my mom and dad, too.

6. YOU KNOW HOW YOU COULD DO THAT?

This is a game I play with my family. We eat a chef's restaurant creation or read a recipe, mull it over for a moment, then say, "You know how you could do that?" and come up with variations. It's a way to make the recipes flexible and personal.

7. COOKUP TIPS

If you're in the habit of doing a Weekly Cookup, these recipes can be broken into components that fit into a batch cooking session. Every recipe includes tips for how to break it down into parts, so you can prepare some of it in advance, then bring it all together at meal time.

ABOUT THE RECIPES

Good news! With the exception of coconut aminos, all of the ingredients used in these recipes can be found in most neighborhood grocery stores. That means you don't have to schlep to multiple shops for supplies (which leaves more time for reading, walking, yoga, and planning your world domination).

Here are some things to keep in mind about ingredients and tools as you read the recipes. Pro tip: Read the entire recipe before you start cooking; you'll be so much happier.

HIGH-QUALITY PROTEIN

It's a blessing and a curse to be at the top of the food chain. We are fortunate to have access to a wide variety of animal proteins, and I honor and respect those animals for making us stronger and healthier. But factory farming damages the environment and manufactures animals that are not optimally healthy—which means they make us less healthy than we could be. I know money is always part of the equation, so I don't specify organic, grass-fed, pastured, or wild-caught protein in my recipes, but I do encourage you to buy the highest-quality protein your budget can manage. If you can't invest in grass-fed, buy lean cuts, remove excess fat before cooking, and drain the fat after cooking.

ORGANIC PRODUCE

It's preferable to eat local produce that's in season, for the health of both your body and your wallet—but it's also OK to occasionally eat produce that's not grown locally or is out of season. My recommendation is to buy local, organic versions of the produce on the "dirty dozen" list. Produced by the Environmental Working Group, the list identifies the fruits and vegetables that retain the most pesticide residue from commercial production. (Find it here: www.ewg.org/foodnews/dirty_dozen_list.php).

For the rest of your produce needs, you can feel comfortable buying conventionally grown produce. Be sure to wash it well under running water to remove dirt and pesticides.

COOKING FATS

Fat is where it's at! It's an essential component for good health, and it taste so (so so so) good. But there's no reason to go overboard. I'm not afraid of fat, but I'm also not on the team that thinks paleo requires us to dive face-first into a vat of pastured lard. My recipes include enough fat to appropriately cook and flavor the food. Feel free to increase the amount of fat if you'd like, but I don't recomend that you reduce the amount of fat listed in the recipes because that will also reduce the flavor.

The majority of my recipes use extra-virgin olive oil for convenience: It's reasonably priced, it's widely available, and it's liquid at room temperature, which makes measuring easy. The latest research debunks the idea that cooking with extra-virgin olive oil is ill-advised. If you cook at medium-high heat, as my recipes suggest, extra-virgin olive oil retains its healty fatty acids and does *not* undergo substantial structural changes.

If you prefer to use ghee, coconut oil, or animal fats, they will all work, too. All fats can be swapped with each other in a 1:1 ratio, so you can use your favorites. In some recipes, I've specified ghee or coconut oil for its flavor; again, that's a suggestion, and you can use what you like. Pro tip: You can't ever go wrong cooking potatoes in duck fat or pastured lard.

A few words about homemade mayo and creamy dressings: For these recipes, it's essential that you use either light-tasting olive oil or avocado oil. The flavor of extra-virgin olive oil is far too strong for mayo and overpowers creamy dressings.

SEASONING WITH SALT

American table salt is devoid of trace minerals; sea salt is a slightly superior option. Most sea salt, however, doesn't include the iodine found in table salt. I don't specify the type of salt to be used in these recipes, but I recommend iodized sea salt. All measurements refer to fine (not coarse) salt.

It's important to taste food for salt levels throughout the cooking process. I always specify a good starting amount of salt, and I recommend that you taste your dish and adjust seasonings just before the end of cooking. With salt—and all spice quantities—feel free to adjust down or up according to taste.

In recipes that begin with sautéed onions—and, really, don't all great recipes begin with sautéed onions?!—I recommend that you add a pinch of salt to the pan with the onion and fat. This salt is not listed in the ingredients list, but surely you have a salt shaker next to your stove. You do, right?

COOKING TEMPERATURES

If you're using grass-fed meats, you'll get the best results when you cook with medium-high (or even medium) heat. High heat can make leaner, high-quality meats toughen up. You'll also notice that most of my recipes instruct you to preheat the pan before cooking. This is an important step in cooking the food well and provides valuable time for ingredient prep.

OMITTING INGREDIENTS

Some ingredients, including sweeteners, are listed as optional. Keep in mind that in all recipes, flavoring ingredients are always optional. Rather than skip an entire recipe because it includes something that's not your favorite, simply omit the element you don't like. For example, none of these recipes will fail if you omit hot peppers or skip the cumin. (Although why anyone would want to eliminate cumin is beyond me.)

SMASH, PEEL, CRUSH.

I'm terrible at mincing garlic, so I've eliminated this technique from the recipes. There are two garlic treatments in this book, and neither requires you to have master knife skills.

PRO TIP: READ THE ENTIRE RECIPE BEFORE YOU START COOKING; YOU'LL BE SO MUCH HAPPIER.

Smash and peel: That means just what it sounds like it means. Place the garlic clove on a cutting board, place the blade of your knife flat against the clove, and then lightly smash your fist against the blade to break the clove. Remove the husk and proceed. You can also just give the garlic clove a light thwack with the bottom of a ramekin or can, or gentle tap it with a meat hammer. For a video demo, visit www.meljoulwan.com/wellfedweeknights.

Peel and crush: Lightly smash the clove as above, remove the peel, then use a garlic press to crush the garlic.

MISE EN PLACE

In my previous cookbooks, I made the case for setting up a *mise en place* before starting a recipe. Chef-talk for "everything in place," it means you measure and prep the ingredients you need in advance.

With these recipes, I instead recommend that you preassemble everything you need for the recipe—fresh ingredients, bottles, canned foods, spices, cooking tools—but don't do any prep or measurement. The preparation of ingredients is built into the recipe to take advantage of "down time" while pans heat or sauces simmer.

If you gather your ingredients and tools on your countertop, then follow the instructions as written, you shouldn't experience any surprises and your meal should be ready in the time listed at the top of the recipe.

AUTOIMMUNE PROTOCOL (AIP) AND WHOLE30® COMPLIANCE

Some of my recipes are compliant with the Autoimmune Protocol of paleo, and most of them can be adapted to be AIP-friendly. Visit www.meljoulwan.com/wellfed weeknights to download a free PDF that provides detailed AIP modifications for all of the recipes.

I kept the Whole30 guidelines in mind while I developed these recipes. If a recipe includes a non-compliant ingredient, it's clearly marked, along with suggestions to make the recipe fit within the Whole30 template.

YOU'RE GONNA NEED A BIGGER BOWL

This advice from my dad is included in both of my previous cookbooks and will certainly appear in any future volumes I write: Always, always use a bowl that's bigger than you think you need. (Thanks, Dad!)

COOKING & STORAGE TIPS

I started this cookbook project with more than 300 recipe ideas! When the time came to filter the possibilities, it wasn't enough for the dish to taste really good—it had to be fast and easy, too.

I tested these recipes over and over again to find the quickest way to achieve the most flavor. My methods might not stand up to Cordon Bleu–level scrutiny, but I guarantee that if you follow my recommendations, you'll be eating in under 45 minutes, and you'll relish every bite.

COOKUPS VERSUS MADE-TO-ORDER

My previous cookbooks advocated for the idea of a Weekly Cookup: one big cooking session that would fill the refrigerator with cooked raw materials to build meals quickly throughout the week. It's an easy way to make a large quantity of food at once, and it works great... until you don't have two or three hours to spend in the kitchen. Then batch cooking becomes a dreaded chore, instead of a stress reducer.

In contrast, the recipes in this book are based on the assumption that you've done no preparatory cooking—all of your ingredients are raw and, maybe, you're ready to eat *right now*. This approach is great for people who like to buy fresh veggies or a beautiful cut of meat that catch their eye at the market. But if you're in the habit of a Weekly Cookup (good for you!), don't fret: These recipes can be broken into components that can be prepped in advance for quick assembly at meal time. Each recipe outlines how to prep and how to finish the dish when you're ready to eat.

Loving reminder: The times specified apply only to the recipe as written; if you double the recipe, it will take a bit longer to prepare. For example, when I cooked a double batch of Taco Night (p. 93) for a party, it took an hour, rather than the 45 minutes listed on the recipe.

QUICK COOKING TIPS

Fast-cooking proteins

Sure, a slow-braised pork shoulder is one of the sexiest hunks on the planet—but weeknights are not the time to be messing around with slow and low. Getting dinner on the table fast requires proteins that cook quickly, so these recipes rely on chicken breasts and thighs, pork loin, thin steaks, shrimp, and ground meats. They're all loaded with flavor, very versatile, and transform from raw to done in a flash.

The right tools in the right place

Unless you practice your knife skills like Julia Child in that memorable scene from *Julie & Julia*, there's no way you can julienne or mince as quickly as a gadget can. I recommend that you invest in a few essential tools if you're serious about getting meals on the table as quickly as possible. A stick blender and pint-size Mason jar are essential for making the sauces and dressings in this book, and a mandoline or a food processor with a slicing blade will save you precious minutes.

To speed up the process of cooking, I've listed the non-standard cooking tools you need on each recipe page, so you can rummage around in the cabinet to find what you need *before* you start cooking.

Pro tip: If you can give up a corner of counter space to your food processor and stick blender, you will be so much happier. Cooking is far more pleasant when the tools you need are *right there*, instead of tucked away in a drawer or cabinet. On weeknights, you are essentially a head chef, and you deserve a kitchen that's as efficient as possible.

No mise en place

In my previous cookbooks, I made the case for setting up a *mise en place* before starting a recipe. Chef-talk for "everything in place," it means you measure and prep the ingredients you need in advance.

With these recipes, I instead recommend that you preassemble everything you need for the recipe—fresh ingredients, bottles, canned foods, spices, cooking tools—but don't do any prep or measurement. The preparation of ingredients is built into the recipe to take advantage of "down time" while pans heat or sauces simmer.

If you gather your ingredients and tools on your countertop, then follow the instructions as written, you shouldn't experience any surprises and your meal should be ready in the time listed at the top of the recipe.

Clean up later

I get antsy when my kitchen is disorganized, and I usually clean up along the way when I cook. With these recipes, I let some of that slide. To be clear, I'm not advocating that you cook in the midst of mayhem, but to cook the recipe in the time indicated, you'll need to set aside used equipment to be cleaned later—or recruit an assistant to wash while you cook! Some of the recipes include hands-off time, which is an excellent opportunity to restore order to the kitchen. A side bonus of salad for dinner is that you can assemble the salads and set them aside while you tidy up. Then you can relax and enjoy dinner, with just the salad bowls to wash when you're finished.

FOOD STORAGE

Leftovers—and the results of a Weekly Cookup—are like treasures left behind in the fridge by someone who loves you. Nothing feels more caring to me than a refrigerator stacked with matching containers that are stuffed with healthy food.

But let's talk about how long that food can hang around before it's worn out its welcome. Different types of food age in different ways, as they are slowly attacked by microbes or enzymes and gradually become less desirable and nutritious. It's important to keep food cold and stored in airtight containers because the microbial activity increases in warm air and in the presence of oxygen. Keep a dry-erase marker or peel-and-stick labels in the kitchen and mark the "toss by" date on your food containers for a handy reminder. Whether it's raw or cooked, food shouldn't be left at room temperature for more than four hours.

Cooked food: 5–6 days

Cooked foods that you prepared yourself can be kept in the fridge in an airtight container for five to six days.

Prepared salads: 3–4 days

Mixed salads—like tuna (p. 229), egg (p. 199), Chinese Chicken Salad (p. 195), or Thai Yummy Salad (p. 237)—can be stored in the fridge in an airtight container for three to four days. After that, they start to lose their fresh appeal.

Salad dressings: 7–10 days

Vinaigrettes, in theory, are timeless—but they start to lose their zing after about 10 days, and might begin to grow mold eventually. Creamy dressings made with homemade mayo have the same expiration date as the egg you used to make them, so indicate that date on the dressing jar.

Raw meat: varies

The color of meat changes when it's exposed to air and light, so it's not unusual for meat to be purplish red, cherry red, or brownish. With ground meat, the outside of the ball of meat might fade to a dull brown while the inside retains a bright red hue. This is all totally OK. The only time to be suspicious of raw meat is if has an off smell or a sticky/slimy surface. (Gross. Sorry.)

Raw veggies: varies

Vegetables are remarkably resilient. Surface changes like browning, bruising, or wilting are generally cosmetic and don't mean you can't eat the produce. Simply remove the offending bit with a knife and move on with your life. Wilted produce—especially greens, broccoli, carrots, and celery—can be revived by a quick soak in cold water, but if you're going to cook the vegetables anyway, wilting probably doesn't matter. Vegetables like tomatoes and bell peppers may show wrinkly spots as they age, the result of moisture loss; they, too, can be revived in a cold water bath.

Mold. Ew.

Keep an eye out for mold, especially on cooked food and dressings. Some types of mold produce toxins that can lead to foodborne illness, and they can't be "killed" through cooking. It's a good rule of thumb that if something is moldy, it's time to toss it.

DINING OUT

I'm my own favorite cook in a restaurant that only serves foods I like and prepares them just the way I want them. But sometimes I don't want to cook. Maybe I've already spent too much time cooking that day, or I'm tired and pouty. On those evenings, I need a break from the responsibility of planning and cooking a meal that pleases me and my dining companions. That's when I comb my hair, jump in the car, and head out to a previously-scouted, paleo-friendly-enough restaurant.

You probably want a respite from the kitchen sometimes, too!

Here are tips to help you navigate restaurant menus on your night off from cooking duties. With these guidelines you can enjoy restaurant meals without abandoning your good habits or ruining your good time.

Disclaimer: I'm not sharing this information because I want you to be paranoid or freaked out about eating in restaurants. I want you to feel empowered to step outside your kitchen. There are three things to keep in mind as you read this:

1. I eat strict paleo at home 100 percent of the time so that when I eat in a restaurant, I don't have to stress too much about what might be in the food. I almost always avoid gluten, but I sometimes indulge in rice at our local Thai place or not-pastured, probably-includes-some-sugar bacon at the diner up the hill.

2. It's counter-productive to get *so* stressed out about what you're eating that you undo the health benefits of eating well. These tips are guidelines to make your life easier, not rules to make you feel shame or fear about food.

3. You're an adult, and the Food Police don't exist. Eat what you like. You don't need to explain yourself to anyone or seek approval for your choices. Just be you.

SCOPE IT OUT

Your delicious restaurant meal starts at home. With a bit of online recon, you can review menus in advance to make sure you can find food that fits into your eating plan. And by deciding in advance what you'll order, you can prevent temptation from derailing your good intentions.

Chain restaurants and most locally-owned restaurants usually share their menus online, and by being a little bit of a detective on Yelp, you can get valuable insight into the menu and quality of the food.

Your best bets are restaurants that serve meat and produce from nearby farms. The phrase "farm to table" is usually a reliable indicator that the quality of the ingredients will be first rate, and restaurants that concern themselves with ingredient quality are usually open to accommodating "picky eaters." You don't have go totally upscale to eat well; neighborhood joints can be good choices, too.

If I review a menu online and decide what I'm eating before I get to the restaurant, I don't even look at the menu when I get there. Why make myself feel bad about the fried macaroni-and-cheese balls I won't eat? If I'm not able to review the menu before I get there, I scan it to find the "not for me" areas—like pasta, sandwiches, deep-fried things—and I don't read them. Key words to look for when scanning a menu: salads, meat, entrées, and vegetable sides. The daily specials are also a good choice because they're often made to order, which means you can be specific about how they're prepared for you.

MAKE FRIENDS WITH THE SERVER

The first task when you arrive at the restaurant is to enlist the server as your partner-in-crime. Your server can help you understand everything that might end up on your plate. (And this is made easier by the online recon you did to review the menu in advance.)

It can feel uncomfortable to ask for what you need at a restaurant, but remember that you're paying the tab, and you have the right to get exactly what you want on your plate (within reason). Here are some tips and questions to help you team up

THIS MIGHT SEEM LIKE A LOT OF BAD NEWS ABOUT RESTAURANTS, BUT REALLY, IF YOU'RE DILIGENT, EATING IN A RESTAURANT CAN BE NO BIG DEAL. REMEMBER: YOU'RE NOT AIMING FOR PERFECTION.

a warning siren. Anything battered and crispy is most likely rolled in flour and deep-fried in canola oil.

When you see the following adjectives on the menu, ask questions and be prepared to take a pass on foods that don't meet your standards.

* Deep-fried
* Crispy
* Battered
* Coated
* Breaded
* Sauced
* Meatballs, Meatloaf, Croquettes (probably include bread crumbs)
* Sausage
* Fritter
* Dumpling

SO ... WHAT ARE YOU GONNA HAVE?

This might seem like a lot of bad news about restaurants, but really, if you're diligent, eating in a restaurant can be no big deal. Remember: You're not aiming for perfection. Do your best, then relax and savor your food. Here are some suggestions for good choices in different types of restaurant.

AMERICAN RESTAURANTS, DINERS AND CAFÉS

Diners and cafés are among the most paleo-friendly restaurants. Here are the best options you can usually find on the menu.

Eggs: Scrambled, poached, fried, hard-boiled, or in omelet form, eggs are a protein-packed choice that can be found just about everywhere. Be sure to clarify if the chef includes dairy, wheat, or soy in the scrambled eggs and omelets. Most kitchens will honor your request to cook

eggs without added ingredients. When in doubt, poached eggs are a solid choice because they're made with only eggs and water.

Bunless burgers: With a salad and a side of vegetables, a burger *sans* bun makes a great meal. Some restaurants have gotten hip to the trend and offer burgers wrapped in fresh lettuce leaves instead of buns.

Protein and vegetables: When in doubt, a steak and a salad is a pretty safe bet. Other good options are salmon, grilled or roasted chicken, roasted turkey, grilled or broiled pork chops, or any variety of fish or seafood. Ask questions about the preparation, request sauces/gravy on the side, and dig in!

BBQ: Smoked beef, pork, chicken, and turkey are all good choices. Although most BBQ rubs contain sugar, it's a trace amount and probably not worth too much concern unless you're doing a Whole30. Beware of BBQ sauce, though; it usually includes a lot of sugar as an ingredient and may also pack some soy sauce. For side dishes, go for braised greens and tossed salad, but avoid the mayo-based coleslaw and potato salad unless you're OK with canola oil mayo.

Salads: A big salad is another reliable choice: lots of fresh veggies topped with protein and drizzled with quality fat. Always request dressings on the side so you can control the amount that's added to your vegetables, or bring a small container of homemade dressing with you. (What?! Doesn't everyone carry a plastic container of dressing in their bags?) Don't forget to ask your server if the salad includes grated cheese and/or croutons and request yours without them.

INTERNATIONAL CUISINE

As you've probably guessed from my recipes, I love international food! Here are the most paleo-friendly dishes I've found while eating out.

Greek/Mediterranean: Grilled fish, Greek salad (minus the feta cheese), gyro meat (as long as it doesn't contain grains as fillers), roasted chicken, shish kebabs, and olives are all paleo-friendly choices. Take a pass on pita bread, as well as casseroles like moussaka, which will include dairy and flour.

Middle Eastern: Look for beef, lamb, pork, and chicken shawarma, baba ghanoush, and shish kebabs made from lamb, beef, chicken, and vegetables. Tahini dressing—made from lemon juice, sesame seed paste, and olive oil—is a great choice for dipping or drizzling over salads.

Mexican: Focus on meat, salsa, and guacamole. Take a pass on the chip basket and avoid tortillas, gorditas, enchiladas, and other dishes that may be wrapped in tortillas or buried under cheese. In place of rice and beans, request a side of vegetables or grilled jalapeños, if you like it hot. Look for dishes like steak, shrimp, or chicken fajitas; carnitas; carne asada; barbacoa;

and rotisserie chicken. You can even enjoy tacos and burritos—just eat the fillings and leave the rest (or have the insides piled on a bed of lettuce to make a salad).

Italian: You're not eating pasta or garlic bread, but that doesn't mean you can't enjoy Italian food. Look for roasted chicken and grilled fish. Remember to ask questions about preparation; pan-sautéed meats are often dusted in flour before cooking. Your order can probably be made without flour, so ask nicely. A big antipasto platter with olives, peppers, and Italian meats is a good choice. As a side, order grilled vegetables or a green vegetable, like broccoli or spinach, topped with marinara sauce.

Thai: Thai stir-fries often contain soy, and rice noodle dishes can include a lot of added sugar (although they are usually gluten-free). Instead, go for curries made with coconut milk, protein, and vegetables, and request that the cook double the vegetables in your dish. (I always ask for extra eggplant!) If you're sensitive to peanuts, skip the peanut sauce, but you can still enjoy satay with cucumber salad. Request that green papaya and other salads be made without chopped peanuts on top.

Indian: Grilled and roasted meats and vegetables—especially tandoori—are usually a safe bet. Tandoori meats may be marinated in yogurt, so clarify with the server if you're sensitive to dairy. Avoid creamy Indian curry sauces because they usually contain yogurt and may also include flour. Avert your eyes from the naan.

Japanese/Sushi: With a little preparation, these restaurants can be a great place to eat paleo. Bring a bottle of coconut aminos with you and use it instead of soy sauce. When ordering maki or hand rolls, ask that they're made without rice; sashimi is always an excellent option. Avoid tempura rolls and ask about sauces that might be included in rolls or drizzled over the top, as they probably include soy and/or sugar. Appetizers like dumplings and edamame are out, but seaweed salad can be a good choice.

Chinese: Unless you have a relationship with the chef at your local Chinese restaurant, eating Chinese out can be pretty tough. Most recipes include soy, cornstarch, rice and rice flour, and added sugars. If you find yourself in a Chinese restaurant and have no other options, the "cleanest" choices are steamed vegetables and roasted meats—like barbecued spareribs or chicken wings—but even those will probably include soy sauce and sugar. If you're particularly sensitive to gluten and/or soy, you should probably avoid Chinese restaurants and reserve stir-fries for home cooking.

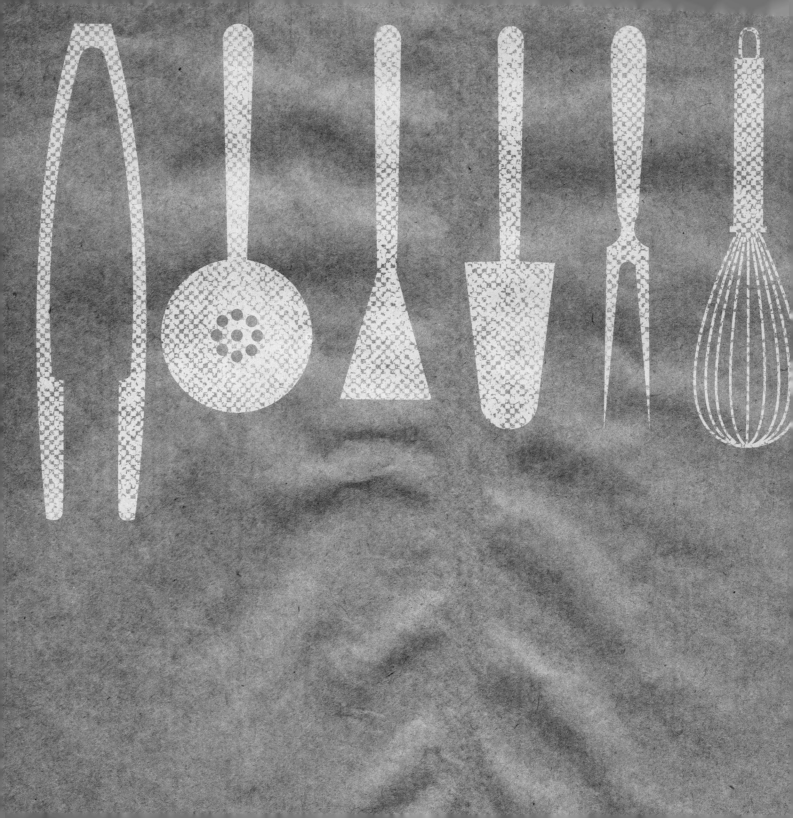

YOUR **PALEO KITCHEN**

ESSENTIAL KITCHEN TOOLS

These are the gadgets I use to cook all of the recipes in this book—and many of them are essential for preparing the recipes quickly. If you don't have something listed, that's OK, but it might take you a little bit longer to make the recipe. For my recommendations on specific pieces of equipment, along with buying information, visit www.meljoulwan.com/wellfedweeknights

LARGE CUTTING BOARD

Almost every recipe begins with chopping. A hefty cutting board protects the knife, your counter top, and you. I have a heavy wooden board that could double as a weapon. I recommend that you use the largest board that will comfortably fit in your work space.

A SHARP KNIFE

In the kitchen, your knife is an extension of you. Choose a knife that feels comfortable in your hand. I like an 8-inch blade; it works well on both meat and produce. Don't forget a good knife sharpener, too!

BENCH SCRAPER/ BOWL SCRAPER

You can get a plastic one for about four bucks and it saves so much hassle! Very useful for scooping up chopped veggies and herbs and safer than using the blade of your knife.

GARLIC PRESS

Not required, but a real time saver unless you're adept at mincing with a knife. When I say "peel and crush" in a recipe, that's code for "remove the peel and crush it in a garlic press to save time."

GRATER/ZESTER

You're not grating cheese anymore, but citrus zest is a transformative ingredient on veggies, salads, meats, and stews.

FOOD PROCESSOR / MANDOLINE

Helpful for chopping and thinly slicing veggies in a fraction of the time it will take you to cut them by hand with a knife. Plus, food processors—little robots that they are—produce more consistent, uniform pieces.

STICK BLENDER

Makes mayo and creamy sauces in a flash! You can use a food processor, but it takes longer and is a little bit more challenging. Even a cheap stick blender—I have one that cost just eight dollars—does the trick. Highly recommended for fast cooking!

PINT-SIZED WIDE- MOUTH MASON JARS

The partner to the stick blender for making mayo and creamy sauces. It's the perfect size for emulsifying and storing in one container. Buy a case of 12 and make your kitchen more efficient.

JULIENNE PEELER OR SPIRALIZER

Super handy for turning vegetables like zucchini into noodles. I recommend the spiralizer because it's faster, but a peeler will work, too.

MINI SCOOP

A 1-tablespoon scoop, intended for cookies but repurposed for meatballs, is just the right size for shaping meatballs quickly.

MEAT HAMMER

This is optional, but it definitely speeds up the process of making Chicken Paillard (p. 167), Pork Medallions with Blackberry Compote (p. 109) and Chicken Caesar Salad (p. 171). You can also release frustrations by using it to bash garlic cloves.

WOODEN SPOONS

My preferred tool for sautéing, mixing, and tossing.

7-QUART DUTCH OVEN

Ideal for delicious, simmered things. I like one with a nonstick interior and heavy bottom.

3- TO 4-QUART NONSTICK SAUCEPAN

Great for jobs that are too small for the Dutch oven. Again, I recommend nonstick.

12-INCH NONSTICK SKILLETS

For most of the recipes in this book, you'll need one large skillet, and a few of the recipes require two. I like one that's fairly deep with curved sides. You may also use a cast-iron skillet, if you prefer.

COLANDER OR WIRE STRAINER

For washing produce and sweating raw vegetables.

TWO RIMMED (13x18-INCH) BAKING SHEETS

Rimmed baking sheets prevent juices and fats from burning in the bottom of the oven. A few recipes require two pans in the oven at once.

2-QUART BAKING DISH

Glass or ceramic, a baking dish is ideal for finishing meats and casseroles in the oven.

PARCHMENT PAPER AND/OR ALUMINUM FOIL

Invaluable for keeping food from sticking to pans and minimizing clean-up time.

IF YOU DON'T HAVE SOMETHING LISTED, THAT'S OK, BUT IT MIGHT TAKE YOU A LITTLE BIT LONGER TO MAKE THE RECIPE.

STURDY MIXING BOWLS

Graduated sizes ensure that you have a bowl for larger projects and spice-sized bowls to keep your workspace tidy.

MEASURING CUPS & SPOONS

For measuring cups, you'll have everything you need if you invest in a 2-cup liquid measuring cup and a set of dry measuring cups that range in size from ¼ cup to 1 cup. For spoons, look for a set that includes 1 tablespoon, ½ tablespoon, 1 teaspoon, ½ teaspoon, and ¼ teaspoon. Bonus points if you also get a ⅛ teaspoon.

RUBBER SCRAPER

I don't like to leave even one drop of my food in mixing bowls, and a scraper is great for gently mixing tender ingredients. Look for a scraper that's both sturdy and flexible.

BPA-FREE STORAGE CONTAINERS

Critical for stocking up on paleo ingredients. You'll need more than you think, and there is acute satisfaction in a fridge filled with ingredients and homemade food.

KITCHEN TIMER(S)

I have three kitchen timers (microwave, stove, free-standing), plus my iPhone, and I've been known to use them all at once. A timer is essential for timing potentially tricky-picky foods like eggs.

HERBS AND SPICES

How much do I love spices? I own a board game called *Spices of the World*, keep a battered copy of *The Complete Book of Spices* on my cookbook shelf, and let it be known often and loudly that cumin is my all-time favorite seed spice.

With the right spices and seasonings, you can go on an adventure anywhere in the world without leaving your kitchen, and you won't get bored eating protein and veggies multiple times every day.

Both herbs and spices originate as plants and are used in cooking, but there are distinct differences. Herbs are the green leaves used for flavor and garnish. They can be eaten fresh or dried, and I use both in my recipes. Spices are made from the dried seed, fruit, root, or bark of plants. You've probably eaten the leafy part of the cilantro plant in Mexican salsa or Thai curry, and enjoyed the seeds—a.k.a. coriander—in chili or Indian curry.

These pages list the herbs and spices you'll need to cook the recipes in this book. You aren't obligated to stock up on all of them at once, but if you gradually build up your supply, your taste buds will reap the benefits. I often buy my spices online for convenience—and because it's a treat to receive a big box of fragrant powders in the mail—but these seasonings can be found in most grocery stores.

ALEPPO PEPPER
Used in Middle Eastern food to add a fruity kick of moderate heat. Named after the city of Aleppo, located along the Silk Road in northern Syria.

ALLSPICE, GROUND
Prevalent in Caribbean cuisine, it combines the flavor of cinnamon, nutmeg, and cloves. Also known as Jamaican pepper, although it's flavorful, not hot.

BASIL, DRIED
Fresh basil is the star of pesto—and a key supporting player in Italian tomato sauce—but dried basil has its place, too. In its dry form, it develops a minty, licorice-y vibe with a nice snap.

BAY LEAF
Adds a mildly sweet, herbiness and depth of flavor. According to legend, the oracle at Delphi chewed bay leaves to promote her visions. Store fresh and dried leaves in the freezer.

BLACK PEPPER, GROUND & WHOLE
Important for just about everything. For optimal flavor, buy it whole and crush or grind it just before using.

CARAWAY SEEDS, WHOLE
The caraway plant looks similar to the carrot plant with fine, feathery leaves. Used in European, Balkan, and Middle Eastern cuisine, its dried seeds impart a decidely anise flavor.

CARDAMOM, GROUND
A member of the ginger family, cardamom releases aromatic notes of eucalyptus and florals. Used in savory and sweet Indian dishes.

CAYENNE PEPPER
Adds a little heat to just about anything. Named for the city of Cayenne in French Guiana.

CELERY SEED
This is going to blow your mind. It's the seed of a plant related to the celery plant, and it has a celery-like flavor.

CHILI POWDER
Used in Tex-Mex, Indian, Chinese, and Thai cuisines. A blend of dried chiles, cumin, oregano, garlic, and salt. Heat varies based on the type of chiles used.

CHINESE FIVE-SPICE POWDER
Balances the yin and yang in Chinese food with star anise, Szechuan peppercorns, cinnamon, cloves, and fennel seeds. In Hawaii, it's used as a table-top condiment along with salt and pepper.

CHIPOTLE CHILI POWDER
Made of only dried and ground chipotle chiles (as compared to chili powder, which is a spice blend). Moderate heat, fruity and smoky undertones.

CHIVES, DRIED
The smallest species of edible onion, chives have a mild flavor. Ideal for seasoning scrambled eggs, steamed veggies, and creamy salad dressings.

CINNAMON, GROUND & STICK
A must-have for sweet and savory foods in just about every ethnic cuisine. In ancient times, it was prized as a gift fit for the gods.

CLOVES, GROUND & WHOLE

Used in sweets, as well as Indian, Vietnamese, Mexican, and Dutch cooking. Eaten on their own, cloves will numb your tongue!

COCOA, UNSWEETENED

The secret ingredient for adding richness and umami to savory dishes.

CORIANDER, GROUND

Common in Middle Eastern, Asian, Mediterranean, Indian, Mexican, Latin American, African, and Scandinavian foods. Coriander is the seed of the cilantro plant.

CRUSHED RED PEPPER FLAKES

Made from a combination of dried red peppers including ancho, bell, cayenne, and others. Adds a gentle kick to Italian and Asian dishes.

CUMIN, GROUND

Used in North African, Middle Eastern, Mexican, and Chinese dishes. The Greeks used cumin as a table seasoning and that habit continues today in modern Morocco.

CURRY POWDER

Essential for curries, egg or tuna salad, and vegetable dishes. My favorite is Penzeys salt-free Maharajah Style Curry Powder.

FENNEL SEED, WHOLE

Another anise-flavored seed, fennel is slightly sweeter than caraway. One of nine Anglo-Saxon sacred herbs, it symbolizes longevity, courage, and strength.

GARLIC POWDER, GRANULATED

Fresh is best for cooking, but dried is useful for homemade spice blends. Confession: Sometimes I just reach for the powder when I don't feel like dealing with fresh cloves. I'm a culinary pragmatist.

GINGER, POWDERED & FRESH

A necessity for Indian curries and Asian dishes. Scrambled with eggs, it's a paleo home remedy for a cough.

ITALIAN HERB BLEND, DRIED

Enormously helpful for adding a taste of Italy to vegetables, soups, stews, and sautés.

MARJORAM, DRIED

Slightly sweeter than oregano, but related. Used in the cuisine of the Middle East, Mediterranean, and Eastern Europe.

MINT, DRIED & FRESH

A powerful flavor in Middle Eastern and Mediterranean cooking.

MUSTARD, POWDERED & WHOLE

Used in homemade mayo, salad dressings, and piquant spice blends. Jewish texts compare the knowable universe to the size of a mustard seed to teach humility.

OREGANO, DRIED

The "pizza herb" for everything Italian, also good in Turkish, Syrian, Greek, and Latin American foods.

PAPRIKA

Adds a peppery bite and rich color to Moroccan, Middle Eastern, and Eastern European dishes.

PARSLEY, DRIED

Poor parsley! It's usually banished to the edge of the plate as garnish, but its bright, somewhat grassy flavor wakes up everything it touches.

POPPY SEEDS

Produced by the opium poppy. There are more than 46,000 blue-black poppy seeds in 1 tablespoon. They're oily with a slightly nutty flavor.

SAGE, RUBBED

It's the Thanksgiving herb! I prefer rubbed sage, made by massaging whole, dried sage leaves to produce a light, fluffy powder. If you use ground instead, reduce the amount by about half.

SEA SALT, FINE

Salt brings out the best in everything we eat. I like fine sea salt for cooking, preferably iodized.

THYME, DRIED

Used in Middle Eastern, Indian, Italian, French, Spanish, Greek, Caribbean, and Turkish cuisines. The ancient Greeks believed thyme was a source of courage.

TURMERIC

Brilliant yellow, turmeric adds the tang and immediately identifiable color to curry powder.

WASABI POWDER

Powerful, green horseradish with a singular bite (and sinus-clearing properties). Essential to recreate the sushi experience at home.

ZA'ATAR SPICE BLEND

A classic Middle Eastern finishing seasoning—made from sesame seeds, dried sumac, salt, and thyme—to sprinkle on salads and cooked vegetables.

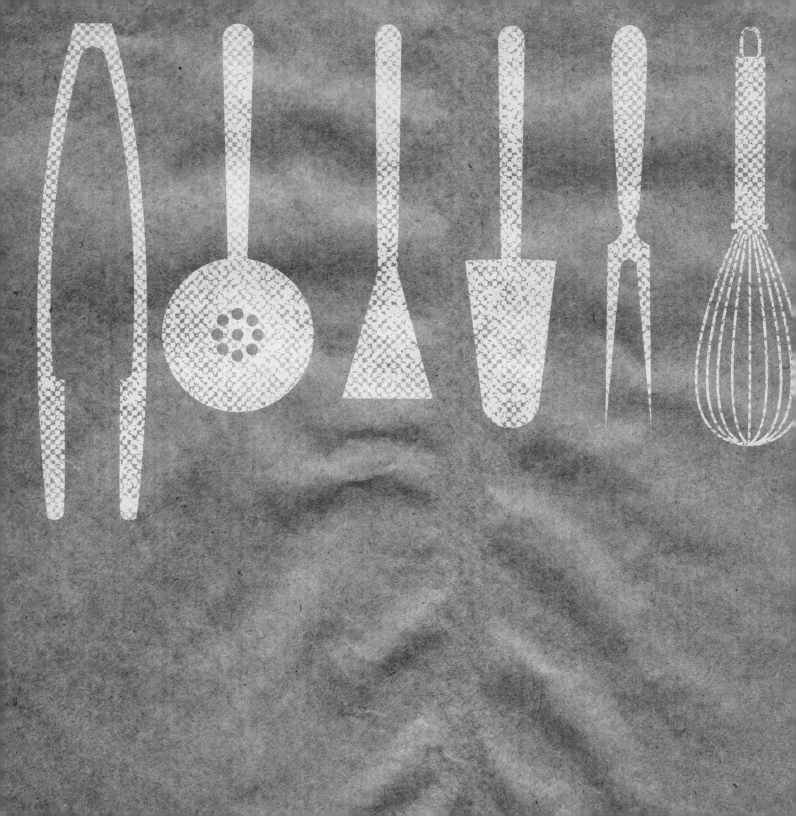

RECIPES

MINI COOKUP

make your week a little easier

In my cookbooks *Well Fed* and *Well Fed 2*, I advocate for a Weekly Cookup: a big, batch cooking session that ensures you have cooked food in your fridge for the week. Even though the recipes in this book are designed to be cooked at meal time, you can give yourself a head start and save time with this Mini-Cookup. In just about an hour, you can prep some of your favorite paleo staples that can be used in the recipes throughout this book. Like Samuel Taylor Coleridge said, "He who is best prepared can best serve his moment of inspiration." I like to pretend that when he said "inspiration," he meant "dinner."

HERE'S HOW IT WORKS

This is a speed round! You'll crank up a bunch of appliances at once to bust out some of the basic building blocks of satisfying, nutritious paleo meals: potatoes, hard-boiled eggs, zucchini noodles, cauliflower rice, roasted chicken, olive oil mayo, and salad dressing. I've included my recommendations for quantities, but you can easily cut them in half or double them. (Except for the mayo; you should make that exactly as prescribed.)

ROASTED CHICKEN BREASTS
- 3 pounds boneless, skinless chicken breasts
- 1 tablespoon salt
- 1 teaspoon ground black pepper

POTATOES
- 4-6 medium, any variety

HARD-BOILED EGGS
- 4 cups water
- 1 dozen large eggs

ZUCCHINI NOODLES
- 2-3 pounds zucchini
- 1 tablespoon salt

CAULIFLOWER RICE
- 2 large heads cauliflower

OLIVE OIL MAYO
- 1 large egg
- 2 tablespoons lemon juice
- ½ teaspoon mustard powder
- ½ teaspoon salt
- 1¼ cups light-tasting olive or avocado oil

SALAD DRESSING
- Ingredients TBD! Turn to page 65 and pick out a salad dressing— or two. Five minutes of work now means tons of flavor later.

1 PREHEAT THE OVEN TO 425F

Line a large rimmed baking sheet with parchment paper. Lay out the chicken in a single layer and sprinkle both sides with salt and pepper. Set aside while the oven preheats.

2 BOIL WATER FOR THE EGGS

Place the water in a medium saucepan over high heat, cover, and bring to a rolling boil.

Total time: 40–60 minutes (plus 8–10 hours for slow cooker potatoes)
Tools: rimmed baking sheet, slow cooker, pint-size Mason jar, stick blender, food processor, spiralizer, colander, 2 timers

3 START THE POTATOES

Scrub the potatoes.

To bake: Place the potatoes directly on the oven rack when the oven is preheated.

To slow cook: Place the potatoes in the slow cooker on low for 8–10 hours.

To boil: Peel and cut the potatoes into 2-inch chunks, place them in a large sauce-pan, and cover them with cold water. Add 2 teaspoons salt, bring to a boil over high heat, then reduce heat to low and simmer about 20 minutes, until a knife slides easily into the potato without resistance.

ALERT! Is the oven preheated?

If no, proceed to Step 4.

If yes, slide the tray of chicken into the oven and, if you're baking potatoes, place the potatoes directly on the oven rack. Set a timer for 25 minutes.

ALERT! Is the water boiling for the eggs?

If no, proceed to Step 4.

If yes, proceed to Step 5, then come back to Step 4.

4 SPIRALIZE THE ZUCCHINI

Julienne the zucchini and place the noodles in a colander. Toss them with the salt until the strands are lightly coated. Set the colander in the sink to drain.

Burger Deluxe
p.45

MEAT & POTATOES

the ultimate comfort food

The phrase "meat and potatoes" stands for everything that's good. Who doesn't want to be besties with at least one meat-and-potatoes kinda guy? For centuries, a nutritious meal was defined by roasted meat for strength and tubers for energy. As cooking evolved, so did this basic meal. Meat and potatoes were transformed into classic comfort foods like shepherd's pie and meatloaf with mashed potatoes—then pub menus and food trucks gave us sexy, multiple-napkin, shareable eats like stuffed potato skins, poutine, and street fries.

All recipes serve 2-4
Total time: 20-40 minutes, see
    individual recipes

With these meat-and-potato recipes, you can assemble a satisfying stuffed baked potato or crispy-messy street fries that are paleo approved and crazy-good in under 40 minutes, no deep-frying required. You start by plopping potatoes into the slow cooker and finish by sautéing savory meats and chopping garnishes.

HERE'S HOW IT WORKS:

1. Cook white or sweet potatoes in the slow cooker for 8-10 hours.

2. Choose your potato style: baked, street fries, or home fries.

3. Prep the meat toppings, garnishes, and sauce.

4. Devour.

1 MAKE SLOW COOKER POTATOES

The slow cooker potato is the foundation of these recipes. The advantage of cooking the potatoes in the slow cooker is that it doesn't require your time or attention. You can:

* Cook the potatoes overnight and toss them in the fridge in the morning.

* Cook them during the day while you're going about your business and they'll be ready by dinner time.

A few things to keep in mind:

This technique works for both sweet and white potatoes.

Wash the potatoes, but don't poke, wrap, or otherwise molest them. Just place them in the slow cooker and forget about them for 8-10 hours.

The flesh of the potato turns a caramel color as the potatoes cook. (This Maillard reaction results when starches cook without liquid. *Science!*) This gives the potatoes a slightly dense texture and nutty flavor.

Potatoes that are cooked, cooled, and reheated are an excellent source of resistant starch, so you can feel confident about their nutrition while you snarf their deliciousness. (Resistant starches feed your good gut bacteria to improve insulin resistance and boost immunity.)

For slow cooker potatoes

Place scrubbed white or sweet potatoes in the slow cooker. Cover and cook on low for 8-10 hours. To store for later, place the cooked potatoes in an airtight container in the fridge until you're ready for Step 2.

2 CHOOSE YOUR POTATO STYLE

When the potatoes are tender, it's time to transform them. If you're going to eat them in the stuffed-baked form and you haven't cooled them, you can skip ahead to Step 3. For all other potato styles, follow these instructions. The quantities listed here are for four medium potatoes, so adjust accordingly.

For stuffed baked potatoes

Preheat the oven to 450F and line a rimmed baking sheet with parchment paper. While the oven heats, cut the slow-cooked potatoes in half lengthwise. Place them in a single layer on the baking sheet and cover the pan with aluminum foil. Slide it into the oven—it doesn't matter if the oven temperature hasn't yet reached 450F. While the potatoes reheat, make the meat topping.

For street fries

Preheat the oven to 450F and line a rimmed baking sheet with parchment paper. While the oven heats, cut the cooked potatoes into french fry strips. Place the fries in a large bowl and toss them with 1 tablespoon extra-virgin olive oil until coated. Spread

How to: Meat and Potatoes

1. COOK

slow cooker

2. CUT

hash browns

street fries

baked

3. TOP

vegetables

sauce

at

4. EAT

dinner!

the fries in a single layer on the prepared baking sheet and sprinkle them generously with salt. Slide the pan into the oven—it doesn't matter if the oven temperature hasn't yet reached 450F. Set a timer for 10 minutes and check the fries to make sure they don't burn! While the fries bake, make the meat topping.

A few words about fries: White potatoes get quite crispy and brown with this technique, but sweet potatoes do not. The sweets achieve a caramelized outside and tender inside, but don't get crisp. Just wanted to let you know.

For home fries

Heat 2 tablespoons extra-virgin olive oil in a large, nonstick skillet over medium-high, 2 minutes. While the pan heats, cut the slow-cooked potatoes into ½-inch cubes. Add the cubes to the pan in a single layer. Cook the spuds without stirring until the cubes are golden brown on the bottom, about 5 minutes, then flip them with a large spatula and make another single layer. Repeat this process until the cubes are browned on most sides, about 15 minutes total. Sprinkle the potatoes generously with salt. While the home fries brown, cook the meat topping in another pan.

3 MAKE THE TOPPINGS.

These meat toppings are like a tasting tour around the international food court of your dreams. They combine seasoned proteins with vibrant, fresh garnishes and creamy sauces. The resulting flavors are bold and complex, but the preparations are easy and fast.

BURGER DELUXE

Time: 25–30 minutes
Tools: pint-size Mason jar, stick blender
Best on: white potato

BEEF:
    4 slices nitrate-free bacon
    1 medium sweet onion
    2 cloves garlic
    1 teaspoon salt
    ½ teaspoon ground black pepper
    ½ teaspoon paprika
    1½ pounds ground beef
    1 medium tomato
    ¼ head iceberg lettuce
    dill pickles, pickled jalapeños

GARLIC MAYO:
    1 clove garlic
    1 large egg
    1¼ cup light-tasting olive or
        avocado oil
    2 tablespoons lemon juice
    ½ teaspoon mustard powder
    ½ teaspoon salt

Fry the bacon. Cut the bacon crosswise into ¼-inch pieces. Place the chopped bacon in a large, cold skillet, turn the heat to medium-high, and fry the bacon until it's crisp, about 3–4 minutes. While it cooks, dice the onion; set aside. Peel and crush the garlic and place in a small bowl with salt, pepper, and paprika.

Cook the beef. Remove the pan from the heat and transfer the bacon to a paper towel-lined plate. Remove all but about 1 tablespoon of the bacon fat from the skillet. Reheat the skillet over medium heat and add the onion. Cook until the

onion is translucent, 7 minutes. Add the garlic-spice mix and cook 30 seconds. Add the beef to the skillet and cook, breaking it up with a wooden spoon, until it is no longer pink, 5–7 minutes.

Prep the veggies & mayo. While the beef cooks, dice the tomato, shred the lettuce, and make the mayo: Smash and peel the garlic and place in a pint-size Mason jar. Add the remaining mayo ingredients and whirl with a stick blender until thickened.

To serve, pile the beef on potatoes and top with bacon, raw veggies, and a dollop of mayo.

SAUSAGE & PEPPERS

Time: 20–25 minutes
Tools: nothing special
Best on: white potato

    2 teaspoons extra-virgin olive oil
    1 medium yellow onion
    ½ large red bell pepper
    ½ large green bell pepper
    1½ pounds ground pork
    2 cloves garlic
    1 teaspoon salt
    1 teaspoon dried parsley
    ¾ teaspoon dried Italian herbs
    ¼ teaspoon ground black pepper
    ¼ teaspoon coarse (granulated)
        garlic powder
    ¼ teaspoon paprika
    ¼ teaspoon fennel seeds
    ⅛ teaspoon crushed red pepper
        flakes
    2 tablespoons tomato paste
    ⅓ cup water
    2 ounces Applegate Farms Uncured

POTATO COOKUP TIPS

If you don't have a slow cooker but do have time during a Cookup, all of these methods work well. Use one of these techniques to cook the potatoes, then follow the instructions in Step 2 for stuffed bakers, street fries, or home fries.

Stovetop: Bring salted water and whole, peeled potatoes to a boil, then simmer for 20–30 minutes until a knife can be inserted into the center with no resistance.

Microwave: Wash each potato, poke holes all over it with a fork, wrap it in a paper towel, and microwave it on high for 5–10 minutes, until tender. This works best if you zap the potatoes one at a time.

Oven: Wash the potatoes and bake the potatoes at 425F, directly on the wire rack in the oven, for 45–60 minutes, until a knife can be inserted into the center with no resistance.

MAKE IT A BOWL

When you're not in the mood for potatoes, pile meat and garnishes onto these satisfying, non-starchy alternatives:

* cauliflower rice
* zucchini noodles
* baby spinach
* spring mix

Pork Pepperoni (omit for Whole30)

Prep the veggies. Heat the oil in a large, nonstick skillet over medium-high heat, 2 minutes. While the oil heats, slice the onion and cut the bell peppers into ¼-inch strips. Add the onion and peppers to the pan and cook until they are crisp-tender, 2 minutes. Transfer the veggies to a bowl.

Cook the pork. Return the pan to medium-high heat and add the pork to the skillet, breaking it up with a wooden spoon. While the pork cooks, peel and mince the garlic, then place it in a small bowl with the salt, parsley, Italian herbs, pepper, garlic powder, paprika, fennel seeds, and red pepper flakes; stir with a fork to combine. Add the spices and tomato paste to the skillet; cook for 1–2 minutes, until the tomato paste darkens a bit. Add the water and simmer. While the sauce thickens, cut the pepperoni slices in half. Add the pepperoni to the skillet and stir-fry for 1 minute.

To serve, pile the sausage and peppers on the potatoes, then eat with gusto.

BEEF BURRITO

Time: 20–25 minutes
Tools: pint-size Mason jar, stick blender
Best on: white or sweet potato

BEEF:
    2 teaspoons extra-virgin olive oil
    1 medium sweet onion
    3 cloves garlic
    1 tablespoon ground cumin
    1 teaspoon salt
    1½ teaspoons chipotle chile powder
    ½ teaspoon dried oregano
    1½ pounds ground beef
    3 tablespoons tomato paste
    1 (4-ounce) can diced green chiles
    ½ cup water
    a handful pitted black olives
    1 avocado

CUMIN-LIME DRESSING:
    1 clove garlic
    1 large egg yolk
    3 tablespoons lime juice
    ¼ teaspoon salt
    2 tablespoons plus ½ cup light-
        tasting olive or avocado oil
    1 teaspoon ground cumin
    1 tablespoon fresh cilantro leaves
    3-5 pickled jalapeño rings

Cook the beef. Heat the oil in a large, non-stick skillet over medium-high heat, 2 minutes. While the oil heats, finely dice the onion. Add the onion to the pan and cook until translucent, 5–7 minutes. While the onion cooks, peel and crush the garlic and place it in a small bowl with the cumin, salt, chipotle powder, and oregano. Add the beef to the skillet and cook, breaking up the meat with a wooden spoon, until it loses some pinkness. Stir in the spices and cook until fragrant, about 30 seconds. Push the meat to the side of the pan and drop in the tomato paste, frying until it darkens a bit, about 1 minute. Add the green chiles and water and stir. Bring to a simmer over low heat and cook uncovered until thickened.

Prep the garnishes and dressing. While the beef cooks, slice the olives, dice the avocado, and make the dressing: Smash and peel the garlic and place it in a pint-size Mason jar. Add the egg yolk, lime juice, salt, 2 tablespoons of the oil, cumin, cilantro, and jalapeños. Purée with a stick blender until smooth. Then, with the blender running inside the jar, slowly pour in the remaining

Beef Burrito
p. 46

oil until the dressing is smooth and thickened.

To serve, pile the beef on the potatoes, top with olives and avocado, then drizzle with the dressing.

HARVEST

Time: 15–20 minutes
Tools: nothing special
Best on: white or sweet potato

PORK:
- 1 Granny Smith or other tart apple
- 2 teaspoons grass-fed ghee
- 2 tablespoons dried cranberries
- 2 tablespoons dry-roasted pepitas
- 1½ pounds ground pork
- 1 teaspoon salt
- ½ teaspoon ground cinnamon
- ¼ teaspoon powdered ginger
- pinch ground nutmeg
- pinch ground cloves
- pinch ground allspice
- 2 scallions

Cook the apples. Heat the ghee in large, nonstick skillet over medium heat, 2 minutes. While it heats, cut the apple into ¼-inch dice. Add the apple, cranberries, and pepitas to the pan with a pinch of salt and cook until the apples are golden and tender, about 5 minutes. While the apple cooks, mix together the salt, cinnamon, ginger, nutmeg, cloves, and allspice in small bowl; set aside.

Cook the pork. When the apples are done cooking, transfer them to a bowl then place the pork in the skillet, breaking up the meat with a wooden spoon. Add the spices and stir to combine. Continue to cook until the pork is no longer pink. While the pork cooks, slice the scallions and set them aside. Return the apples to

the skillet and stir.

To serve, pile the pork on the potatoes, then top with sliced scallions.

STEAK HOUSE

Time: 20–25 minutes
Tools: nothing special
Best on: white potato

STEAK:
- 2 tablespoons extra-virgin olive oil
- 8 ounces sliced white mushrooms
- 1 medium yellow onion
- 1½ pounds beef sirloin
- 1 teaspoon salt
- ¼ teaspoon ground black pepper
- 1 tablespoon dried chives

Prep the steak. Heat 2 teaspoons of the oil in a large, nonstick skillet over medium-high heat. While it heats, slice the onion and cut the steak into strips. Toss the steak with salt and pepper; set aside.

Cook the mushrooms. Toss the sliced mushrooms into the hot pan with a pinch of salt, and stir to evenly coat them with oil. You'll hear them sizzle! Continue to cook them for 1–2 minutes, stirring frequently, until the mushrooms release their moisture. Cook over medium heat, stirring occasionally, until all the moisture has evaporated and the mushrooms begin to brown, about 5–8 more minutes. Transfer the mushrooms to a plate.

Prep the onions. Add 2 teaspoons of oil to the pan, increase the heat to medium-high, and let it heat for 2 minutes. Add the onion and cook until just crisp-tender, 1–2 minutes. Transfer the onion to the plate

with the mushrooms.

Cook the steak. Add 2 teaspoons of oil to the pan, increase the heat to medium-high, and let it heat up for 2 minutes. Add the steak in a single layer and cook it undisturbed for 2 minutes, then flip it, and cook it for an additional 2 minutes. Return the mushrooms and onion to the pan, add the chives, and toss to mix with the steak.

To serve, pile the steak and veggies on the potatoes.

SLOPPY JOES

Time: 30–35 minutes
Tools: nothing special
Best on: white or sweet potato

- 1 tablespoon extra-virgin olive oil
- 1 medium yellow onion
- ½ medium green bell pepper
- 2 cloves garlic
- 1 teaspoon salt
- ¾ teaspoon chili powder
- ¼ teaspoon ground black pepper
- ¼ teaspoon ground cinnamon
- 1½ pounds ground beef
- 1 cup tomato purée
- ½ cup water
- 2 teaspoons coconut sugar (omit for Whole30)
- 1½ teaspoons cider vinegar
- ¼ teaspoon hot sauce
- 2 scallions

Prep the veggies. Heat the oil in a large nonstick skillet over medium-high heat, 2 minutes. While the oil heats, finely dice the onion and pepper. Add the vegetables to the skillet with a pinch of salt and stir until coated with oil. Reduce the heat to

Spicy Nigerian Beef
p. 50

Chicken Shawarma
p. 53

Cook the chicken. Place 2 teaspoons of the ghee in a large, nonstick skillet and heat over medium-high heat, 2 minutes. In a small bowl, combine the arrowroot, salt, and pepper; set aside. Add the chicken to the skillet and cook, breaking it up with a wooden spoon, until it starts to lose its pinkness, about 3 minutes. Add the spiced arrowroot to the chicken and stir. While the chicken cooks, slice the carrots, celery, and scallions very thinly with a mandoline or the slicing blade of a food processor. When the chicken's cooked, add the hot sauce and remaining 1 tablespoon ghee; stir to combine. Add the carrots and celery to the pan, toss with two wooden spoons to mix, then remove the pan from the heat.

To serve, pile the chicken and veggies on the potatoes, then drizzle with ranch dressing and sprinkle with scallions.

CHICKEN SHAWARMA

Time: 35–40 minutes
Tools: food processor
Best on: white potato

CHICKEN:
- 1 teaspoon extra-virgin olive oil
- 4 boneless, skinless chicken breasts (about 4–6 ounces each)
- ¼ cup water

SPICE BLEND:
- 1 teaspoon salt
- ½ teaspoon ground cumin
- ½ teaspoon ground cardamom
- ¼ teaspoon smoked paprika
- ¼ teaspoon ground coriander
- ¼ teaspoon coarse (granulated) garlic powder
- ⅛ teaspoon ground black pepper
- ⅛ teaspoon cayenne pepper

SALAD:
- ¼ small head red cabbage
- 1 large carrot
- 1 tablespoon lemon juice
- 1 tablespoon extra-virgin olive oil
- ¼ teaspoon salt
- ¼ teaspoon ground black pepper
- a handful fresh mint leaves

TAHINI DRESSING:
- 1 clove garlic
- ⅓ cup tahini
- ⅓ cup water
- 2 tablespoons lemon juice
- pinch salt
- pinch ground black pepper

Cook the chicken. Heat the oil in a large, nonstick skillet over medium-high heat, 2 minutes. While it heats, make the spice blend: mix together all the spices in a small bowl. Rub the spice blend on both sides of the chicken, then place it in the pan and cook it undisturbed, 5 minutes. Flip the chicken and cook for 2 minutes, then add the water, cover the skillet, and reduce the heat to medium-low. Cook until the chicken is no longer pink inside, about 10–15 minutes.

Make the salad. Use the slicing blade on a food processor to thinly slice the cabbage and carrot. Place the vegetables in a large mixing bowl and toss with the lemon juice, olive oil, salt, pepper, and mint; set aside.

Make the tahini dressing: Smash and peel the garlic, then place it in the bowl of the food processor. Add the remaining ingredients and whirl until smooth.

To serve, cut the chicken into thin slices and pile it on the potatoes, then top with salad and drizzle with tahini dressing.

COOKUP TIPS

If you're doing a Cookup, you can prep the meat and garnishes in advance, then bring it all together quickly at meal time.

Full-blast: Cook the meat completely and prep all the garnishes during your Cookup, then when you're ready to eat, reheat the meat in a nonstick skillet over low heat while you finish the potatoes.

Halfway: During Cookup, prep your veggies, garnishes, and sauces. When you're ready to eat, cook the meat according to the recipe and finish the potatoes.

TO REHEAT

PROTEIN
Heat a large, nonstick skillet over medium-high heat. Add your protein to the pan and stir-fry until hot.

POTATOES

Oven: Wrap the potatoes (fries, home fries, or halved, slow-cooked potatoes) in aluminum foil and warm in a 350F oven until heated through. For fries and home fries, you can zap them under the broiler if you want to make them crisper.

Stove: Heat a large, nonstick skillet over medium-high heat. Add the potatoes and cook, mostly undisturbed, until hot.

Hoisin Pork
p. 58

Orange Beef & Walnut
p. 58

Velvet Stir-Fry

Cashew Chicken, p. 58

Sesame Beef p. 58

Hoisin Mushroom Chicken
p. 59

Beef & Snap Peas
p. 59

Sesame Pork & Bok Choy
p. 59

Hoisin Shrimp
p. 59

How to: Velvet Stir-Fry

1. VELVET — marinate the meat

2. CUT — lots o' veggies

3. SAUCE — mix the sauce

4. MINCE — garlic & ginger

5&6. HEAT — cook the meat

7. VEGGIES — cook the veggies

8. AROMATICS — cook the garlic — veggies to one side

9&10. STIRY-FRY — add sauce — everything together

EAT!

VELVET STIR-FRY

so satiny, so plush

It's time for some real talk about homemade stir-fry. I'm sure at some point or another you've asked yourself, "Why doesn't stir-fry at home taste as good as the stir-fry at Red Dragon Chinese Restaurant?" Two reasons: (1) No offense meant, but you're probably making a kitchen-sink stir-fry. You know what I mean: It's the one where you throw in all the odds-and-ends of vegetables in your fridge and hope for the best. (2) Restaurant cooks probably use corn starch, sugar, soy sauce, and MSG to give their stir-fries that indescribable, unrepeatable *something*.

All recipes serve 2–4
Total time: 25–35 minutes,
    depending on your chopping speed
Tools: pint-size Mason jar

I've got great news for you! With these recipes, I can teach you how to make a stir-fry at home that has a mouth-pleasing texture and tastes bright. It's a stir-fry with more restraint and intention, lightly seasoned with ginger and garlic to let the flavor of high-quality ingredients shine.

The key to a good stir-fry is to quickly cook the ingredients separately, then combine them in a high-heat, high-velocity crescendo. This requires you to prep all the ingredients in advance and then systematically stir fry in the proper order. It's fast and uncomplicated, and the results are even better than a restaurant.

HERE'S HOW IT WORKS:
This is a 10-step process, but each step lasts just a few minutes, and at the end, you will be rewarded with a stir-fry that rivals the colorful plates of your favorite Chinese restaurant.

1 VELVET THE MEAT
This is key! Mix the velveting ingredients in a medium bowl with a fork. Thinly slice your protein—about ¼-inch thick—and toss it in a bowl with the velveting liquid, then set it aside. That's it! (For shrimp stir-fry, leave the shrimp whole.)

VELVETING INGREDIENTS
    2 tablespoons coconut aminos
    1 tablespoon arrowroot powder
    1 teaspoon unseasoned rice
        vinegar
    ¾ teaspoon salt

2 CUT THE VEGGIES
Cut all the vegetables into similar shapes and sizes for consistent cooking. I've recommended shapes in the recipes, but you can slice, julienne, cut into batons or cubes… whatever you like as long as the pieces are the same width and thickness.

3 MAKE THE SAUCE
Combine the sauce ingredients in a pint-size Mason jar and whisk with a fork.

4 PREP THE AROMATICS
Crush the garlic, peel and grate the ginger, and mix in a small bowl with the oil.

5 HEAT THE PAN
Place 1 tablespoon oil in a large, non-stick skillet (or wok) and warm it over medium-high heat, 2 minutes.

6 COOK THE PROTEIN
Add the velveted protein to the pan and cook, undisturbed, 1–2 minutes. Stir and cook another 1–2 minutes. Transfer to plate.

7 COOK THE VEGGIES
Reheat the pan with another 1 tablespoon oil, 30 seconds. Stir-fry the veg until just tender, 1–4 minutes, depending on the vegetables.

8 COOK THE AROMATICS
Push the veggies to the side of the pan, add the aromatics, and stir-fry them for about 15 seconds. Toss the veggies and aromatics together.

9 RECOMBINE
Return the meat to the pan and toss with the veggies.

10 FINAL STIR-FRY
Add the sauce and toss to combine. Stir-fry until it looks so good you can't wait to eat it, 30–90 seconds.

Blueberry Pie Salad
p. 62

THE ULTIMATE SALAD BAR

lettuce romaine friends forever

Ever wondered why salads in a restaurant taste better than the ones you make at home? (I mean besides the obvious: Everything tastes better when someone else makes it for you.) It's probably because the salads in restaurants are made with intention—deliberate choices about ingredients and dressings. Like a sculpture, a novel, or a compelling argument, a memorable salad is as much about what you leave out as what you put in.

And, believe it or not, there is technique involved. It *looks* like all you need to do is throw fresh ingredients in a bowl and call it done, but a salad with impact requires a few specific—but very easy—tricks.

I've compiled 10 tips to help you edit your salads and toss them like a pro. Your vegetable creations will embody mouth-pleasing contrasts in texture and flavor, take advantage of surprising ingredients, and employ the perfect amount of salt, a.k.a. the chef's secret to an fantastic salad. This section also includes six salad dressing recipes and 25 salad combo ideas—it's the ultimate salad bar, in *your* kitchen.

1 WASH AND DRY THE GREENS

Yes, even if you buy the pre-washed greens, you need to wash them. The best way to wash is in your salad spinner! Place the greens in the spinner, cover them with cold water, swish the leaves around, and let them soak for a minute (this freshens and crisps them). Lift the strainer basket of greens out of the base bowl, empty and rinse the bowl, then re-assemble it and use the spinner to totally dry the leaves. This is not me being overly-picky: Wet greens don't hold dressing, and that means they don't hold the dressing flavor. No one wants flavor-repelling greens!

2 BECOME A MIX MASTER

Some salads demand one particular type of greens. A Caesar, for example, would feel all wrong without romaine. But it's also appetizing—and nutritious—to mix greens of contrasting flavor and texture. The most intuitive way is to mix light and dark greens: lighter greens like romaine, iceberg, and Boston/butter lettuce tend to be sweeter and pair well with the mildly bitter or peppery taste of darker greens like spring mix, watercress, and baby spinach.

3 USE A BIGGER BOWL

Salads taste best when every element is lightly coated in dressing, and the easiest way to achieve that is to toss in a large bowl. Lots of surface area means lots of room for the elements of your salad to jostle against each other and roll in the oil of the dressing.

4 EMBRACE CONTRASTS

In salads, as in romance, opposites attract. You'll love your salads if you balance ingredients that are hot and cold, sweet and savory, chewy and crunchy. You can also change the mouth-feel of the ingredients with the size and shape of the cuts: shaved versus chopped versus thinly sliced. A chopped salad—all ingredients chopped to ¼-inch dice—is one of my favorites.

5 GO RAW (AND COOKED)

We tend to think of salads as piles of raw veggies, but roasted, grilled, or caramelized vegetables are sweeter and more yielding than their raw counterparts and are welcome additions to raw greens. Try warm roasted Brussels sprouts or butternut squash with dark greens and cool sliced apples—or hot, golden sautéed mushrooms and/or caramelized onions with baby spinach and cold sliced steak.

6 PUT THE DRESSING IN THE BOWL

This might blow your mind because you've probably been doing the opposite your entire salad-eating life: Place dressing in the bottom of the salad bowl before tossing, rather than drizzling dressing over the top. When dressing is in the bottom, you essentially roll the ingredients through a dressing bath with each toss—much more effective than when the dressing gets stuck in the nooks and crannies of the ingredients in the top-down method.

Sesame-Ginger

Greek Lemon

"Good Seasons" Italian

Creamy Italian

Smoky Peach

SALAD DRESSINGS

These dressings all make enough for several salads and can be stored for 7–10 days in an airtight jar in the fridge before they start to lose their freshness. Use them on whatever salad combos you like, or check out the 25 Super Salad Combos (p. 66) for specific ideas.

"GOOD SEASONS" ITALIAN DRESSING

- 1½ teaspoons coarse (granulated) garlic powder
- 1½ teaspoons coarse (granulated) onion powder
- 1½ teaspoons dried parsley
- 1½ teaspoons salt
- 1½ teaspoons dried oregano leaves
- ½ teaspoon ground black pepper
- ½ teaspoon dried basil leaves
- ¼ teaspoon dried thyme leaves
- ⅛ teaspoon celery seeds
- 2 tablespoons water
- ¼ cup red wine vinegar
- ⅔ cup extra-virgin olive oil

In a pint-size Mason jar, combine the dry spices, water, and vinegar; whirl with a stick blender until combined; the liquid will turn opaque and a little frothy. With the blender running inside the jar, slowly add the oil and blend until emulsified.

SMOKY PEACH VINAIGRETTE

- 4 slices canned peaches, packed in juice
- ¼ cup unseasoned rice vinegar
- 1 tablespoon water
- ½ teaspoon smoked paprika
- 1 clove garlic
- ¼ cup fresh parsley
- ⅛ teaspoon salt
- pinch ground black pepper
- ¼ cup extra-virgin olive oil

Smash and peel the garlic and place in a pint-size Mason jar. Add the remining ingredients except the oil and whirl with a stick blender until smooth. Then, with the blender running inside the jar, slowly add the oil until combined.

TAHINI-GARLIC DRESSING

- 1 clove garlic
- ¼ cup fresh parsley
- ¼ cup water
- 3 tablespoons tahini
- 2 tablespoons lemon juice
- 1 tablespoon coconut aminos
- 1 tablespoon minced chives
- 1 teaspoon cider vinegar
- 1 teaspoon honey (omit for Whole30)
- ¼ teaspoon salt
- ⅛ teaspoon ground black pepper
- ⅓ cup extra-virgin olive oil

Smash and peel the garlic clove and place it in a pint-size Mason jar. Add the remaining ingredients except the oil and whirl with a stick blender until smooth. Then, with the blender running inside the jar, slowly add the oil until combined.

CREAMY ITALIAN DRESSING

- 1 clove garlic
- 1 large egg yolk
- 2 tablespoons plus ½ cup light-tasting olive or avocado oil
- 2 tablespoons red wine vinegar
- 1 tablespoon lemon juice
- 1 tablespoon dried Italian herb blend
- ¼ teaspoon salt
- ⅛ teaspoon ground black pepper

Smash and peel the garlic clove and place it in a pint-size Mason jar. Add the egg yolk, 2 tablespoons of the oil, the vinegar, lemon juice, Italian herb blend, salt, and pepper. Whirl with a stick blender until puréed, then with the blender running inside the jar, add the remaining ½ cup oil and blend until thickened.

SESAME-GINGER DRESSING

- 3 cloves garlic
- 1-inch piece fresh ginger
- 4 scallions
- ¼ cup coconut aminos
- 2 tablespoons unseasoned rice vinegar
- 2 teaspoons toasted sesame oil
- 2 teaspoons maple syrup (omit for Whole30)
- ⅓ cup light-tasting olive or avocado oil

Smash and peel the garlic cloves and place them in a pint-size Mason jar. Peel and chop the ginger and slice the scallions; add them to the jar. Pour the coconut aminos, rice vinegar, sesame oil, and syrup into the jar. Whirl with a stick blender until puréed and a little frothy. Then, with the blender running inside the jar, add the oil and blend until smooth.

GREEK LEMON VINAIGRETTE

- 1 clove garlic
- 2 tablespoons red wine vinegar
- grated zest and juice of 1 lemon
- 2 teaspoons dried oregano
- 1 teaspoon coconut sugar or honey (omit for Whole30)
- ½ teaspoon salt
- ¼ teaspoon ground black pepper
- ½ cup extra-virgin olive oil

Smash and peel the garlic clove and place it in a pint-size Mason jar. Add the vinegar, lemon zest, lemon juice, oregano, sugar,

KOREAN BEEF WITH KIMCHI RELISH

K is for kimchi

This recipe is a riff on Korean BBQ, which is usually cooked on a table-side grill. To keep it fast and simple any time of year, I opted for pan cooking, but you could fire up the grill for a more leisurely cookout vibe. The strips of beef are made spicy and special with a piquant relish of kimchi and sweet pear. When it's doused with the creamy sauce, the whole shebang becomes a study in delicious contrasts: hot/cool, spicy/sweet, crispy/tender.

BEEF:
- 3 cloves garlic
- 3 tablespoons coconut aminos
- 1 tablespoon toasted sesame oil
- 1½ pounds skirt or sirloin steak
- 8 scallions

RELISH:
- 1 cup kimchi
- 1 firm pear
- 1 tablespoon toasted sesame oil

SPICY SAUCE:
- 2 cloves garlic
- 1 large egg yolk
- 2 tablespoons plus ½ cup light-tasting olive or avocado oil
- 1 tablespoon lemon juice
- 1 tablespoon hot sauce
- 1 teaspoon coconut aminos
- ¼ teaspoon salt

Marinate the meat Peel and crush the garlic; place in a medium bowl with the coconut aminos and sesame oil; whisk to combine. Slice the steak across the grain into ¼-inch-wide strips and add them to the marinade. Toss to coat and set aside at room temperature while you prepare the other ingredients.

Prep the relish. Coarsely chop the kimchi and core and cut the pear into ¼-inch dice. Place both in a medium bowl, add the sesame oil, and toss to combine. Set aside.

Make the sauce. Smash and peel the garlic cloves and place them in a pint-size Mason jar. Add the egg yolk, 2 tablespoons olive oil, the lemon juice, hot sauce, coconut aminos, and salt to the jar and whirl with the stick blender until puréed. With the blender running inside the jar, add the remaining ½ cup oil and blend until thickened.

Cook the meat. Heat a large, nonstick skillet over high heat, 2 minutes. Remove the steak from the marinade with tongs and place it in the hot pan in a single layer—you will need to do this in at least 2 batches. Cook undisturbed for 1 minute, then flip and brown the other side. Transfer the cooked meat to a bowl and repeat until all the meat is browned. While the meat browns, split the scallions lengthwise and cut into 2-inch-long batons. Pour any remaining marinade into the skillet, add the scallions, and toss them vigorously in the pan to scrape up any brown bits. Add the scallions to the bowl with the meat and toss to combine.

To serve, place the meat on a plate, top with relish, and drizzle with sauce.

Serves 2–4
Total time: 30–35 minutes
Tools: pint-size Mason jar, stick blender

YOU KNOW HOW YOU COULD DO THAT?
This is crazy-good on street fries, so if you have some slow-cooker potatoes on hand (p. 43), go for it. You could also turn this into tacos by wrapping the meat in butter lettuce leaves.

COOKUP TIPS
You can marinate the meat overnight. The relish and spicy sauce will hold up in the fridge in separate airtight containers for up to 5 days.

SICILIAN CAULIFLOWER WITH BEEF

a simple, savory secondi

With its vinaigrette-style dressing and simple preparation, this recipe flirts with being a salad. But to think of it as such is to do it a disservice. It's rustic, sure, but the flavors are simultaneously complex and comforting. Sicilian cooks love cauliflower—pairing it with pasta, olives, and anchovies—and their cuisine incorporates Arab influences like nuts and raisins, embracing the allure of sweet-savory contrasts. If you can find it, the pale green cauliflower from the farmers' market is the most similar to the variety found in Sicily, but any kind will do.

Serves 2–4
Total time: 25–30 minutes
Tools: rimmed baking sheet, pint-size Mason jar, stick blender

CAULIFLOWER:
1 large head cauliflower
1 tablespoon extra-virgin olive oil
1 teaspoon salt

DRESSING:
2 cloves garlic
2 anchovy fillets
⅛ teaspoon crushed red pepper flakes
2 tablespoons red wine vinegar or balsamic vinegar
3 tablespoons extra-virgin olive oil
½ cup fresh parsley

BEEF:
3 tablespoons pine nuts
1½ pounds ground beef
1 teaspoon salt
½ teaspoon ground black pepper
¼ cup raisins or currants
½ lemon

Preheat the oven to 450F.

Roast the cauliflower. Separate the cauliflower into florets and toss them with the oil and salt. Spread them in single layer on a baking sheet and roast until brown in some spots, but still crunchy, 10–15 minutes. Meanwhile...

Make the dressing. Smash and peel the garlic. Place the garlic, anchovies, red pepper flakes, red wine vinegar, olive oil, and parsley in pint-size Mason jar and blend with a stick blender. Set aside.

Cook the beef. Heat a large, nonstick skillet over medium heat. Toast the pine nuts in the pan until golden brown, 4–5 minutes. Transfer the pine nuts to a large mixing bowl. Return the skillet to the stove and increase the heat to medium-high. Crumble the ground beef into the skillet and cook, breaking up the meat with a wooden spoon. Season with the salt and pepper and add the raisins; cook until the meat is no longer pink. Transfer the meat to the mixing bowl with the pine nuts and cover with aluminum foil. Cut the ½ lemon into wedges.

Bring it home. When the cauliflower is done roasting, add it to the bowl with the meat. Add the dressing and toss to coat everything with flavor.

To serve, spoon the cauliflower and beef into bowls and spritz with fresh lemon juice.

YOU KNOW HOW YOU COULD DO THAT?
Replace the ground beef with ground pork or lamb.

COOKUP TIPS
Roast the cauliflower and make the dressing in advance; store both in separate airtight containers in the fridge. When it's time to eat, cook the meat, adding the cauliflower to the pan when the meat is browned. Cook until heated through, then toss with dressing and serve.

BEEF MILANESA WITH PEACH SALSA AND SPINACH

crispy, crunchy cutlets

Milanesa is a popular dish in Latin American countries, but just about every cuisine has its own version of breaded meat cutlets fried to crisp perfection. In the United States, we've got chicken-fried steak, and there's Austrian Wiener Schnitzel, Italian scaloppine, and Japanese tonkatsu. No matter what name you apply, it's irresistible. This version uses a small amount of paleo-friendly starch and a pan sauté to create a crisp crust. The bold, colorful peach salsa on top? That's just bonus awesome.

SALSA:
- 1 (14.5-ounce) can sliced peaches, packed in juice
- 1 cup cherry tomatoes
- ¼ medium red onion
- 1 clove garlic
- ¼ cup fresh mint leaves
- ½ jalapeño
- 1 tablespoon lime juice
- 1 tablespoon extra-virgin olive oil

BEEF:
- 1 large egg
- ½ cup tapioca starch or arrowroot powder
- 1 teaspoon salt
- 1 teaspoon ground black pepper
- 1–2 tablespoons extra-virgin olive oil
- 4 thin-cut slices beef top round or sirloin (1½ pounds)
- 1 (5-ounce) package baby spinach

Make the salsa. Drain the peaches over a bowl to catch the juice and set the juice aside. Cut the peaches into ½-inch dice and slice the tomatoes in half; place in a large mixing bowl. Finely mince the onion, garlic, mint leaves, and jalapeño; add them to the peaches. Add the lime juice, 1 tablespoon peach juice, and olive oil. Toss gently with a rubber scraper to combine.

Make the beef. In a shallow bowl, beat the egg; set aside. In a second shallow bowl, mix together the tapioca starch, salt, and pepper with a fork. Place 1 tablespoon olive oil in a large, nonstick skillet and heat it over medium-high heat, 2 minutes. While the oil heats, dip the beef slices in the egg, one at a time, then dredge each in the tapioca. Cook the beef on both sides, about 3 minutes per side, until well browned and sizzling.

To serve, divide the baby spinach leaves among individual plates, top with the hot beef milanesa, and spoon peach salsa over the top.

YOU KNOW HOW YOU COULD DO THAT?

Use fresh peaches in summer, if you're lucky enough to have them. You can also replace the beef with thin-cut pork or chicken cutlets. Make it Italian with marinara sauce instead of peaches, or top it with a fried egg for Argentinian flair.

Serves 2–4
Total Time 30–35 minutes
Tools: nothing special

Weird
p. 81

Breakfast
p. 81

Hawaiian
p. 80

Apple Pie
p. 81

Tropical
p. 80

Sweet & Savory
p. 81

Burger Night

California
p. 80

Greek
p. 82

How to: Burger Night

1. CUT

veggies

2. SHAPE

make an indent with your thumb!

3&4. COOK

hot pan

delicious toppings

5&6. EAT!

BUT NOT IN ONE BITE...

that would be rude to the cook.

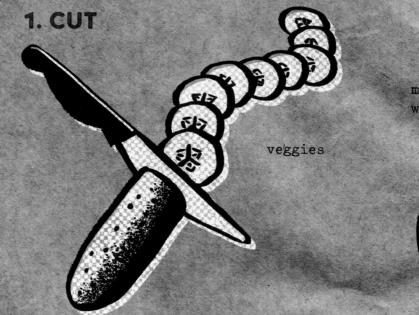

BURGER NIGHT

I'm into fitness*

Hamburgers are the quintessential American food: easy to cook, filling, portable, and equally appealing to kids and adults. With these recipes, we're ditching the bun and going back to the hamburger's German roots. The original Hamburg steak was popularized in the city of Hamburg, way back in the early 1700s. Crafted from ground beef—sometimes with the addition of eggs, bread, or onions—it was roasted or fried in a little butter.

Which bring us to this collection of ground meat patties heaped with globally-inspired toppings: crisp vegetables and fruits, smoked meats, fresh herbs, and creamy sauces. Think of it as a revolution in burger-dom, an uprising against the nutritional wasteland of the bun, and a return to the proud roots of quality meat cooked to juicy perfection.

HERE'S HOW IT WORKS:

1. Cut raw veggies.
2. Season and shape burgers.
3. Brown the burgers and prep the toppings.
4. Flip the burgers and continue to prep the toppings.
5. Rest the burgers and finish the toppings.
6. Eat!

1 CUT RAW VEGGIES.

2 large carrots
2 large stalks celery
1 large seedless cucumber
2 bell peppers

Wash the veggies and cut them into eye-pleasing shapes.

2 SEASON AND SHAPE BURGERS.

1½ pounds ground beef
1 teaspoon salt
½ teaspoon ground black pepper

Divide the ground meat into four equal 6-ounce portions and loosely shape each portion into a ball. Gently flatten the ball into a 4½-inch-wide patty, about ¾ inch thick. Try not to overwork the meat; just pat it gently and quickly into shape. Press your thumb into the center of each patty to make a ½-inch-deep indentation. This prevents them from turning into bulbous hockey pucks when they cook. Sprinkle the patties on both sides with salt and pepper, then move on to Step 3.

3 BROWN THE BURGERS AND PREP THE TOPPINGS

On the stove: Heat a little extra-virgin olive oil in a nonstick skillet over medium heat for 2 minutes. Add the patties, indentation-side up, and cook until brown, about 4 minutes. Flip the burgers with a spatula and continue to cook: about 3 minutes for rare, 4 minutes for medium, 5 minutes for well done.

On the grill: Preheat a gas grill with all burners on high and the lid closed for 15 minutes. Grill the patties, uncovered, until they're seared on one side, about 3 minutes. Flip and continue to grill: 3 minutes for rare, 4 minutes for medium, 5 minutes for well done.

In the oven: Line a rimmed baking sheet with parchment paper. Preheat the oven to 400F, then bake the patties for 20 minutes or until brown and cooked to your liking.

PRO TIP: Slide a spatula under the burger: If it releases easily from the pan or grill, it's time to flip. If it's stuck, let it keep cooking.

4 CONTINUE TO PREP THE TOPPINGS

While the burgers cook, prep the toppings. See the recipes on the pages that follow for ingredients and instructions.

5 REST THE BURGERS AND FINISH THE TOPPINGS

When the burgers are done cooking, let them rest about 5 minutes before adding toppings and eating. This allows the juices to redistribute throughout the meat. You will be rewarded for your patience!

6 EAT!

Serve the burgers on a plate with crudité—forks optional.

* fit'ness this burger in my mouth

DINER-STYLE CHOPPED STEAK

Craving a more traditional chopped steak dinner? This recipe is inspired by the retro-cool chopped steaks found on the menus of roadside diners. Serve these meaty patties alongside cauliflower mash (p. 123) and your favorite green veggie for an old-school dinner.

- ½ medium sweet onion
- 1 ½ pounds ground beef
- 2 large eggs
- ½ cup almond flour
- 1 tablespoon coconut aminos
- 1 teaspoon salt
- ½ teaspoon ground black pepper

Grate the onion into a large mixing bowl, then add the remaining ingredients. Mix with your hands until just combined, then shape into four oval-shaped patties, about 1/2-inch thick. Fry in a large nonstick skillet over medium-high heat for 5-7 minutes per side.

DINER LINGO

"Burn one, take it through the garden and pin a rose on it." (Make a burger with lettuce, tomato, and onion.)

"Gimme a hockey pock." (I'd like my burger well done, please.)

HAMBURGERS! THE CORNERSTONE OF ANY NUTRITIOUS BREAKFAST. -QUENTIN TARANTINO

to medium-high, and fry the bacon until it's crisp, 3–4 minutes. While it cooks, peel, core, and slice the apples. When the bacon is ready, transfer it to paper towels to drain. Add the apples to the skillet and toss to coat them with the bacon fat. Add the apple pie spice, lemon zest, and salt. Stir-fry until the apples are tender, about 5 minutes. While the apples cook, chop the pecans. Add the bacon and pecans to the pan and toss to combine.

MAPLE MUSTARD:
- ¼ cup Dijon mustard
- 2 tablespoons maple syrup (omit for Whole30)

Whisk mustard and syrup together in a small bowl until smooth.

To serve, pile some fried apples on top of each burger and drizzle it with the maple mustard.

GREEK

Tools: pint-size Mason jar, stick blender
YKHYCDT: ground lamb

OLIVE-TOMATO RELISH:
- ¼ cup pitted black olives
- 1 medium tomato
- pinch salt
- pinch dried oregano leaves

Cut the olives in half and dice the tomato. Mix all the ingredients in a small bowl and set aside.

TZATZIKI:
- 1 clove garlic
- 1 large egg yolk
- 2 tablespoons plus ½ cup light-tasting olive or avocado oil
- 2 tablespoons lemon juice
- ¼ teaspoon salt
- 1 medium seedless cucumber
- ¼ medium sweet onion
- ⅓ cup fresh mint leaves

Smash and peel the garlic clove and place it in a pint-size Mason jar. Add the egg yolk, 2 tablespoons of the oil, the lemon juice, and salt to the jar. Whirl with the stick blender until puréed. Then, with the blender running inside the jar, pour in the remaining ½ cup oil and blend until smooth.

Dice the cucumber and mince the onion and mint; place them in a medium mixing bowl. Add a few spoonfuls of the garlic mayo and gently mix with a spatula. Store any leftover garlic mayo in the fridge.

To serve, spoon some olive-tomato relish on top of each burger, then add a dollop or two of tzatziki.

Sweet and Savory
p. 81

BBQ MEATBALLS AND SESAME COLESLAW

a tiny taste of Texas

When I lived in Austin, Texas, eating BBQ was a weekly event. There were in-town joints for quick fixes, but my favorite was The Salt Lick BBQ out in the Hill Country. The meat is slow-smoked and literally falls apart when poked with a fork. But beyond the meat, I fell in love with their sesame coleslaw. The founder's wife is Hawaiian, and he combined her food traditions with his to make The Salt Lick a special place.

Serves 2–4
Total time: 40–45 minutes
Tools: rimmed baking sheet, 2-quart baking dish, food processor or mandoline

MEATBALLS:
  1½ pounds ground beef
  1 teaspoon salt
  ½ teaspoon ground black pepper
  ½ teaspoon paprika
  ½ teaspoon ground cumin
  ¼ teaspoon onion powder
  2 tablespoons warm water
  ½ teaspoon cream of tartar
  ¼ teaspoon baking soda

BBQ SAUCE:
  1 cup tomato sauce
  2 tablespoons cider vinegar
  ½ cup unsweetened apple sauce
  1 tablespoon coconut aminos
  1 tablespoon maple syrup (omit for Whole30)
  1 tablespoon Dijon mustard
  ½ teaspoon salt
  ½ teaspoon chili powder
  ½ teaspoon hot sauce
  ¼ teaspoon ground black pepper
  ⅛ teaspoon cayenne pepper
  ⅛ teaspoon ground cinnamon
  ⅛ teaspoon ground cloves
  ⅛ teaspoon ground allspice

SESAME COLESLAW:
  2 tablespoons sesame seeds
  ½ medium head green cabbage
  ¼ cup unseasoned rice vinegar
  ¼ cup white vinegar
  1 tablespoon coconut sugar (omit for Whole30)
  1 teaspoon salt
  ½ teaspoon ground black pepper
  pinch celery seeds
  1 tablespoon toasted sesame oil
  2 tablespoons light-tasting olive or avocado oil
  4 scallions

Preheat the oven to 425F. Line a rimmed baking sheet with parchment paper.

Make the meatballs. In a large mixing bowl, combine the ground beef, salt, pepper, paprika, cumin, and onion powder. In a small bowl or measuring cup, mix the water, cream of tartar, and baking soda with a fork until combined. When it fizzes, add the liquid to the meat and mix with your hands until all the ingredients are evenly distributed.

Roll the meatballs. Moisten your hands and scoop 1 tablespoon of the meat and roll it into a ball between your palms. Line up the meatballs on the prepared baking sheet and place in the oven. Bake 10 minutes. Meanwhile…

Make the BBQ sauce. In a medium bowl, whisk together all of the sauce ingredients. Pour the sauce into the baking dish. When the meatballs have baked for 10 minutes, remove them from the oven and transfer to the dish with the sauce. Roll them to coat with the sauce and return to the oven for 10–15 minutes, until the sauce is bubbly. Meanwhile…

Make the slaw. Heat a large, nonstick skillet over medium heat and toast the sesame seeds for 3–5 minutes; set aside. Use the slicing blade of a food processor to shred the cabbage. In a large bowl, whisk together the vinegars, sugar, salt, pepper, and celery seeds. Continue to whisk as you add the sesame oil and olive oil. Slice the scallions and add them to the bowl, along with the cabbage. Toss well, add the sesame seeds, and toss again.

To serve, tuck the meatballs next to a pile of slaw and drizzle with extra BBQ sauce.

YOU KNOW HOW YOU COULD DO THAT?
Use ground pork, chicken, or turkey—or a combo!—in place of the beef.

COOKUP TIPS
Make the BBQ sauce, bake the meatballs, then combine them in an airtight container. Cut the veggies for the slaw. Store everything in the fridge. To cook, place the meatballs and sauce in a baking dish, cover with aluminum foil, and bake at 400F until hot. While the meatballs bake, toss the slaw with the dressing.

GROUND BEEF & GRAVY WITH RICE

school lunch grows up

When I was a kid, our elementary school lunch menus were a collection of weird combos and overcooked vegetables. No pizza day was complete without a plateful of baked beans alongside the frozen pizza, and I probably shouldn't elaborate too much on Tuna Surprise. But I looked forward to lunch when Ground Beef and Gravy was on the schedule. Gloppy, saucy, and kind of bland in a good way, it was a comfort in the middle of the day. This version is seasoned just right with thyme and the umami of coconut aminos, and it's as reassuring as afternoon naptime.

Serves 2–4
Total time: 25–30 minutes
Tools: food processor

CAULIFLOWER RICE:
- 1 large head cauliflower
- 1 tablespoon extra-virgin olive oil
- ¾ teaspoon salt

GROUND BEEF & GRAVY:
- 2 teaspoons extra-virgin olive oil
- ½ medium sweet onion
- 3 tablespoons potato starch or arrowroot powder
- 1 teaspoon salt
- ½ teaspoon ground black pepper
- ⅛ teaspoon dried thyme leaves
- 1½ pounds ground beef
- 2 cloves garlic
- ¾ cup water or chicken broth
- 1 teaspoon coconut aminos
- garnish: fresh parsley leaves

Rice the cauliflower. Break the cauliflower into florets, removing the stems. Place the florets in the food processor bowl and pulse until the cauliflower looks like rice, about 10 pulses. You may need to do this in batches.

Cook the rice. Warm the oil in a large, nonstick skillet over medium-high heat, 3 minutes. Add the cauliflower and salt. Toss with two wooden spoons to coat the cauliflower with the oil. Cover, reduce the heat to low, and cook undisturbed for 10 minutes while you prep the meat.

Cook the onion. Place the olive oil in another large, nonstick skillet and warm over medium-high heat, 2 minutes. While the oil heats, very finely mince the onion. Add the onion and a pinch of salt to the pan and cook until the onion is translucent, about 5 minutes. While the onion cooks, combine the potato starch, salt, pepper, and thyme in a small bowl; set aside.

Cook the meat. Crumble the beef into the skillet with the onion and cook, breaking up the meat with a wooden spoon. While it cooks, peel and crush the garlic cloves and add them to pan. When the meat is beginning to lose its pink color, add the starch-spice mixture. Stir to combine, then add the water and coconut aminos. Stir again and simmer, uncovered, until the sauce is thickened and bubbly. Mince the parsley and set it aside.

Finish the rice. Remove the lid from the cauliflower, stir, and let it cook uncovered while the beef gravy thickens.

To serve, divide the cauliflower rice among individual bowls, then top with ground meat and sprinkle with parsley.

YOU KNOW HOW YOU COULD DO THAT?
Make a quasi-Hawaiian-style loco moco: Add a few fried eggs to the top of your ground beef and gravy pile.

COOKUP TIPS
Cook the cauliflower rice and store it in an airtight container in the fridge. Make the arrowroot spice blend. When it's time to eat, reheat the rice and cook the meat and gravy.

MOROCCAN STEAK SALAD WITH FIG & PISTACHIO DRESSING

rock the casbah, rock the casbah

This salad is as pleasing as a major chord, with its slinky dressing—studded with figs and pistachios—and the harmony of orange, cilantro, and red bell pepper. The spice blend on the steak is based on one of the most popular spice blends from my previous cookbooks. Called ras el hanout, it's practically a magic powder, giving everything it touches a seductive spiciness. If you have a commercial blend or homemade ras el hanout on hand, you can use 1 to 1½ teaspoons in place of the spice blend listed here.

Serves 2–4
Total time: 30–35 minutes
Tools: nothing special

SIRLOIN:
2 teaspoons ghee
4 small sirloin steaks, 4–6 ounces each

SPICE BLEND:
1 teaspoon salt
¼ teaspoon ground cumin
¼ teaspoon powdered ginger
¼ teaspoon ground cinnamon
⅛ teaspoon ground coriander
⅛ teaspoon ground black pepper
⅛ teaspoon ground allspice
pinch ground cloves

FIG & PISTACHIO DRESSING:
3 tablespoons ghee
3 tablespoons balsamic vinegar
4 dried figs
2 tablespoons shelled pistachios
1 clove garlic

SALAD:
2 heads butter lettuce
a handful cilantro leaves
½ medium red onion
1 large seedless cucumber
1 medium green bell pepper
1 large navel orange

Cook the steak. Warm the ghee in a large, nonstick skillet over medium-high heat, 2 minutes. While it heats, make the spice blend by combining all the spices in a small bowl. Rub the steaks with the spice blend, and place them in the skillet. Cook undisturbed for 5 minutes, then flip and cook for another 3 minutes. Cover the skillet, reduce the heat to medium low, and cook 5–10 minutes for medium doneness.

Make the dressing. While the steak cooks, place the ghee and balsamic vinegar in a small saucepan over low heat. Dice the figs, chop the pistachios, and peel and crush the garlic, adding each to the saucepan as you go.

Prep the salad. Wash and tear the lettuce into bite-sized pieces. Coarsely chop the cilantro. Thinly slice the red onion, cucumber, and bell pepper. Peel the orange and divide it into segments.

To serve, divide the veggies and orange among individual serving plates. Slice the steak crosswise and place the slices on each bed of greens, then drizzle with the hot dressing.

YOU KNOW HOW YOU COULD DO THAT?

Replace the spice blend, herbs, and nuts with the following seasonings:

Make it Italian:
1 teaspoon dried Italian herb blend; basil instead of cilantro; pine nuts instead of pistachios.

Make it Mexican: ½ teaspoon chili powder, ½ teaspoon ground cumin, ¼ teaspoon ground coriander; add avocado; raisins and dry-roasted pepitas instead of pistachios and figs.

COOKUP TIPS

Make the spice blend and dressing and prep the veggies; store everything separately in airtight containers in the fridge. When it's time to eat, cook the steak and reheat the dressing.

Taco Night

How to: Taco Night

1&2. RICE

3. PLANTAINS

preheat
oven to
425F

roast
rice
20–25 min.

boil plantains
10–12 min.

green
is best

4&5. COOK

EAT!

the
taco meat

DIA
DE LOS
MUERTOS
IS
NOVEMBER
2nd.

but
Taco
Tuesday
is
EVERY
TUESDAY!

TACO NIGHT

every-thing is awesome

I'm not saying you're required to institute Taco Tuesday in your house like President Business does in *The Lego Movie*, I'm just saying it's a pretty damn good idea. Why not turn a regular old week night into a fiesta?! Imagine a good-time party in the kitchen as you all snag a plate and load up on spicy meat, creamy avocado, crunchy pepitas, and a mess of other bunch times. Bonus: The prep is dead-easy. A simple sauté and a little chopping you can serve up colorful bowls of toppings in no time. Serve recruit knife-wielding amigos to assist ('cause you're totally a team).

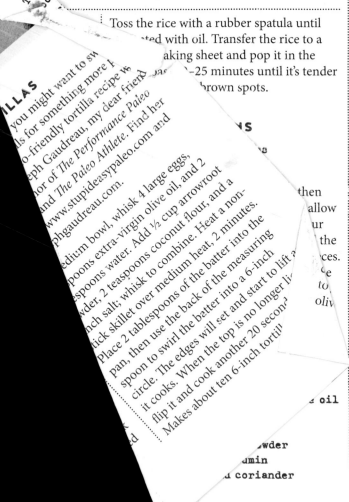

Toss the rice with a rubber spatula until ...ted with oil. Transfer the rice to a ...aking sheet and pop it in the ...-25 minutes until it's tender ...brown spots.

...ILLAS

...you might want to sw... ...s for something more ...-friendly tortilla recipe v... ...ph Gaudreau, my dear frien... ...or of *The Performance Paleo*... ...nd *The Paleo Athlete*. Find her ...www.stupideasypaleo.com and ...phgaudreau.com.

...edium bowl, whisk 4 large eggs, ...spoons extra-virgin olive oil, and 2 ...spoons water. Add ½ cup arrowroot ...der, 2 teaspoons coconut flour, and a ...nch salt; whisk to combine. Heat a non-...tick skillet over medium heat, 2 minutes. Place 2 tablespoons of the batter into the pan, then use the back of the measuring spoon to swirl the batter into a 6-inch circle. The edges will set and start to lift a... it cooks. When the top is no longer li... flip it and cook another 20 secon... Makes about ten 6-inch tortil...

...wder
...min
...coriander

½ teaspoon dried oregano leaves
¼ teaspoon cayenne pepper
1 teaspoon salt
1½ pounds ground beef
2 tablespoons tomato paste
½ cup water
2 teaspoons cider vinegar

Warm the oil in a large, nonstick skillet over medium heat, 2 minutes. While it warms, finely mince the onion. Add the onion to the skillet and cook until softened, about 7–10 minutes. While the onion cooks, peel and crush the garlic, then place it in a small bowl with the chili powder, cumin, coriander, oregano, cayenne, and salt. Add the spices to the onion and cook until fragrant, about 30 seconds.

Crumble the beef into the skillet and cook, breaking up the meat with a wooden spoon, until it is no longer pink, about 5 minutes. Push the meat to the side of the pan and drop in the tomato paste, frying until it darkens a bit, about 2 minutes. Add the water and vinegar to the pan and stir to combine. Bring to a boil, reduce the heat to low, and simmer, uncovered, for 10 minutes or until the liquid has reduced and thickened to your liking. Meanwhile...

5 PREP THE TOPPINGS

½ head iceberg lettuce
a handful fresh cilantro
1 avocado
6 scallions
½ cup pitted black olives
½ cup green olives
1 (8-ounce) can pineapple chunks, packed in juice
1 lime
¼ cup dry-roasted pepitas
your favorite salsa
pickled jalapeño slices (replace with fresh for Whole30)

While the meat simmers, chop the lettuce and cilantro. Dice the avocado. Slice the scallions and black olives. Drain the pineapple. Cut the lime into wedges. Arrange all of the ingredients in individual bowls.

6 COMMENCE TACO NIGHT

When the meat is cooked, transfer it to a serving bowl, then drain the plantains and sauté them in the pan you used for the meat, about 2–3 minutes or until slightly browned. Transfer the cauliflower rice and plantains to serving bowls. Arm your dining partners with plates and dig in!

YOU KNOW HOW YOU COULD DO THAT?

Replace the ground beef with ground pork or turkey, whole shrimp, or white fish.

COOKUP TIPS

Rice the cauliflower, boil the plantains, and prep the taco meat in advance. When it's time to eat, roast the cauliflower rice, reheat the meat, brown the plantains, and prepare the toppings.

TO REHEAT

Heat two large, nonstick skillets over medium-high heat. Reheat the cauliflower rice in one pan and toss the taco meat and plantains into the other. Stir-fry the contents of both skillets until the food is heated through.

TACO NIGHT: IT'S IN YOUR HANDS

There are times when embracing the spirit of Taco Tuesday means putting down the fork and eating with your hands. Here are some nutrient-dense taco shells to add more food fun to Taco Tuesday. They increase your prep time, but some days, it's worth a little extra effort.

JICAMA TACOS

Also known as the "Mexican potato," jicama is crisp and cool once you get past that tough, dusty-brown skin. Choose a small-ish jicama for the best texture, then peel and slice it on the mandoline to create flexible tostoda shells.

BUTTER LETTUCE

The sweet, coolness of the lettuce complements the spicy meat, and the leaves are sturdy enough to handle plenty of toppings.

BELL PEPPER CUPS

Slice off the top of large bell peppers, then cut them in half lengthwise and remove the ribs and seeds. You've got a sturdy, flavorful cup to stuff full of taco goodness.

COLLARD GREENS

Go big! Roll your taco meat and toppings in collard greens to turn Taco Tuesday into burrito night.

GET FUNGI!

Place a little extra-virgin olive oil in a large, nonstick skillet over medium-high heat, 2 minutes. While it warms, remove the stems from Portobello mushroom caps and sprinkle the caps with salt and pepper. Place them smooth-side down in the skillet and cook 5 minutes, then flip and cook them another 1–2 minutes, until brown and tender. Fungi taco shell!

STREET FRIES

Use slow-cooker potatoes (p. 43)—white or sweet—to make oven fries or home fries, then turn them into loaded street fries that are good and good for you.

PALEO TORT

Once in a while
veggie taco she
able. This pale
created by S
and the aut
Cookbook
online at
www.st

In a m
2 tea
tabl
po
p

THAI BASIL BEEF

sour-sweet-salty-bitter-spicy

This easy stir-fry packs a punch of umami flavor, thanks to fish sauce, lime juice, and fragrant basil. Traditional Thai cuisine is built on the interplay of the five fundamental tastes: sour, sweet, salty, bitter, and spicy. Although the ingredients and technique here are pretty straight forward, the result is an explosion of flavor and texture that's anything but simple. This recipe calls for the sweet basil variety you find in most grocery stores, but if you can find Thai basil, use it! You will be so happy.

Serves 2–4
Total time: 35–40 minutes
Tools: nothing special

VEGGIES:
- ⅓ cup water
- ½ pound green beans
- ¾ pound Japanese eggplant
- 2 teaspoons coconut oil
- 1 large red bell pepper
- 4 scallions
- a generous handful fresh basil leaves

BEEF:
- 1½ pounds ground beef
- 1 small jalapeño
- 1 teaspoon salt

SAUCE:
- 3 cloves garlic
- 1 lime
- 1 tablespoon fish sauce
- 2 tablespoons coconut aminos

Cook the beans and eggplant. Heat the water in a large, nonstick skillet over medium heat. While the water heats, wash the vegetables, then cut the green beans in half cross-wise, cut the eggplant into strips, and thinly slice the bell pepper. Increase heat to high, and when the water boils, add the green beans and eggplant to the skillet, cover the pan, and steam the veggies until they're just tender, about 4 minutes. Transfer the vegetables to a large bowl; set aside.

Cook the peppers. Place the coconut oil in the same skillet you used for the beans and warm the pan over medium-high heat, 2 minutes. Add the bell pepper and cook, stirring occasionally, until just soft and beginning to get brown spots, about 2 minutes; transfer the pepper to the bowl with the green beans.

Brown the meat and make the sauce. Return the skillet to the heat and add the ground beef. Slice the jalapeño and add it to the skillet, along with the salt. Cook, breaking up the meat with a wooden spoon, until it's browned and sizzling. Meanwhile, peel and crush the garlic and place it in a small bowl. Squeeze the juice of the lime into the bowl and add the fish sauce and coconut aminos. Whisk with a fork to combine.

Final stir-fry. Return the veggies to the skillet and use two wooden spoons to toss them with the meat. Add the sauce to the pan and stir to coat the meat and veggies. Allow the stir-fry to caramelize while you slice the scallions. Turn off the heat, add the scallions and basil to the pan, and toss to combine.

To serve, divide the stir-fry among individual serving bowls and spritz the top with a little more lime juice for extra punch.

YOU KNOW HOW YOU COULD DO THAT?

Replace the green beans with snow or snap peas, or swap ground pork or chicken for the beef. Place the finished stir-fry in a bowl and add homemade beef broth for quick soup. Garnish your plate with a sliced hard-boiled egg or sprinkle it with crushed cashews. For a quick curry, add 1 cup unsweetened, canned coconut milk to the sauce.

COOKUP TIPS

Steam the raw veggies and make the sauce in advance; store both separately in airtight containers in the fridge. When you're ready to eat, follow the stir-fry instructions.

BACON-JALAPEÑO BALLS WITH EVERYTHING CARROTS

the best of the burger in a ball

These meatballs take all the best parts of a standard diner burger—crispy bacon, spicy jalapeños, juicy beef, secret sauce, seeded bun—and deliver them in an easy-to-make, pop-'em-in-your-mouth meatball. It's a burgers-and-fries combo that makes you feel good, inside and out! The "everything" blend on the carrots works equally well on parsnips or slow cooker potatoes (p. 43).

Serves 2–4
Total time: 45 minutes
Hands-off time: 15 minutes
Tools: 2 rimmed baking sheets, grater, pint-size Mason jar, stick blender

BALLS:
    4 strips nitrate-free bacon
    ¼ medium yellow onion
    ½ medium jalapeño
    1½ pounds ground beef
    1 teaspoon salt
    ¼ teaspoon ground black pepper
    ¼ teaspoon paprika

"EVERYTHING" CARROTS:
    4 teaspoons olive oil
    1½ teaspoon poppy seeds
    1½ teaspoon sesame seeds
    1½ teaspoon caraway seeds
    1 teaspoon coarse salt
    ¼ teaspoon ground black pepper
    3 cloves garlic
    1½ pounds carrots

SPECIAL SAUCE:
    2 cloves garlic
    1 large egg yolk
    2 tablespoons plus ½ cup light-tasting olive or avocado oil
    2 tablespoons lemon juice
    1 tablespoon cider vinegar
    1 teaspoon tomato paste
    ½ teaspoon paprika
    ½ teaspoon mustard powder
    ¼ teaspoon ground cumin
    ¼ teaspoon salt
    ⅛ teaspoon cayenne pepper
    ¼ yellow onion
    ¼ cup pickle slices

Prep. Preheat the oven to 450F and line two large, rimmed baking sheets with parchment paper.

Cook the bacon. Cut the bacon crosswise into ¼-inch-wide pieces. Place it in a cold, nonstick skillet, and fry over medium-high heat until crisp, 3–4 minutes. While it cooks, grate the onion and mince the jalapeño. Remove bacon from the pan and drain on paper towels. Pour the grease out of the pan, leaving whatever clings to it, and return it to the heat. Add the onion and jalapeño to the skillet; sauté until the jalapeño is soft, 1–2 minutes. Set the skillet aside to cool.

Prep the carrots. In a large mixing bowl, combine the olive oil, poppy seeds, sesame seeds, caraway seeds, salt, and pepper. Peel and crush the garlic and add it to the bowl. Cut the carrots into ⅛-inch-thick strips and add to the bowl. Toss until the carrots are coated with seasonings. Spread carrots on a baking sheet and pop it into the oven. Set a timer for 10 minutes.

Roll the meatballs. In a large bowl, combine ground beef, salt, pepper, paprika, bacon, and the cooked onion and jalapeño. Measure a 1-tablespoon scoop of meat and roll it into a ball. Place the meatballs on the second baking sheet. When the timer rings, reduce the oven to 425F and slide the meatballs into the oven. Bake 10–15 minutes, until meatballs are browned and carrots are crisp-tender.

Make the sauce. Smash and peel the garlic cloves and place in a pint-size Mason jar. Add the egg yolk, 2 tablespoons of oil, the lemon juice, vinegar, tomato paste, paprika, mustard powder, cumin, salt, and cayenne. Whirl with a stick blender until puréed. Then, with the blender running inside the jar, add the remaining ½ cup oil; blend until smooth. Mince the onion and pickles, then stir them into the sauce with a fork.

To serve, pile carrots and meatballs on each plate. Drizzle the meatballs with special sauce.

COOKUP TIPS
Prep the carrots, spice blend, meat dough, and sauce; store them in separate airtight containers in the fridge. To cook, toss the carrots with spices, shape the meatballs, and follow the baking instructions.

YUCATAN GREEN CHILE SAUTÉ WITH CUMIN-LIME SAUCE

eat like a Mayan

I grew up in Pennsylvania in the '70s and '80s, and to me, Mexican food was smothered in orange cheese, always included refried beans, and was seasoned with a heavy hand of red chili powder. To be clear: I will go to town on Americanized Mexican food with glee. But a trip to Playa del Carmen and a particularly memorable pumpkin seed salsa made me curious about the more European flavors of the Yucatan. The cuisine marries the influence of the Dutch, Lebanese, and Spanish with local ingredients. This recipe brings together traditional flavors of the peninsula: chiles, pepitas, lime, and cumin.

Serves 2-4
Total time: 30-35 minutes
Tools: pint-size Mason jar, stick blender

SAUTÉ:
- ½ head cauliflower
- 2 teaspoons extra-virgin olive oil
- 1 medium yellow onion
- 1½ teaspoons salt
- 2 cloves garlic
- 1½ teaspoons ground cumin
- 1½ teaspoons smoked paprika
- ½ teaspoon ground black pepper
- ½ teaspoon dried oregano leaves
- 1½ pounds ground beef
- 2 (4-ounce) cans diced roasted green chiles
- 2 tablespoons tomato paste
- 2 teaspoons red wine vinegar
- ⅓ cup raisins
- ⅓ cup dry-roasted pepitas
- a handful cilantro

CUMIN-LIME SAUCE:
- 2 cloves garlic
- 1 large egg yolk
- 2 tablespoons plus ½ cup light-tasting olive or avocado oil
- 3 tablespoons lime juice
- ¼ teaspoon salt
- 1 teaspoon ground cumin
- 1 tablespoon fresh cilantro leaves
- 3-5 pickled jalapeño rings

Rice the cauliflower. Break the cauliflower into florets, removing the stems. Place the florets in the bowl of a food processor and pulse until the cauliflower looks like rice. This takes about 6 one-second pulses.

Prep the seasonings. Warm the olive oil in a large, nonstick skillet over medium-high heat, 2 minutes. While the oil warms, dice the onion. Add the onion to the skillet with a pinch of salt and cook, stirring occasionally, until soft, about 5 minutes. While it cooks, peel and crush the garlic and place in a small bowl with the salt, cumin, smoked paprika, black pepper, and oregano.

Cook the meat. Crumble the beef into the skillet and cook, breaking up the meat with a wooden spoon. When the meat is no longer pink, add the garlic-spice blend to the pan and stir to combine. Add the tomato paste and cook until it darkens, about 2 minutes. Add the vinegar, raisins, pepitas, riced cauliflower, and chiles; stir to combine and reduce the heat to low.

Make the sauce. Smash and peel the garlic cloves and place them in a pint-size Mason jar. Add the egg yolk, 2 tablespoons of the oil, the lime juice, salt, and cumin to the jar. Whirl with a stick blender until smooth. With the blender running inside the jar, add the remaining ½ cup oil and purée until thickened. Mince the cilantro and jalapeño rings and stir them into the dressing with a fork.

To serve, divide the sauté among serving bowls and drizzle with the dressing.

YOU KNOW HOW YOU COULD DO THAT?

Replace the ground beef with pork. If you're a cilantro fan, you could sprinkle the sauté with minced cilantro just before eating—and if you need more fat in your day, avocado is a lovely addition.

COOKUP TIPS

Rice the cauliflower, prepare the spice blend, and make the sauce in advance; store everything in separate airtight containers in the fridge. When it's time to eat, begin with the "Cook the meat" step.

BUFFALO BEEF SALAD

sorta like wings at midnight

During my freshman year of college, a dorm floormate taught me how to apply appropriately goth-y eyeliner, I spent countless hours weaving thread bracelets when I should have been studying, and I nearly bankrupted myself with delivery orders of hot wings in the middle of the night. I'm still a fan of heavy black kohl liner, and bracelets are my favorite accessory, but the midnight wings have been replaced. This salad is an ode to making better choices.

RANCH DRESSING:
- 1 clove garlic
- 1 large egg yolk
- 2 tablespoons plus ½ cup light-tasting olive or avocado oil
- 2 tablespoons lemon juice
- 1 tablespoon fresh parsley leaves
- 1 tablespoon dried chives
- ½ teaspoon paprika
- ¼ teaspoon salt

BEEF:
- 1½ pounds ground beef
- 1 teaspoon salt
- ½ teaspoon ground black pepper
- ½ teaspoon dried thyme leaves
- ¼ teaspoon mustard powder
- 2–3 tablespoons hot sauce

CHOPPED SALAD:
- ½ head iceberg lettuce
- 1 large seedless cucumber
- ¼ medium head red cabbage
- 3 stalks celery
- 2 large carrots
- ½ medium red onion
- 1 tablespoon cider vinegar

Make the dressing. Smash and peel the garlic clove and place it in a pint-size Mason jar. Add the egg yolk, 2 tablespoons of the oil, lemon juice, parsley, chives, paprika, and salt to the jar and whirl with the stick blender until puréed. With the blender running inside the jar, add the remaining ½ cup oil and blend until thickened.

Cook the meat and prep the veggies. Heat a nonstick skillet over medium-high heat. Crumble the beef into the skillet and cook, breaking up the meat with a wooden spoon. When the meat begins to lose its pinkness, add the salt, pepper, thyme, mustard powder, and hot sauce. Stir to combine and continue cooking until the liquid is absorbed and the meat is cooked through. While the meat cooks, thinly slice the lettuce, cucumber, cabbage, celery, carrots, and onion with a mandoline or food processor.

Make the salad. In a large bowl, toss the salad ingredients with the cider vinegar until they're coated.

To serve, place a serving of veggies on each plate, top with a mound of beef, then drizzle with the dressing.

YOU KNOW HOW YOU COULD DO THAT?
Replace the ground beef with ground chicken or turkey.

COOKUP TIPS
Make the dressing and chop the raw veggies in advance and store them in separate airtight containers in the fridge. Cook the meat and put it all together just before eating.

Serves 2–4
Total time: 20–25 minutes
Tools: pint-size Mason jar, stick blender, mandoline or food processor

PICADILLO WITH PLANTAINS

picar is Spanish for "mince" or "chop"

The piquant hash known as picadillo is found in many Latin American countries, and, like many beloved food traditions, each country and cook puts its own spin on the basics of ground meat, tomatoes, and spices. My version is a nod to the Cuban way, with cumin, raisins, and pimiento-stuffed green olives. The meat is often used as a stuffing for fritters, so I turned that idea inside-out and added cubed plantains for a chewy bite of (resistant) starch.

Serves 2-4
Total time: 30-35 minutes
Tools: nothing special

PLANTAINS:
  2 large green plantains
  2 teaspoons salt

PICADILLO:
  2 teaspoons extra-virgin olive oil
  ½ medium yellow onion
  3 cloves garlic
  2 teaspoons ground cumin
  1½ teaspoons ground coriander
  1 teaspoon salt
  ¾ teaspoon ground black pepper
  ¾ teaspoon ground cinnamon
  ⅛ teaspoon ground cloves
  1 bay leaf
  1½ pounds ground beef
  2 tablespoons tomato paste
  ½ cup water
  1 tablespoon red wine vinegar
  ⅓ cup raisins
  ⅓ cup small pimiento-stuffed green olives
  garnish: 1 lime, fresh cilantro, scallions

Boil the plantains. Cut off both ends of each plantain, then with the tip of a sharp knife, make shallow slits lengthwise along the skin. Use your fingers to pry off the strips and discard the skins. Cut the plantains into ½-inch pieces and place them in a saucepan. Add the salt and enough water to cover the plantains by about two inches. Bring to a boil over high heat, then reduce heat to low and simmer until a knife slides into the plantain with no resistance, about 10-12 minutes. Meanwhile…

Make the picadillo seasoning. Warm the oil in a large, nonstick skillet over medium heat, 2 minutes. While the oil heats, finely dice the onion then add to the pan and cook until softened, 7-10 minutes. Peel and crush the garlic cloves and place in a small bowl with the cumin, salt, coriander, pepper, cinnamon, cloves, and bay leaf. Add the garlic-spice mixture to the pan and stir until fragrant, about 30 seconds.

Cook the beef. Crumble the ground beef into the pan and cook, breaking up the meat with a wooden spoon, until it's no longer pink, about 5 minutes. Push the meat to the side of the pan and drop in the tomato paste; fry for 1 minute, stirring constantly. Add the water, vinegar, and raisins; stir to combine. Bring to a boil, then reduce the heat to low and simmer, uncovered, for 3-4 minutes, until the liquid has reduced and thickened. While it cooks, prep the garnishes: cut the lime into wedges, mince the cilantro, and slice the scallions.

Bring it home. Drain the plantains and add them to the meat, along with the olives. Stir to combine and cook for 1-2 minutes.

To serve, divide the picadillo among individual bowls and top with the garnishes.

YOU KNOW HOW YOU COULD DO THAT?

Replace the beef with ground pork, turkey, or lamb.

Make it Puerto Rican style: add capers and cooked potatoes instead of plantains.

Make it Dominican: add hard-boiled eggs.

Make it Filipino: skip the olives and add a fried egg on top of each serving.

COOKUP TIPS

Boil the plantains, make the spice blend, and prep the garnishes in advance. Store everything in separate airtight containers in the fridge. Just before eating, cook the meat and combine with the plantains. If you made cauliflower rice in your Cookup (p. 39), throw some under your picadillo.

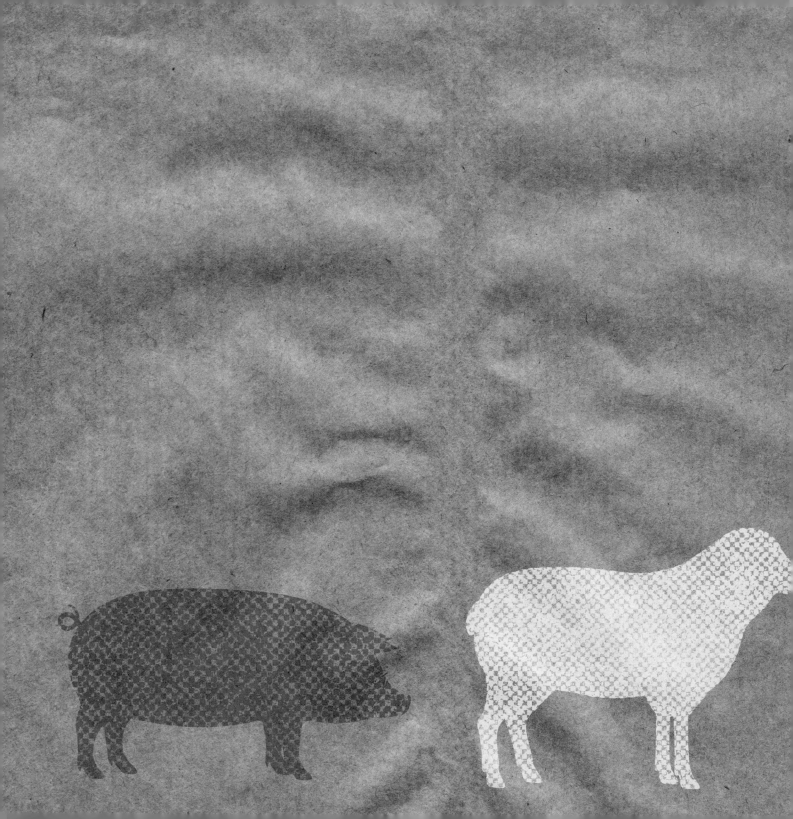

PORK MEDALLIONS WITH BLACKBERRY COMPOTE AND CAULIFLOWER PURÉE

ramble in a bramble

Pork and apples are a classic combination, so I wanted to diverge from the familiar path for something spicier, moodier, and a little syrupy. Blackberries are sweet enough and bring a hint of rose, cedar, and clove mixed with the berriness. When you apply a touch of heat and acid, they acquiesce to become a luxe liquid that's somewhere between a sauce and a glaze. Make a perfect bite—cauliflower mash, pork, and berry compote on the fork all at once—and let the contrasting and complementary textures roll around your tongue.

CAULIFLOWER PURÉE:
- 1–2 cups water
- 1 large head cauliflower
- 2 tablespoons ghee
- ½ teaspoon salt
- ¼ teaspoon ground black pepper

COMPOTE:
- 1 tablespoon ghee
- 2 cups blackberries
- 1 teaspoon arrowroot powder
- 1 teaspoon lemon juice
- ¼ teaspoon powdered ginger
- pinch salt

PORK MEDALLIONS:
- 1 teaspoon extra-virgin olive oil
- 1½ pounds pork tenderloin
- 1 teaspoon salt
- ½ teaspoon ground black pepper

Preheat the oven to 250F.

Steam the cauliflower. Place 1 cup water in a medium saucepan and bring it to a boil. While it heats, coarsely chop the cauliflower. Add the cauliflower to the pan, bring it back to a boil, cover with a lid, and steam it until it's very tender, 10–15 minutes. Check the pan occasionally and add more water, if necessary. Meanwhile…

Make the compote. In a small saucepan, warm the ghee over medium heat, 2 minutes. In a medium bowl, toss the berries with the arrowroot powder, then add the berries, lemon juice, ginger, and salt to the pan. Cook over low heat until the some of the berries have collapsed and the liquid is syrupy, about 10 minutes. While the compote cooks…

Cook the pork. Warm the oil in a large, nonstick skillet over medium-high heat, 2 minutes. While it heats, cut the tenderloin into ½-inch-thick medallions and press them lightly with your palm to flatten them a bit. Season them on both sides with the salt and pepper. Add half the pork to the pan and cook undisturbed 3 minutes, flip and cook the other side, 3 minutes. Transfer the cooked pork to a plate and cover with foil to keep it warm while you cook the remaining pork.

Finish the purée. Add the ghee, salt, and pepper to the steamed cauliflower and purée with a stick blender until very smooth.

To serve, place pork medallions on a bed of cauliflower purée and top with berry compote.

Serves 2–4
Total time: 30–35 minutes
Tools: stick blender

YOU KNOW HOW YOU COULD DO THAT?
Replace the blackberries with raspberries, blueberries, or a mix. You might also toss in a diced fresh peach or apricot!

COOKUP TIPS
Prepare the cauliflower purée and berry compote in advance; store both in separate airtight containers in the fridge. When it's time to eat, reheat the purée and compote while you cook the pork.

GREENS WITH POTATOES & SAUSAGE

slinky and spicy

Confession—This is how I eat most vegetables: I partially steam them and toss 'em in a container in the fridge, and then, when it's time to eat, I throw the cooked vegetables in a pan with hot fat, garlic, and salt. Imagine my delight when I learned there's an Italian term for that kind of cooking! *Ripassare.* Literally, re-passing. The result? Greens that are slinky, not mushy, and a nutritious bed for spicy sausage and tender potatoes.

Serves 2–4
Total time: 30–35 minutes
Tools: nothing special

GREENS & POTATOES:
- 4 medium white potatoes (about 1½ pounds)
- 2 teaspoons salt
- 1 bunch kale (about 1 pound)
- 4 cloves garlic
- 1 cup water
- 1 tablespoon extra-virgin olive oil
- ½ teaspoon crushed red pepper flakes
- garnish: lemon wedges

QUICK SAUSAGE:
- 1 teaspoon dried parsley
- 1 teaspoon salt
- ¾ teaspoon dried Italian herb blend
- ½ teaspoon fennel seeds
- ½ teaspoon crushed red pepper flakes
- ½ teaspoon ground black pepper
- ½ teaspoon coarse (granulated) garlic powder
- ½ teaspoon paprika
- 1½ pounds ground pork

Prep the potatoes. Peel the potatoes and cut them into 1-inch dice. Place them in a medium saucepan, add enough cold water just to cover them, and add the salt. Bring to a boil over high heat, then reduce the heat to low and simmer, uncovered, until the potatoes are tender but not falling apart, about 10 minutes. Meanwhile…

Prep the kale. Remove the tough stems from the kale and cut the leaves into 1-inch-wide strips. Place 1 cup water in a large, nonstick skillet and bring to a boil. Add the kale, cover the pan, and steam until tender, checking it once in a while to stir. While the kale steams…

Make the sausage seasoning. In a small bowl, combine the parsley, salt, Italian herb blend, fennel seeds, red pepper flakes, black pepper, garlic powder, and paprika; set aside. When the kale is tender and the water has evaporated, transfer the kale to a large bowl and set aside.

Cook the sausage. Reheat the same skillet you used for the kale over medium-high heat, 2 minutes. Crumble the pork into the pan and cook, breaking up the meat with a wooden spoon. Add the spices to the pork, stir to combine, and continue to cook until the pork is browned, then add it to the bowl with the kale.

Finish the potatoes. Drain the potatoes in a colander. Smash and peel the garlic cloves; set aside.

Bring it all together. Reheat the skillet over medium-high heat and add 1 the oil, crushed garlic, and red pepper flakes. When the garlic is fragrant, about 30 seconds, add the kale and pork to the skillet. Toss with two wooden spoons to coat everything in oil and cook 1 minute. Add the drained potatoes and toss to combine. Let it cook 2 minutes and taste it, adding additional salt and pepper, if necessary. Toss and cook 1–2 minutes more until it's heated through.

To serve, divide the sauté among individual serving plates and squeeze fresh lemon juice over the top. Drizzle with additional extra-virgin olive oil, if you're feeling fancy.

COOKUP TIPS
Boil the potatoes, wash and cut the kale, and mix and cook the sausage. Store everything in separate airtight containers in the fridge, then follow the instructions to bring it all together.

MOROCCAN CABBAGE SAUTÉ

faster than a tagine

Cabbage is one of my favorite vegetables because when it's cooked just right, it collapses without taking it all the way to mushy, and the flavor goes from nose-crinkling to almost-sweet. This recipe is a fast sauté scented with the perfume of a Moroccan spice market: cumin, cinnamon, coriander, ginger. But these same ingredients can be dressed up with different spices to season this sauté with the local flavors of markets in Italy, Mexico, and Eastern Europe.

2 teaspoons extra-virgin olive oil
1 medium sweet onion
1 teaspoon salt
3 cloves garlic
1 teaspoon ground cumin
1 teaspoon paprika
½ teaspoon ground cinnamon
½ teaspoon ground coriander
¼ teaspoon ground black pepper
⅛ teaspoon powdered ginger
1½ pounds ground lamb
2 tablespoons tomato paste
2 plum tomatoes
½ medium head green cabbage
¼ cup water
garnish: fresh parsley and/or cilantro
    leaves

Cook the aromatics. Warm the oil in a large, nonstick skillet over medium-high heat, 2 minutes. While the oil heats, dice the onion. Add the onion to the pan with a pinch of salt and cook, stirring occasionally, until soft, about 5 minutes. Peel and crush the garlic and place in a small bowl, then add the salt, cumin, paprika, cinnamon, coriander, black pepper, and ginger. Mix with a fork and set aside.

Cook the lamb. Crumble the lamb into the skillet and cook, breaking up the meat with a wooden spoon, until it is just pink, about 3 minutes. While it cooks, dice the plum tomatoes and thinly slice the cabbage. Add the garlic-spice blend to the skillet and stir to combine. Add the tomato paste and cook, stirring often, until it darkens in color, about 2 minutes.

Cook the vegetables. Add the tomatoes, cabbage, and water to the skillet. Stir to combine, then cover with a lid and cook for 4–5 minutes until the cabbage is wilted. Remove the lid, stir-fry vigorously until it begins to dry out and caramelize a bit, about 2–3 minutes. Mince the herbs for garnish.

To serve, spoon the sauté into individual serving bowls and sprinkle with minced herbs.

YOU KNOW HOW YOU COULD DO THAT?

Make these ingredient substitutions and follow the cooking directions above.

Italian: Omit the cumin, paprika, cinnamon, coriander, and ginger; add ½ teaspoon dried Italian herb blend and ¼ teaspoon fennel seeds. Replace ground lamb with ground beef or pork. Garnish with minced fresh basil leaves.

Mexican: Omit the paprika, cinnamon, and ginger; add 1 tablespoon chili powder, ½ teaspoon dried oregano leaves, and ¼ teaspoon cayenne pepper. Replace the ground lamb with ground beef. Garnish with lime wedges and minced fresh cilantro leaves.

Polish: Omit the cumin, cinnamon, coriander, and ginger; add ¼ teaspoon celery seeds. Replace the ground lamb with ground beef. Garnish with minced fresh parsley leaves.

Serves 2–4
Total time:
    25–30 minutes
Tools: nothing
    special

CHINESE BBQ PORK MEATBALLS WITH SNAP PEAS

char siu means "fork roast"

This recipe is like an order of Chinese spare ribs that have been thoughtfully deboned, chopped, and rolled into an amiable, no-chopsticks-needed meatball. The classic Chinese BBQ sauce is usually based on soy and hoisin sauces. This recipe uses just one dried date, a handful of spices, and nut butter to recreate that sticky, tangy-sweet sauce.

Preheat the oven to 450F.

Prep the meatballs. In a large bowl, combine the ground pork, salt, ginger, coriander, and black pepper. Mix well with your hands, then moisten your hands with cold water. and shake them off. With the 1-tablespoon scoop, measure rounded tablespoons of meat, roll it into balls, and place them in the 2-quart baking dish.

Make the sauce. Heat the oil in a medium saucepan over medium-high heat, 2 minutes. While it warms, dice the onion. Add the onion to the pan with a pinch of salt and cook until soft, 5–7 minutes. While the onion cooks, pit and coarsely chop the date, then smash and peel the garlic; set aside. In a small bowl, combine the ginger, Chinese five-spice, salt, red pepper flakes, and black pepper. Add the spices to the onion in the pan and stir-fry for 30 seconds. Add the tomato paste, date, and garlic; stir-fry about 1 minute. Add the coconut aminos, water, sunflower seed butter, rice vinegar, and sesame oil; stir to combine. Simmer 5 minutes, then carefully transfer to a pint-size Mason jar and purée the sauce with a stick blender (or in a food processor or blender).

Make the magic. Pour the sauce over the meatballs and place the pan in the oven. Bake for 20–25 minutes, until the sauce is bubbly and the whole lot is beginning to caramelize.

Make the snap peas. About 5 minutes before the meatballs are ready, heat a large, nonstick skillet over medium-high heat. Add the sesame seeds and stir-fry until golden, 3–5 minutes. Transfer the seeds to a plate to cool and return the skillet to medium-high heat. Wash the snap peas and toss them into the hot pan. Stir-fry until tender, 2–3 minutes. Add the ghee and some of the sesame seeds; toss to coat. Taste and add a little salt and pepper. Thinly slice the scallions and remove the meatballs from the oven.

To serve, divide the snap peas among individual serving plates and top with meatballs; sprinkle with more toasted sesame seeds and the sliced scallions.

YOU KNOW HOW YOU COULD DO THAT?

Replace the ground pork with ground chicken.

Serves 2–4
Total time: 45 minutes
Hands-off time: 15 minutes
Tools: 1-tablespoon scoop, 2-quart baking dish, pint-size Mason jar, stick blender

MEATBALLS:
1½ pounds ground pork
1 teaspoon salt
½ teaspoon powdered ginger
¼ teaspoon ground coriander
¼ teaspoon ground black pepper

SAUCE:
2 teaspoons extra-virgin olive oil
½ medium sweet onion
1 dried medjool date
1 clove garlic
¾ teaspoon powdered ginger
½ teaspoon Chinese five-spice powder
¼ teaspoon salt
⅛ teaspoon crushed red pepper flakes
⅛ teaspoon ground black pepper
2 tablespoons tomato paste
⅓ cup coconut aminos
¼ cup water
2 teaspoons sunflower seed or almond butter
1 teaspoon unseasoned rice vinegar
1 teaspoon toasted sesame oil

SNAP PEAS:
2 teaspoons sesame seeds
1 pound snap peas
2 teaspoons ghee
garnish: a few scallions

COOKUP TIPS

Prep the sauce and store it in the Mason jar in the fridge. When you're ready to eat, roll the raw meatballs and follow the directions, starting with "Make the magic."

SCHNITZEL MEATBALLS WITH PARSLEY POTATOES

(guten tag and guten appetit)

You know how a song you loved as a teenager is somehow always a favorite? I have a similar experience with food. Sixteen-year-old me was a member of the American Music Abroad Choir, a traveling group of singing nerds who performed in red-white-and-blue outfits in town halls across Europe in the summer of 1985. In all of the German-speaking countries we visited, our hosts wanted to serve us a traditional meal, so night after night, we dug into Weiner Schnitzel and french fries at dinner. This recipe is like a (healthier) time machine back to that summer (without the dorky uniform and four-part harmony).

POTATOES:
- 4 medium white potatoes
- 4 cups water
- 2 teaspoons salt
- ¼ cup fresh parsley

MEATBALLS:
- 1½ pounds ground pork
- 1 teaspoon salt
- ½ teaspoon ground black pepper
- 1 tablespoon lemon juice
- ½ cup fresh parsley
- 1 large egg
- 3 ounces pork rinds
- garnish: lemon

Prep. Preheat the oven to 425F and line a large, rimmed baking sheet with aluminum foil (for easy cleanup).

Boil the potatoes. Peel the potatoes and cut them into 2-inch pieces. Place them in a saucepan, add the water and salt, and bring the water to a boil. Reduce the heat to low and simmer, uncovered, until tender, about 15 minutes. Meanwhile…

Prep the meatballs. In a large bowl, combine the ground pork, salt, black pepper, and lemon juice; mince the parsley and add it to the bowl. Mix all the ingredients with your hands until combined.

Crush the pork rinds. You have a choice: (a) Place the pork rinds in a resealable bag, seal it, then smash them with the smooth side of a meat hammer or (b) crush them in a food processor. Transfer the porky dust to a plate or shallow bowl.

Roll the meatballs. Beat the egg in a shallow bowl, then set up your work space with the pork dust, beaten egg, and prepared baking sheet. Measure a rounded tablespoon of meat and roll it into a ball; repeat with the remaining pork, lining up the meatballs on the baking sheet as you go. Next, gently roll each meatball in egg, then pork dust, and return it to the baking sheet. Roast the meatballs until they're sizzling and crisp, 20–25 minutes.

Finish the potatoes. When the meatballs are almost finished, drain the potatoes and toss them with ghee. Mince the parsley and sprinkle it over the potatoes. Taste and add salt and pepper as needed. Cut the lemon into wedges.

To serve, place meatballs and potatoes on individual serving plates, then squeeze lemon juice over the meatballs.

Serves 2–4
Total time: 40–45 minutes
Hands-off time: 10 minutes
Tools: rimmed baking sheet, meat hammer or food processor, 1-tablespoon scoop

YOU KNOW HOW YOU COULD DO THAT?
Replace the ground pork with ground veal.

COOKUP TIPS
Boil the potatoes in advance and store them in an airtight container in the fridge. Gently reheat them in a saucepan with ghee just before eating. To save time, you can use Bacon's Heir Pork Dust instead of crushing your own pork rinds.

VIETNAMESE LAMB WITH SCALLION RICE

it's all about balance

I sing the General Public song "Hot You're Cool" when I make this dish—it's the yin/yang principle in Vietnamese cooking that makes me do it. Vietnamese meals balance the five flavors (sour, bitter, sweet, spicy, salty), colors (green, red, yellow, white, black), nutrients (carbs, fat, protein, minerals, water), and the five senses—all while paying attention to the contrast between hot and cool. In this recipe, "hot" is represented by the pork and jalapeño, while the mint, cilantro, and lime juice are "cool." So cool, they're hot.

SCALLION RICE:
- 1 large head cauliflower
- 4 scallions
- 1 tablespoon extra-virgin olive oil
- ¾ teaspoon salt
- ½ teaspoon ground black pepper

LAMB:
- 1 cup fresh cilantro
- 1 cup fresh mint
- 2 limes
- 1 tablespoon fish sauce
- 1 tablespoon coconut sugar (omit for Whole30)
- ½ teaspoon ground black pepper
- ½ medium jalapeño
- 1½ pounds ground lamb
- 2 cloves garlic
- ¼ cup cashews
- garnish: 1 cucumber, 2 carrots

Preheat the oven to 425F.

Make the cauliflower rice. Break the cauliflower into florets, removing the stems. Place the florets in the food processor bowl and pulse until the cauliflower looks like rice, about 10 pulses. You may need to do this in batches. Thinly slice the scallions and place them in a large mixing bowl. Add the cauliflower, olive oil, salt, and pepper to the bowl. Toss with a rubber spatula until the veggies are coated in oil. Spread the mixture on a large, rimmed baking sheet and pop it in the oven. (It's OK if the temperature hasn't reached 425F yet.) Roast for 20–25 minutes, until the cauliflower is tender and starting to look toasty. Rinse the food processor with water, then slice the cucumber and shred the carrots; set aside.

Prep the lamb seasonings. Coarsely chop the cilantro and mint. Place the herbs in a medium mixing bowl and squeeze the juice from the limes into the bowl. Add the fish sauce, sugar, and pepper. Finely mince the jalapeño and add it to the bowl, then mix with a fork and set aside.

Cook the lamb. Warm a large, nonstick skillet over medium-high heat, 2 minutes. Crumble the lamb into the skillet and cook, breaking up the meat with a wooden spoon, until it is just pink, about 3 minutes. While the lamb cooks, peel and crush the garlic cloves, then add them to the pan; continue to cook until the meat is browned and sizzling. Remove the pan from the heat and add the herb mixture. Stir until combined. Chop the cashews.

To serve, divide the rice among individual serving bowls and top with the lamb and a sprinkling of chopped cashews. Garnish with raw veggies.

Serves 2–4
Total time: 30–35 minute
Tools: food processor, rimmed baking sheet

YOU KNOW HOW YOU COULD DO THAT?
To transform this dish into Thai larb instead, replace the lamb with ground pork, reduce the cilantro and mint to ½ cup each, and add ¼ cup fresh basil leaves.

COOKUP TIPS
Prep the cauliflower rice in advance and store it in an airtight container in the fridge. When it's time to eat, roast the cauliflower rice and proceed with the lamb.

TROPICAL TACOS WITH JICAMA SLAW

it's tiki time

I can hold two conflicting thoughts with equal conviction: I like using language properly, but I have a soft spot for cussing. I prefer to dress in black, but I can't resist the colors pink and orange together. And while I detest hot, humid weather, I'm a sucker for tiki culture and recipes from my vintage Trader Vik cookbooks—which were the inspiration for this recipe. The tacos are a balance of sweet and hot, just like a day on the beach. Don't be frightened of the jalapeño, it's more flavorful than fiery, and the sweet-cool mango, carrots, and jicama keep the spiciness of the pepper in check.

SLAW:
- 1 large carrot
- ½ small jicama
- 1 lime
- ¼ cup fresh cilantro

TACOS:
- 2 teaspoons coconut oil
- 1 medium yellow onion
- 1 medium jalapeño
- 2 cloves garlic
- 1 teaspoon powdered ginger
- 1 teaspoon salt
- ½ teaspoon ground black pepper
- ½ teaspoon ground allspice
- 1½ pounds ground pork
- 1 ripe mango
- 4 scallions
- 1 tablespoon coconut aminos
- 1 head butter or Boston lettuce

Make the slaw. Peel the carrot and jicama. Use the shredder attachment of a food processor to grate the vegetables, then place them in a large bowl. Zest and juice the lime; add to the bowl. Mince the cilantro; add it to the bowl and toss to mix the slaw. Set aside.

Cook the pork. Warm the oil in a large, nonstick skillet over medium-high heat, 2 minutes. While it heats, mince the onion and jalapeño. Add the onion and jalapeño to the pan with a pinch of salt, toss to coat them in oil, and cook until soft, 5–7 minutes. While the onion cooks, peel and crush the garlic, then place it in a small bowl with the ginger, salt, pepper, and allspice. Crumble the pork into the skillet and cook, breaking up the meat with a wooden spoon, until it's no longer pink. While the meat cooks, peel and dice the mango. Add the spices to the meat and stir to combine. Slice the dark green part of the scallions and set aside. Add the mango and coconut aminos to the pan and stir again. Let the meat flavors meld, about 5 minutes, while you wash and separate the lettuce leaves.

Serve the ingredients in big bowls, family style, letting your dining companions make their own tacos with the lettuce leaves.

YOU KNOW HOW YOU COULD DO THAT?
Replace the ground pork with ground chicken or turkey.

COOKUP TIPS
Shred the veggies for the slaw in advance and store them in an airtight container in the fridge. When it's time to eat, add the lime and cilantro to the slaw and cook the pork.

Serves 2–4
Total time:
  30–35 minutes
Tools: grater, food
  processor

DECONSTRUCTED SHEPHERD'S PIE

turn that casserole upside down

Casseroles are the comfie blanket of food, but between us friends, the idea of preparing one on a weeknight makes me feel a little overwhelmed: Cook the components, layer them in a dish, bake them in the oven—it seems like so much work! This recipe is an inversion of a casserole. It takes the essential parts of paleo Shepherd's Pie—creamy mashed cauliflower and lamb seasoned with the herbs of the British Isles—and gets them onto your plate in less than half an hour. No casserole dish or baking required.

CAULIFLOWER MASH:
- ½ cup water
- 1 large head cauliflower
- 2 tablespoons ghee
- ¾ teaspoon salt
- ¼ teaspoon ground black pepper

LAMB:
- 2 teaspoons extra-virgin olive oil
- ½ medium yellow onion
- 1 teaspoon salt
- 1 clove garlic
- ½ teaspoon ground black pepper
- ½ teaspoon dried rosemary leaves
- ¼ teaspoon dried thyme leaves
- 1½ pounds ground lamb
- 1 tablespoon tomato paste
- ½ cup water or chicken broth
- 1 teaspoon coconut aminos

garnish: a handful fresh parsley

Start the mash. Place the water in a medium saucepan and bring it to a boil. Break the cauliflower into florets and add them to the pot, cover with a lid, and steam the cauliflower for about 10 minutes or until tender, adding more water if necessary. Remove the pan from heat, cover to keep hot, and set aside.

Cook the meat. Warm the oil in a large, nonstick skillet over medium-high heat, 2 minutes. While the oil heats, finely dice the onion. Add the onion and a pinch of salt to the pan and cook until the onion is tender and translucent, 5–7 minutes. While the onion cooks, peel and crush the garlic and combine it with 1 teaspoon salt, pepper, rosemary, and thyme in a small bowl; set aside. Crumble the lamb into the skillet and cook, breaking up the meat with a wooden spoon, until it is just pink, about 3 minutes. Add the spices and stir to combine. Push the meat to the side of the skillet and drop in the tomato paste; fry it about 2 minutes. Add the water and coconut aminos, then stir to combine and reduce the heat to low. Simmer, uncovered, until the water is mostly gone and the meat is saucy, about 10 minutes. Meanwhile…

Finish the mash. Place about half of the steamed cauliflower into a food processor bowl and purée until smooth. Add the rest of the cauliflower and purée again. With the motor running, add the ghee, salt, and pepper through the feed tube. Taste and adjust the seasonings. Mince the parsley.

To serve, divide cauliflower mash among individual serving bowls, then top with ground meat and sprinkle with parsley.

Serves 2–4
Total time: 25–30 minutes
Tools: food processor

YOU KNOW HOW YOU COULD DO THAT?

Replace the ground lamb with ground beef (a.k.a. cottage pie), or try the Chilean version called "pastel de papa" by adding raisins, black olives, and chopped hard-boiled eggs to the ground meat.

COOKUP TIPS

Make the cauliflower mash and store it in an airtight container in the fridge. When it's time to eat, reheat the cauli mash in a small saucepan while you cook the lamb.

CRISPY PORK CUTLETS WITH RED CABBAGE

Well Fed is dobře živeni in Czech

It's no secret to readers of my blog that Prague is one of my favorite cities. My husband Dave and I have visited there on vacation several times, and our ritual when we land at the airport never wavers. We catch a ride into town, drop our bags at the hotel, and walk directly around the corner to Restaurant U Provaznice (a.k.a. The Rope-Maker's Wife) for a plate of schnitzel and red cabbage. This is a healthier version of that pub classic. *Dobrou chut'!*

Serves 2–4
Total time: 40–45 minutes
Tools: rimmed baking sheet, meat hammer. food processor (maybe)

PORK:
- 1 large egg
- 1 tablespoon coconut aminos
- 1 teaspoon Dijon mustard
- 1 teaspoon salt
- 1 teaspoon ground black pepper
- 3 ounces pork rinds
- 8 thin, boneless center-cut pork chops (1½ pounds)
- 2–3 tablespoons extra-virgin olive oil
- a handful fresh parsley

RED CABBAGE:
- 1 tablespoon extra-virgin olive oil
- ½ medium yellow onion
- 1 small head red cabbage (about 1 pound)
- 1 large Granny Smith apple
- 1 tablespoon cider vinegar
- ½ navel orange
- 1 teaspoon salt
- ¼ teaspoon ground black pepper
- ½ teaspoon caraway seeds

Preheat the oven to 325F. Line a large, rimmed baking sheet with parchment paper.

Prep the pork coating. In a shallow bowl, beat the egg with coconut aminos, mustard, salt, and pepper; set aside. Crush the pork rinds. You have a choice: (a) Place the pork rinds in a resealable bag, seal it, then smash them with the smooth side of a meat hammer or (b) crush them in a food processor. Transfer the magical piggy dust to a plate or shallow bowl.

Make the cutlets. Dip the pork chops in egg, then dredge them in the pork dust and place them on the prepared baking sheet. Place 2 tablespoons oil in a large, nonstick skillet and warm it over medium-high heat for 2 minutes. Working in batches, brown the pork chops for 2 minutes on each side, adding more oil, if necessary. Return the cutlets to the baking sheet as they're finished, then slide the sheet into the oven. Set a timer for 20 minutes.

Cook the cabbage. Reheat the skillet over medium-high heat, and add the oil. While the fat heats, slice the onion very thinly. Add it to the pan and cook until it's translucent and slightly golden, 5–7 minutes. While the onion cooks, core the cabbage and apple. Slice both very thinly, then add them to the pan along with the vinegar, juice of the ½ orange, salt, pepper, and caraway seeds. Toss with two wooden spoons to combine, then cover and cook over medium heat, stirring occasionally, until the cabbage is very soft, 5–10 minutes. If the oven timer rings while the cabbage is still cooking, remove the pork from the oven and cover loosely with foil. Mince the parsley and set it aside. Taste the cabbage and add more salt, if necessary; remove the pork from the oven.

To serve, divide the cabbage among individual serving plates and top with pork cutlets. Sprinkle with parsley.

YOU KNOW HOW YOU COULD DO THAT?

This is one recipe where pastured lard is a spectacular replacement for extra-virgin olive oil. You can replace chops with thinly-sliced pork loin. To save time, you can use Bacon's Heir Pork Dust instead of crushing your own pork rinds.

DAN DAN NOODLES

"noodles carried on a pole"

These noodles are one of the most popular street foods in Sichuan (a.k.a. Szechuan) province of southwestern China. The cuisine of this region is beloved for its bold flavors, with lots of garlic, chiles, and Sichuan pepper. The name "dan dan" refers to the pole that noodle vendors used to sell their wares. It was carried across the shoulders, a basket of noodles on one end and the spicy sauce on the other. Traditionally, the noodles swim in a face-tingling broth and are topped with minced pork and preserved vegetables. This version uses zucchini noodles for slurping, cornichons for an acidic tang, and a separate chili oil so you can customize the heat.

Make the noodles. Julienne the zucchini with the spiralizer. Place the noodles in a colander and toss them with the salt until the strands are lightly coated. Set the colander in the sink to drain while you prep the other ingredients.

Make the chili oil. In a small saucepan, combine the oil, peppercorns, cinnamon, and red pepper flakes. Warm the oil over medium-low heat while you cook.

Cook the pork. Warm the oil in a large, nonstick skillet over medium-high heat, 2 minutes. While the oil heats, peel and grate the ginger, mince the jalapeño, and peel and crush the garlic. Add the aromatics to the oil and cook until fragrant, about 1 minute. Crumble the pork into the pan, season with the salt and pepper, and cook, breaking up the meat with a wooden spoon, until it's browned, 7–10 minutes.

Make the sauce. While the pork cooks, place the tahini, sesame oil, Chinese five-spice, and black pepper in a small bowl and mix with a fork. Add the coconut aminos, vinegar, and sugar; stir until combined. Chop the cornichons and set them aside.

Put it together. Add the sauce to the meat in the skillet and stir to coat the meat. Add the cornichons to the skillet, toss to combine, and transfer the meat mixture to a large bowl. Reheat the skillet over medium-high heat. Rinse the zucchini noodles under running water, drain well, and squeeze them dry in a clean dish towel. Add the noodles to the heated pan and stir-fry for 2–3 minutes until hot. Return the meat to the pan and toss with two wooden spoons to combine; allow it to heat through. Use a slotted spoon to remove the cinnamon stick from the chili oil and discard it. Set the oil aside to cool. Chop the cashews and scallions.

To serve, divide the noodles among individual bowls and top with a drizzle of chili oil, then sprinkle with cashews and scallions.

Serves 2–4
Total time: 40–45 minutes
Tools: grater, spiralizer, colander

NOODLES:
- 2 pounds zucchini
- 2 teaspoons salt

CHILI OIL:
- ½ cup light-tasting olive or avocado oil
- 1 tablespoon whole black peppercorns
- ½-inch piece of cinnamon stick
- 2 tablespoons crushed red pepper flakes

PORK:
- 1 tablespoon extra-virgin olive oil
- 2-inch piece fresh ginger
- 1 jalapeño
- 3 cloves garlic
- 1½ pounds ground pork
- 1 teaspoon salt
- ½ teaspoon ground black pepper

SAUCE:
- 2 tablespoons tahini or almond butter
- 2 teaspoons toasted sesame oil
- ½ teaspoon Chinese five-spice powder
- ¼ teaspoon ground black pepper
- ¼ cup coconut aminos
- 2 tablespoons unseasoned rice vinegar
- pinch coconut sugar (omit for Whole30)
- ⅓ cup cornichons
- garnish: a handful cashews, 2–3 scallions

COOKUP TIPS

Spiralize the zucchini, make the chili oil, and prep the sauce in advance; store everything in separate airtight containers in the fridge. When it's time to eat, cook the pork and put it all together according to the directions.

DIRTY RICE

Dirty rice is a classic creole dish that gets its "dirty" color from chicken livers. It's big-time in Louisiana, but it's also popular in other areas of the South, where it's often known as rice dressing. But I didn't know any of that the first few times I ate dirty rice as a teenager. All I knew was that the steam wafting out of the take-out bags from Popeye's Fried Chicken smelled like heaven. I wanted that tiny styrofoam container of rice in my hands and opened as soon as possible. This version of dirty rice will treat you more kindly than fast food, but I've kept all the really good bits: chicken livers, cajun spices, and the porkaliciousness of a little bit o' lard.

dirty deeds, done dirt cheap

Serves 2–4
Total time: 40–45 minutes
Hands-off time: 15 minutes
Tools: food processor, rimmed baking sheet

THE RICE:
- 3 pounds cauliflower (about 1½ heads)
- 1 tablespoon extra-virgin olive oil
- 1 teaspoon salt

THE DIRTY:
- 1 small yellow onion
- 2 stalks celery
- 2 cloves garlic
- 1 small jalapeño pepper
- 1 teaspoon dried oregano leaves
- 2 teaspoons extra-virgin olive oil
- ½ pound chicken livers
- 1 pound ground pork
- 1 teaspoon salt
- ¼ teaspoon ground black pepper
- ½ teaspoon chili powder
- 3–4 scallions
- ¼ cup fresh parsley leaves
- 1 tablespoon lard or ghee
- 1 (5-ounce) package baby spinach

Preheat the oven to 425F.

Rice the cauliflower. Break the cauliflower into florets, removing the stems. Place the florets in the food processor bowl and pulse until the cauliflower looks like rice, about 10 pulses. You may need to do this in batches. In a large bowl, combine the riced cauliflower with the olive oil and salt. Spread it evenly on a large, rimmed baking sheet. Roast 15–20 minutes, until tender. While it roasts…

Prep the aromatics. Coarsely chop the onion. Slice the celery. Smash and peel the garlic. Stem and chop the jalapeño. Add the vegetables and the oregano to the bowl of a food processor. Pulse a few times, then run the motor until the veggies form a paste. Warm the 2 teaspoons of olive oil in a large, nonstick skillet over medium-high heat for 2 minutes. When the oil is hot, add the onion mixture. Stir to coat it in the oil, then leave it alone until it begins to dry out a bit, about 4–5 minutes. Meanwhile…

Prep the meats. Add the chicken livers to the food processor bowl (no need to wash it out) and pulse a few times until they're chopped. Add the chicken livers to

the veggies in the skillet and cook, stirring occasionally, 3–4 minutes. Add the ground pork to the skillet and cook, breaking up the meat with a wooden spoon, until it is just pink, about 3 minutes. Add the salt, pepper, and chili powder; stir to combine. Continue to cook until the pan is dry and the meat begins to get crusty brown bits. This takes longer than you might think; you want it to get quite a bit drier and caramelized.

Bring it home. While the meat is browning, mince the dark green tops of the scallions and the parsley. Place the herbs in a very large bowl. When the rice is tender and the meat is browned, add them both to the bowl with the herbs. Toss well with two wooden spoons until all the ingredients are evenly distributed. Plop in the lard and continue to toss until the melted fat coats the rice.

To serve, place a handful of baby spinach leaves in the bottom of individual serving bowls and top with rice. The heat wilts the spinach and—bam!—Dirty Rice and greens, like magic. Bonus points if you add a few shakes of hot sauce to the spinach before burying it under the rice.

COOKUP TIPS

Rice the cauliflower, prep the aromatics, and chop the chicken livers; store everything in separate airtight containers in the fridge. When it's time to eat, roast the cauliflower, cook the meats, and follow the rest of the instructions.

MOO SHU STIR-FRY

don't skip the wood ear mushrooms

Moo shu pork was my "usual" for Chinese take-out until I became a paleo devotee. *Well Fed 2* includes a recipe for this dish that's truer to the original and, therefore, takes far more time. This version is its equal, but uses ground pork and skips the marinating step to expedite the whole process. Moo shu is most fun when it's served family style so everyone can roll their own wraps, but you could also serve it in bowls on a bed of cauliflower rice.

Serves 2–4
Total time: 25–30 minutes
Tools: pint-size Mason jar, stick blender

VEGGIES:
- 1 ounce dried, shredded wood ear (Chinese black) mushrooms
- ½ medium head green cabbage
- 4 scallions
- 1 (8-ounce) can bamboo shoots
- 1 tablespoon extra-virgin olive oil
- 5 ounces sliced shiitake mushrooms
- 2 heads fresh butter or Boston lettuce

PORK:
- 1½ pounds ground pork
- 1 tablespoon arrowroot powder
- 2 cloves garlic
- ¼ cup coconut aminos
- 1 teaspoon toasted sesame oil

HOISIN SAUCE:
- 2 cloves garlic
- 1 medjool date or dried fig
- ½ cup coconut aminos
- ¼ cup sunflower seed butter
- 4 teaspoons unseasoned rice vinegar
- 1 teaspoon toasted sesame oil
- 1 teaspoon hot sauce
- ¼ teaspoon ground black pepper

Prep. Place the wood ear mushrooms in a small bowl and cover with hot water; set aside to rehydrate. Get the veggies ready for the speed round of the stir-fry: Thinly slice the cabbage and scallions. Drain the bamboo shoots.

Start the pork. Heat a large, nonstick skillet over medium-high heat for about 3 minutes. Crumble the pork into the skillet and cook, breaking up the meat with a wooden spoon, until it is just pink, about 3 minutes. While it cooks, make the sauce.

Make the sauce: Smash and peel the garlic and place it in a pint-size Mason jar. Remove the pit from the date and drop the date into the jar, then add the coconut aminos, sunflower seed butter, rice vinegar, sesame oil, hot sauce, and black pepper. Blitz with a stick blender until smooth; set aside.

Finish the pork. Add the arrowroot powder to the pork and stir to combine. Peel and crush the garlic; add it to the pan with the coconut aminos and sesame oil. Stir to combine and continue cooking until the liquid is mostly evaporated and the meat is cooked through, 5–7 minutes. Transfer the meat to a large bowl.

Cook the veggies. Place the oil in the same skillet you used for the pork and reheat it over medium-high, 2 minutes. Add the cabbage and shiitake mushrooms to the pan and toss with two wooden spoons until the cabbage has wilted, 1–2 minutes. Drain the wood ear mushrooms and add them to the skillet along with the bamboo shoots and scallions; toss to combine. Return the pork to the skillet with any accumulated juices and stir-fry until heated through, 1–2 minutes.

Serve family style with a platter of butter lettuce leaves, a big bowl of moo shu, and the hoisin sauce for drizzling.

YOU KNOW HOW YOU COULD DO THAT?
Add eggs: After cooking the meat, beat and fry 4 eggs and add to the meat in the bowl—or replace the ground pork with ground beef or chicken or whole shrimp. If you made Cauliflower Rice during a Mini Cookup (p. 39), this is an excellent deployment.

COOKUP TIPS
Make the hoisin sauce, stir-fry the pork, and cut up the raw veggies in advance; store everything in separate airtight containers in the fridge. When it's time to eat, cook the veggies and follow the instructions for the final stir-fry.

ITALIAN HOAGIE SALAD

this is how we roll

I grew up in eastern Pennsylvania, where hoagies are known as "subs" and homemade rolls from Philadelphia are trucked to local sandwich shops on the regular. These days, I know the best part of the hoagie is the inside: spicy Italian cold cuts, cool-crisp iceberg lettuce with just enough olive oil to make it slinky and vinegar to give it teeth. This recipe relies on Applegate Farms cold cuts and requires nothing more of you than a lot of chopping. It's as close as you can get to running out for a sub on a Saturday afternoon.

DRESSING:
- ¼ cup red wine vinegar
- 3 tablespoons extra-virgin olive oil
- ½ teaspoon dried oregano
- ¼ teaspoon coarse (granulated) garlic powder
- ¼ teaspoon salt
- ¼ teaspoon ground black pepper
- 1 (6-ounce) can anchovies

MEATS:
- 1 (5-ounce) package Applegate Farms Uncured Pork Pepperoni
- 1 (4-ounce) package Applegate Farms Genoa Salami
- 1 (4-ounce) package Applegate Farms Prosciutto

VEGGIES:
- 1 head iceberg lettuce
- a few handfuls baby spinach
- 2 stalks celery
- 1 red bell pepper
- ½ medium sweet onion
- ½ (15-ounce) can red beets
- 1 (14-ounce) can hearts of palm
- 1 (6-ounce) can black olives

Make the dressing. Equip yourself with an enormous mixing bowl. Place the vinegar, oil, oregano, garlic powder, salt, and black pepper in the bowl and whisk to combine. Drain and mince the anchovies and add them to the bowl; whisk one more time to introduce the anchovies to the rest of the crew.

Prep the meats and veggies. Julienne the pepperoni, salami, and prosciutto; add them to the bowl with the dressing. Thinly slice the veggies and add them all to the bowl with the meats.

Toss with intent. When everything is in the bowl, toss the salad again with two spoons while singing a rousing rendition Dean Martin's "That's Amore" or Louis Prima's "Buona Sera." (Seriously. You want to toss for at least 2 minutes.)

YOU KNOW HOW YOU COULD DO THAT?
Make it Whole30 compliant by replacing the deli meats with leftover chicken or steak. You could also add chopped hard-boiled or pickled eggs, if that's your thing.

COOKUP TIPS
Prep the dressing and place it in a jar. Julienne and slice the remaining ingredients, then toss them together in large, airtight container. Store everything in the fridge. Toss the salad with the dressing just before eating.

Serves 2–4
Total Time: 15–20 minutes
Tools: nothing special

MOLE MEATBALLS WITH WILTED CABBAGE

"go to a mole" means "go to a wedding"

Mole is the catch-all term for "sauce" in Mexican cuisine, but the mole most familiar to us gringos is the dark, rich version known as mole poblano. Built on layers of flavor that begin with chiles, mole can be an all-day affair of roasting and grinding each ingredient separately, before combining them with water in a cauldron called a cazuela. The mole bubbles for hours in the pot and is stirred constantly to prevent scorching. You and I don't have that kind of time! This recipe uses shortcuts but keeps key ingredients: chile peppers, nuts, raisins, cocoa.

Serves 2–4
Total time: 40–45 minutes
Tools: 1-tablespoon scoop, stick blender

MOLE SAUCE:
2 teaspoons extra-virgin olive oil
½ medium yellow onion
1 clove garlic
2 teaspoons chili powder
½ teaspoon salt
¼ teaspoon ground cinnamon
⅛ teaspoon ground cloves
¼ teaspoon ground black pepper
1 tablespoon tomato paste
1 tablespoon unsweetened cocoa
2 tablespoons raisins
1 tablespoon sesame seeds
¾ cup tomato sauce or purée
½ cup water or chicken broth
2 tablespoons almond butter

MEATBALLS:
1½ pounds ground pork
1 teaspoon chili powder
1 teaspoon salt
¼ teaspoon ground black pepper
¼ teaspoon ground coriander

WILTED CABBAGE:
1 tablespoon extra-virgin olive oil
½ large head green cabbage

garnish: dry-roasted pepitas, fresh cilantro

Make the sauce. Warm the oil in a nonstick saucepan over medium-high heat, 2 minutes. While it heats, dice the onion. Add the onion to the pan and sauté it until it's soft, 5–7 minutes. While it cooks, peel and crush the garlic and place it in a small bowl with the chili powder, salt, cinnamon, cloves, and pepper. When the onion is soft, add the spices to the pan and stir until fragrant, about 30 seconds. Add the tomato paste, cocoa, raisins, and sesame seeds; stir-fry for about 2 minutes. Add the tomato sauce, water, and almond butter; stir to combine. Simmer over low heat while you prep the meatballs, about 10 minutes.

Prep the meatballs. In a large bowl, combine the ground pork, chili powder, salt, pepper, and coriander; mix well with your hands. Run a dinner plate under cold water, shake off the excess water, and set it near your work space. Moisten your hands with cold water, measure a rounded tablespoon of pork with the scoop, then roll it into a ball and place it on the wet plate; repeat with the remaining pork.

Cook the meatballs. Purée the sauce in the saucepan with a stick blender in the pot (or carefully in a food processor or blender). Bring the sauce back to a simmer and gently place the meatballs in the pot. Cover the pan and cook for 10 minutes, then remove the lid and stir gently to coat the meatballs in sauce. Cover and cook 5 minutes more, then remove the lid and cook an additional 5 minutes uncovered, until the sauce has thickened and the meatballs are cooked through.

Cook the cabbage. During the final 10 minutes of the meatballs' cooking time, place the olive oil in a large, nonstick skillet and warm it over medium-high heat, 2 minutes. While the oil heats, thinly slice the cabbage. Add the cabbage to the pan with a pinch of salt and stir-fry until it's wilted, about 2 minutes.

To serve, divide the cabbage among individual serving plates and top it with meatballs and sauce. Sprinkle with pepitas and cilantro leaves.

YOU KNOW HOW YOU COULD DO THAT?
Replace the ground pork with ground chicken, turkey, or lamb.

COOKUP TIPS
Make the meatballs and sauce in advance; store them together in an airtight container in the fridge. When it's time to eat, sauté the cabbage while the meatballs reheat.

BANH MI BOWL

who needs a baguette ?!

I first learned about the Vietnamese banh mi sandwich while watching a PBS documentary called *Sandwiches That You Will Like*. The show was a culinary tour of memorable sandwiches, and the banh mi sounded like nothing I'd ever tried before. Pork and liver... with pickles and mayo? I decided it was either the weirdest, grossest combo or the most fantastic thing ever. When I finally tried one—on a sunny day in New York from a standing-room-only hole-in-the-wall sandwich shop—I realized it was fantastic. This version keeps all the signature contrasts and ditches the baguette. The bread only gets in the way.

Serves 2-4
Total time: 25-30 minutes
Tools: pint-size Mason jar, stick blender

VEG RELISH:
2 large carrots
1 bunch radishes
½ medium red onion
1 jalapeño
⅓ cup cider vinegar
⅓ cup water
2 teaspoons coconut sugar (omit for Whole30)
½ teaspoon salt
½ teaspoon crushed red pepper flakes

MAYO:
1 large egg
2 tablespoons lemon juice
½ teaspoon mustard powder
½ teaspoon salt
1¼ cups light-tasting olive or avocado oil

PORK:
1½ pounds ground pork
1 tablespoon fish sauce
1 tablespoon lime juice
½ teaspoon salt
½ teaspoon ground black pepper

SALAD:
a handful fresh cilantro
a handful fresh basil
1 large seedless cucumber
4 scallions
1 (5-ounce) package baby spinach
1 lime
coconut aminos (for sprinkling)

Prep the veg relish. Wash the carrots and shave them into ribbons with a vegetable peeler. Wash and thinly slice the radishes. Slice the onion into thin half moons. Cut the jalapeño into thin rings. Place the vegetables in a medium mixing bowl and add the cider vinegar, water, and sugar. Mix to combine and set aside.

Make the mayo. Place all the mayo ingredients in a pint-size Mason jar and whirl with a stick blender for about 30 seconds. Voila! Mayo is done.

Cook the pork. Heat a large, nonstick skillet over medium-high heat for 3 minutes. Add the pork to the skillet and cook, breaking up the meat with a wooden spoon. When it's beginning to lose its pink color, add the fish sauce, lime juice, salt, and pepper. Stir to combine and continue cooking until the liquid is absorbed and the meat is cooked through, about 5 minutes. Turn off the heat.

Prep the salad. Coarsely chop the cilantro and basil. Thinly slice the cucumber and scallions. Wash the spinach. Cut the lime into quarters.

To serve, place a handful of spinach leaves in individual serving bowls, then top with herbs, cucumber, and scallions. Pile some cooked pork on top of the vegetables and use a slotted spoon to add some carrot-radish relish to the bowl. Spoon a dollop of mayo on top, then give the whole thing a squeeze of fresh lime juice and a few shakes of coconut aminos.

YOU KNOW HOW YOU COULD DO THAT?
Make it more traditional with the addition of liver; add ½ pound chopped raw chicken livers to the pork stir-fry. If you made Cauliflower Rice during your Cookup (p. 39), it's a nice addition to the Banh Mi Bowl; just slide the rice into the oven as your first step and let it roast while you prep the rest of the ingredients.

COOKUP TIPS
Make the mayo and cut all the raw veggies and herbs; store everything in separate airtight containers in the fridge. When you're ready to eat, stir-fry the pork and build your bowl.

Hot Dog Night

Thai Dog
p. 143

Tiki Dog
p. 142

Banh Mi Dog
p. 142

Buffalo Dog
p. 143

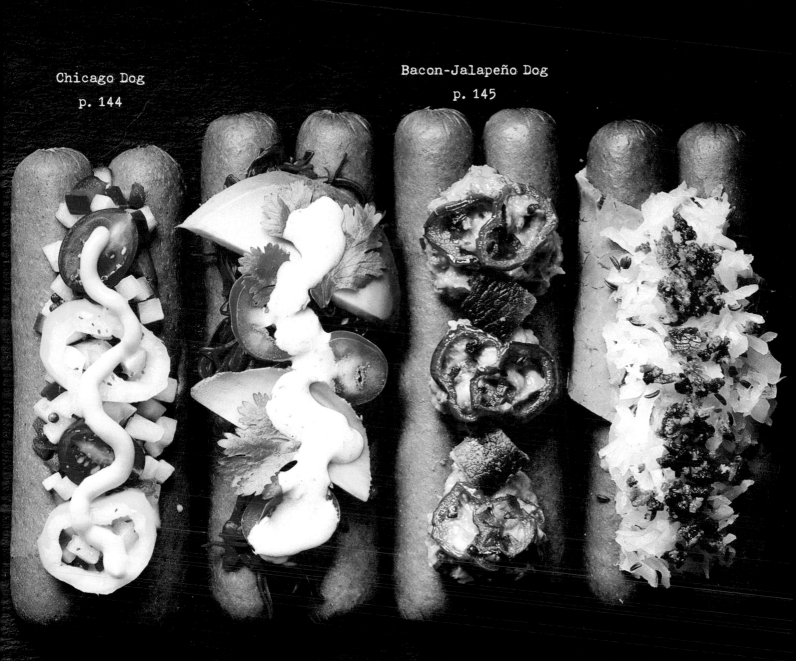

Chicago Dog

p. 144

Bacon-Jalapeño Dog

p. 145

Tex-Mex Dog

p. 144

Deli Dog

p. 145

How to: Hot Dog Night

1. SAUCE

make
the
magic

2. COOK

pan fry

boil

grill

3&4. CHOP

cut crudité

prep toppings.

5. EAT

BUFFALO LOVE
BUFFALO DOGS!

that's
not true.

HOT DOG NIGHT

eat with relish

With all the talk of blood sugar management, anti-inflammatory properties, and nutrient-density, an essential point about food is lost: Food can be fun. Hot dogs are fun.

I mean, when do you ever eat a hot dog in a bad mood? During a ball game? At a cook-out? On the corner at your favorite cart? It's impossible to be grumpy. If you're downing a dog, you're happy, taking in the fresh air, probably hanging out with a favorite friend or family member. It's restorative and enthralling, all the way around.

When you take that first bite, there's the distinctive frankfurter taste, and the distinguishing snap when you sink your teeth into it. But what truly makes the magic happen are the toppings—the little bits of this and that to complement the salty-greasy flavor of the dog. That's where these recipes come in! They're flavorful, creative condiments and veggie combos to boost the nutrient-density of a humble hot dog.

A few words of encouragement: Don't be put off by the long-ish ingredients lists and instructions. These recipes are super simple and fast; I've just provided lots of explanation so your prep can go as quickly as possible.

HERE'S HOW IT WORKS:

1. Make the sauce.
2. Cook the dogs.
3. Prep the other toppings.
4. Cut the crudité.
5. Assemble and dig in.

All recipes serve 2–4
Total Time: 25–40 minutes, depending on chopping speed

1 MAKE THE SAUCE

See the recipes that follow for ingredients and instructions.

2 COOK THE DOGS

You'll want 2–4 hot dogs per person; I recommend Applegate Farms brand. You have a few options for cooking the dogs: simmered (basically just warmed up), pan fried (snappy exterior), or grilled (summertime classic). To make cooking and assembling your fancy dogs a little easier, you can butterfly the dogs: split the hot dog down the middle lengthwise, without cutting all the way through. This provides a flat surface with two advantages: (1) It gets caramelized in a particularly pleasing way and (2) It ensures that your tasty toppings stay put on top of your dog.

Simmered: Place 4–6 cups water in a large saucepan and bring it to a boil. Add the hot dogs, return the water to a boil, then cover the pan and remove it from the heat. Let it stand undisturbed for 7 minutes or until the dogs are heated through.

Pan fried: Warm a nonstick skillet over medium-high heat, 2 minutes. Place the hot dogs in the pan in a single layer and cook, flipping them occasionally, until they're evenly browned, about 7 minutes.

Grilled: Heat a gas grill to medium heat with the lid closed for 10 minutes. Grill dogs for 7 to 9 minutes, turning them occasionally for even browning.

3 PREP THE OTHER TOPPINGS

See the recipes that follow for ingredients and instructions.

4 CUT THE CRUDITÉ

  2 large carrots
  1 large seedless cucumber
  2 bell peppers

Wash the veggies and cut them into eye-pleasing shapes.

5 ASSEMBLE AND DIG IN

Serve the dogs with all the fixings and a few Wet-Naps.

APPLEGATE FARMS HOT DOGS

I recommend Applegate Farms hot dogs because they taste really good, and they're made from high-quality ingredients. They're available in several varieties—including cured and uncured beef, beef and pork, chicken, and turkey—and they can be found in most regular grocery stores.

HOT DOG "SALAD"

Cut your franks into coins or chunks, then place them in a bowl with toppings for the most junk-food-ish salad ever. To cook the hot dogs, slice them into ¼-inch-thick coins or ½-inch-thick chunks. Warm a nonstick skillet over medium-high heat, 2 minutes. Place the pieces cut-side down in a single layer in the pan and cook 2–3 minutes. Use tongs to flip each piece and brown the other side for another 2–3 minutes.

COOKUP TIPS:

Prep the toppings and sauces up to 2 days in advance; store everything separately in airtight containers in the fridge. When it's time to eat, cook the hot dogs and follow assembly instructions.

BANH MI DOG

Tools: mandoline/food processor, pint-size Mason jar, stick blender

QUICK PICKLES:
  1 large carrot
  ¼ medium red onion
  3 tablespoons unseasoned rice vinegar
  3 tablespoons water
  ½ teaspoon coconut sugar (omit for Whole30)
  ⅛ teaspoon salt
  ⅛ teaspoon crushed red pepper flakes

VEGGIE GARNISH:
  1 large seedless cucumber
  1 medium jalapeño
  a handful fresh cilantro

MAYO:
  1 large egg
  2 tablespoons lemon juice
  ½ teaspoon mustard powder
  ½ teaspoon salt
  1¼ cups light-tasting olive or avocado oil

Make the quick pickles. Wash and slice the carrot and red onion with the mandoline or the slicing blade of a food processor. Place in a medium bowl with the remaining ingredients and mix well.

Cook the dogs. See Step 2, page 141.

Prep the veggie garnish. Use the mandoline or food processor to thinly slice the cucumber and jalapeño; set them aside.

Prep the crudité. See Step 4, page 141.

Make the mayo. Place all the mayo ingredients in a pint-size Mason jar and whirl with a stick blender for about 30 seconds. Voila! Mayo is done.

To serve, top the hot dogs with cucumber and jalapeño slices, spoon the pickles over the veggies, and then add a few dollops of mayo and a sprinkle of cilantro.

TIKI DOG

Tools: mandoline/food processor, pint-size Mason jar, stick blender

DUCK SAUCE:
  2 cloves garlic
  10 dried apricots
  ½ cup water
  ¼ cup coconut aminos
  ½ teaspoon powdered ginger
  ¼ teaspoon fish sauce
  ¼ teaspoon crushed red pepper flakes

SLAW:
  ¼ medium head red cabbage
  ¼ cup unseasoned rice vinegar
  1 teaspoon coconut sugar
  ¼ teaspoon salt

  4 strips nitrate-free bacon
  ¼ cup macadamia nuts

Make the sauce. Smash and peel the garlic and place it in a small saucepan with the remaining sauce ingredients. Bring the mixture to a boil, then simmer while you prep the other ingredients.

Cook the dogs. See Step 2, page 141.

Prep the slaw. Use the mandoline or food processor to thinly slice the cabbage and place it in a medium bowl. Add the remaining ingredients and toss to combine.

Prep the crudité. See Step 4, page 141.

Fry the bacon. Cut the bacon crosswise into ¼-inch pieces. Place the chopped bacon in a large, cold skillet, turn the heat to medium-high, and fry the bacon until it's crisp, 3–4 minutes. Remove pan from the heat and use a slotted spoon to transfer the bacon to a paper towel to drain. Coarsely chop the macadamia nuts.

Finish the sauce. Transfer the simmered duck sauce ingredients to a pint-size Mason jar and purée with a stick blender until smooth.

To serve, top hot dogs with the slaw, add a few dollops of duck sauce, and then sprinkle with bacon and macadamia nuts.

THAI DOG

Tools: pint-size Mason jar, stick blender, mandoline/food processor

SUNSHINE SAUCE:
    1 clove garlic
    ¼ cup sunflower seed butter
    2 tablespoons unsweetened canned coconut milk
    2 tablespoons lime juice
    1 tablespoon coconut aminos
    ½ teaspoon crushed red pepper flakes
    ½ teaspoon unseasoned rice vinegar
    ¼ teaspoon powdered ginger

VEGGIE GARNISH:
    ¼ medium head green cabbage
    1 small red bell pepper
    ¼ small red onion
    a handful fresh cilantro

Make the sauce. Smash and peel the garlic and place it in a pint-size Mason

HOW DO YOU LIKE YOUR DOGS COOKED? SIXTY PERCENT OF AMERICANS GO FOR THE GRILL AND TWENTY-ONE PERCENT PREFER BOILED.

jar. Add the rest of the Sunshine Sauce ingredients and purée with a stick blender until smooth.

Cook the dogs. See Step 2, page 141.

Prep the veggie garnish. Use the mandoline or food processor to thinly slice the cabbage, bell pepper, and onion. Coarsely chop the cilantro and place all the ingredients in a large mixing bowl. Toss to mix.

Prep the crudité. See Step 4, page 141.

To serve, make a bed of veggie garnish and place the dogs on top, then drizzle the whole pile with Sunshine Sauce and sprinkle with cilantro.

BUFFALO DOG

Tools: pint-size Mason jar, stick blender, mandoline/food processor

RANCH DRESSING:
    1 clove garlic
    1 large egg yolk
    2 tablespoons plus ½ cup light-tasting olive or avocado oil
    2 tablespoons lemon juice
    1 tablespoon fresh parsley leaves
    1 tablespoon dried chives
    ½ teaspoon paprika
    ¼ teaspoon salt

VEGGIE GARNISH:
    ¼ head iceberg lettuce
    ½ large seedless cucumber
    2 stalks celery
    1 large carrot
    ¼ cup hot sauce

Make the dressing. Smash and peel the garlic clove and place in a pint-size Mason jar. Add the egg yolk, 2 tablespoons olive oil, lemon juice, parsley, chives, paprika, and salt to the jar. Whirl with the stick blender until puréed. With the blender running inside the jar, add the remaining ½ cup oil and blend until smooth.

Cook the dogs. See Step 2, page 141.

Prep the veggie garnish. Thinly slice the lettuce, cucumber, celery, and carrot. Place in a large mixing bowl.

Prep the crudité. See Step 4, page 141.

To serve, make a bed of veggie garnish and place the dogs on top, then add a few shakes of hot sauce and drizzle with the dressing.

AROUND THE WORLD IN 80 (WELL, OKAY, 11) DOGS

And now, in case you love to travel with your taste buds, here's how to say "hot dog" in 11 languages. What?! It could come up!

* Spanish - Perrito Caliente
* Italian - Caldo cane
* French - Chien chaud
* German - Heisser Hund or Wurst
* Portugese - Cachorro quente
* Swedish - Korv or varmkorv
* Norwegian/Danish - Grillpolser
* Latin - Pastillum botello fartum
* Czech - Park v rohliku
* Dutch- Worstjes
* Finnish - Makkarat

YOU WANT FRIES WITH THAT?

These recipes are a complete meal just as they are, but if you want to go for big bonus points, you could use slow cooker potatoes to make oven fries; find the instructions on page 43. DISCLAIMER: Fries will add about 20 minutes to your cooking time, so choose wisely.

TO REHEAT:

Bring 2 tablespoons water to a boil in a nonstick skillet, add leftover hot dogs, return the water to a boil, then cover and steam until the hot dogs are hot.

CHICAGO DOG

Tools: grater

CUCUMBER RELISH:
  1 teaspoon extra-virgin olive oil
  1-inch piece fresh ginger
  1 teaspoon whole mustard seeds
  ⅛ teaspoon ground nutmeg
  ¼ cup unseasoned rice vinegar
  1 teaspoon coconut sugar (omit for Whole30)
  ½ cucumber
  ¼ red bell pepper
  a few sprigs fresh dill

VEGGIE GARNISH:
  1 medium tomato
  ½ small sweet onion

  a handful banana peppers
  celery seeds
  yellow mustard

Make the cucumber relish. Warm the oil in a nonstick skillet over medium-high heat, 2 minutes. While it heats, peel and grate the ginger. Add the mustard seeds to the pan and cook until they begin to pop, then add the ginger and nutmeg; stir and cook for 1 minute. Add the vinegar and sugar, stir, and cook 2 minutes. While it cooks, finely mince the cucumber, pepper, and dill. Add them to the skillet, stir to combine, then remove the skillet from the heat and allow it to cool to room temp.

Cook the dogs. See Step 2, page 141.

Dice the veggie garnish. Cut the tomato and onion into ½-inch dice.

Prep the crudité. See Step 4, page 141.

To serve, top hot dogs with cucumber relish, tomato, and onion. Add a few banana peppers, sprinkle with a pinch of celery seeds, and add a line of yellow mustard.

TEX-MEX DOG

Tools: pint-size Mason jar, stick blender, mandoline/food processor

CUMIN-LIME DRESSING:
  2 cloves garlic
  1 large egg yolk
  2 tablespoons plus ½ cup light-tasting olive or avocado oil
  3 tablespoons lime juice
  a few sprigs fresh cilantro leaves
  1 teaspoon ground cumin
  ¼ teaspoon salt
  3-5 pickled jalapeño rings

MEXICAN RELISH:
  ¼ medium head red cabbage
  ¼ cup fresh cilantro
  4 scallions
  1 teaspoon lime juice
  2 teaspoons extra-virgin olive oil
  ¼ teaspoon salt

VEGGIE GARNISH:
  1 avocado
  1 jalapeño

Make the dressing. Smash and peel the garlic cloves and place them in a pint-size Mason jar. Add the egg yolk, 2 tablespoons of the olive oil, the lime juice, cilantro, cumin, salt, and pickled jalapeños to the jar and whirl with the stick blender until puréed. With the blender running inside the jar, add the remaining ½ cup oil and blend until smooth.

Cook the dogs. See Step 2, page 141.

Make the Mexican relish. Use the mandoline or food processor to thinly slice the cabbage and place it in a large mixing bowl. Coarsely chop the cilantro and thinly slice the scallions; add them to the bowl. Add the lime juice, oil, and salt, then toss to mix.

Prep the veggie garnish. Thinly slice the avocado and jalapeño.

Prep the crudité. See Step 4, page 141.

To serve, make a bed of Mexican relish and place the dogs on top, then add avocado and jalapeño and drizzle with dressing.

BACON-JALAPEÑO DOG

Tools: nothing special

GUACAMOLE:
   1 ripe avocado
   ¼ cup cilantro leaves
   ¼ medium red onion
   ¼ medium jalapeño
   ¼ lime
   ⅛ teaspoon salt

   4 strips nitrate-free bacon
   1 medium jalapeño
   your favorite salsa

Make the guacamole. Cut the avocado in half, remove the pit, and scoop the flesh into a medium mixing bowl. Very finely mince the cilantro, onion, and jalapeño; add them to the bowl and mix with a fork

to combine. Squeeze the juice from ¼ lime into the bowl and add the salt; mix again.

Cook the dogs. See Step 2, page 141.

Fry the bacon & jalapeño. Cut the bacon crosswise into ¼-inch pieces and thinly slice the jalapeño. Place both in a large, cold skillet, turn the heat to medium-high, and fry until the bacon is crisp and the jalapeño is just tender, 3–4 minutes. Remove pan from the heat and use a slotted spoon to transfer the bacon and peppers to a paper towel-lined plate to drain.

Prep the crudité. See Step 4, page 141.

To serve, top hot dogs with guacamole, add a few spoonfuls of salsa, and sprinkle with bacon and jalapeños.

DELI DOG

Tools: pint-size Mason jar, stick blender, mandoline/food processor

THOUSAND ISLAND DRESSING:
   ¼ small white onion
   1 large egg yolk
   2 tablespoons plus ½ cup light-
      tasting olive or avocado oil
   1 tablespoon lemon juice
   1 tablespoon tomato paste
   ½ teaspoon cider vinegar
   ½ teaspoon hot sauce
   ½ teaspoon coconut aminos
   ½ teaspoon paprika
   ¼ teaspoon salt
   ¼ teaspoon mustard powder
   ⅛ teaspoon garlic powder
   ¼ cup dill pickle chips

   2 slices nitrate-free bacon

CARAWAY KRAUT:
   2 cups sauerkraut
   1 teaspoon caraway seeds
   4 slices pastrami or corned beef

Make the dressing. Chop the onion and place it in a pint-size Mason jar. Add the egg yolk, 2 tablespoons of the olive oil, the lemon juice, tomato paste, vinegar, hot sauce, coconut aminos, paprika, salt, mustard powder, and garlic powder to the jar. Whirl with the stick blender until puréed. With the blender running inside the jar, add the remaining ½ cup oil and blend until smooth. Mince the pickles, add them to the jar, and stir with a fork to combine.

Cook the dogs. See Step 2, page 141.

Fry the bacon. Cut the bacon crosswise into ¼-inch pieces. Place the chopped bacon in a large, cold skillet, turn the heat to medium-high, and fry the bacon until it's crisp, 3–4 minutes. Remove pan from the heat and use a slotted spoon to transfer the bacon to a paper towel-lined plate to drain. Discard all but 1 teaspoon of the bacon fat.

Heat the kraut. Place the skillet you used for the bacon over medium heat and reheat the reserved bacon fat. Add the sauerkraut and caraway seeds to the pan and sauté until warm, about 5 minutes. Cut the slices of pastrami in half.

Prep the crudité. See Step 4, page 141.

To serve, make a bed of sauerkraut. Wrap a slice of pastrami around each hot dog and place it on top of the sauerkraut. Sprinkle bacon over the top and drizzle with dressing.

CREOLE HAM & RICE

a taste of the bayou

This recipe is based on a one-pot meal for creole ham and rice with kidney beans. I found the original in a magazine when I was in college, and I've been carting it around on an index card for nearly 25 years. I realized recently that I could make a paleo-friendly version to get this old favorite back on the menu. I ditched the beans, replaced the rice with cauliflower, and added peppers for color and sweetness. The thyme, cayenne, and celery seed are flavorful without being overwhelming, and the cauliflower rice becomes the ideal combination of tender and caramelized in the oven.

Preheat the oven to 425F.

Prep the rice: Break the cauliflower into florets, removing the stems. Place the florets in the bowl of a food processor and pulse until the cauliflower looks like rice. This takes about 10 one-second pulses. You may need to do this in multiple batches to avoid overcrowding. Place the cauliflower in a VERY large mixing bowl.

Add the meat and veggies. Dice the ham, onion, and peppers, then them add to the bowl with the cauliflower. Toss with two wooden spoons until everything is evenly distributed.

Make the spice blend. Peel and crush the garlic; place it in a small bowl, then add the oil, salt, thyme, black pepper, cayenne, and celery seed; mix with a fork to combine. Pour the seasoning over the cauliflower. Toss for at least 1 full minute so the cauliflower and mix-ins are evenly coated with the flavored oil.

Bake it. Divide the rice between two large, rimmed baking sheets and roast it in the oven for 30–35 minutes, 'til the cauliflower is tender and brown bits are beginning to appear. OPTIONAL: For added caramelization, zap each tray under the broiler for about 2 minutes after the roasting time is up.

To serve, divide the rice among shallow bowls and grab a fork.

HAM AND RICE:

- 3 pounds cauliflower
- 1½ pounds nitrate-free ham
- 1 medium sweet onion
- 1 large green bell pepper
- 1 large red bell pepper
- 3 cloves garlic
- 2–3 tablespoons extra-virgin olive oil
- 1 teaspoon salt
- 1 teaspoon dried thyme leaves
- ½ teaspoon ground black pepper
- ¼ teaspoon ground cayenne pepper
- ⅛ teaspoon celery seed

YOU KNOW HOW YOU COULD DO THAT?

Replace the ham with diced pork loin or pork chops and add a ¼ teaspoon liquid smoke to the oil and spices before tossing with the cauliflower. Look for liquid smoke that contains only smoke and water.

COOKUP TIPS

Rice the cauliflower, dice the meat and veggies, prep the spice blend, and toss everything together, then store the mixture in an airtight container in the fridge. When it's time to eat, divide the rice between two baking sheets and roast according to the directions.

Serves 2–4
Total time:
   35–40 minutes
Tools: food
   processor, 2
   rimmed baking
   sheets

WEEKNIGHT ROGAN JOSH WITH SWEET POTATO HOME FRIES

spicy-not-hot curry from Kashmir

Whenever I mention the Indian dish rogan josh to my friend Stacey, I accidentally call it Josh Rogan, and she says, "Who? What?" because she knows it's called rogan josh. We finally realized I was reversing the names because of Seth Rogen—and then Stacey was confusing him with Josh Groban. And maybe there really is something in a name. "Rogan" means oil in Persian and "josh" means heat or passionate. Perhaps rogan josh is an aphrodisiac? I know it makes me feel good all over, and it's so luxurious, it makes me want to marry myself.

Serves 2–4
Total time: 35–40 minutes
Tools: nothing special

SWEET POTATO HOME FRIES:
- 2 pounds sweet potatoes
- 1 tablespoon extra-virgin olive oil
- ½ teaspoon salt
- ¼ teaspoon ground cinnamon
- 2 scallions

LAMB:
- 1 tablespoon extra-virgin olive oil
- 1 medium sweet onion
- 1 clove garlic
- 1 tablespoon paprika
- 2 teaspoons ground cumin
- 2 teaspoons ground coriander
- 1 teaspoon chili powder
- 1 teaspoon ground cinnamon
- 1 teaspoon salt
- ½ teaspoon powdered ginger
- ¼ teaspoon ground cardamom
- ¼ teaspoon ground cloves
- ⅛ teaspoon cayenne pepper
- 1½ pounds ground lamb
- 1 tablespoon tomato paste
- ½ cup canned unsweetened coconut milk
- ¼ cup water

Cook the potatoes. Wash and peel the sweet potatoes, then cut them into ½-inch cubes. Place the oil in a large nonstick skillet and warm it over medium-high heat, 3 minutes. Add the sweet potatoes and toss to coat them in the oil, then sprinkle them with the salt and cinnamon. Reduce the heat to low, cover the skillet, and cook without stirring, 5 minutes. Remove the lid, stir, cover again, and continue to cook until tender. Meanwhile…

Prep the lamb seasonings. Warm the oil in another large, nonstick skillet over medium-high heat, 2 minutes. While the oil heats, dice the onion. Add the onion to the pan with a pinch of salt and cook, stirring occasionally, until soft, about 5 minutes. While the onion cooks, peel and crush the garlic and place it in a small bowl. Add the paprika, cumin, coriander, chili powder, cinnamon, salt, ginger, cardamom, cloves, and cayenne. Mix with a fork and set aside.

Cook the lamb. Crumble the lamb into the skillet with the onion and cook, breaking up the meat with a wooden spoon, until it is just pink, about 3 minutes. Add the garlic-spice blend and stir to combine. Add the tomato paste and cook until it darkens in color, about 2 minutes. Add the coconut milk and water. Stir to combine, then reduce the heat to low, cover, and simmer for 5 minutes.

Bring it home. While the lamb cooks, thinly slice the scallions and sprinkle them over the potatoes, toss, and let them continue to cook uncovered. Remove the lid from the lamb, stir, and cook uncovered until it begins to thicken a bit, 2–3 minutes.

To serve, snuggle the rogan josh and home fries together in a shallow bowl.

YOU KNOW HOW YOU COULD DO THAT?

If you want to add a green veggie, put a handful of baby spinach at the bottom of each bowl. Make it a little more lavish with toasted, sliced almonds on top.

COOKUP TIPS

Peel, cut, and cook the sweet potatoes and make the garlic-spice blend; store both in separate airtight containers in the fridge. When it's time to eat, reheat the potatoes while you cook the lamb.

PIZZA NOODLES

(make me one with everything)

Legendary punk rocker Henry Rollins said, "Pizza makes me think that anything is possible." These zucchini noodles—topped with a quick, homemade Italian sausage, plus pepperoni, jalapeños, and olives—will make you feel like you can conquer the world. Pile it in a big bowl and daydream about all you'll conquer, fueled by vegetables and spices.

Serves 2–4
Total time: 30–35 minutes
Tools: spiralizer, colander

NOODLES:
- 2–2½ pounds zucchini
- 1 tablespoon salt

TOPPINGS:
- ¾ pound ground beef
- ¾ pound ground pork
- 1 teaspoon salt
- 1 teaspoon dried parsley
- ¾ teaspoon dried Italian herbs
- ¼ teaspoon ground black pepper
- ¼ teaspoon coarse (granulated) garlic powder
- ¼ teaspoon paprika
- ¼ teaspoon fennel seeds
- ⅛ teaspoon crushed red pepper flakes
- 1 (4-ounce) package Applegate Farms Uncured Pork Pepperoni (omit for Whole30)
- ½ cup pitted black olives
- a few pickled jalapeño slices

SAUCE:
- 1 tablespoon extra-virgin olive oil
- 2 cloves garlic
- 1 (28-ounce) can fire-roasted diced tomatoes
- ½ teaspoons dried oregano
- ½ teaspoons dried basil
- ½ teaspoon dried parsley
- ⅛ teaspoon salt
- ⅛ teaspoon coarse (granulated) garlic powder
- ⅛ teaspoon onion powder
- pinch crushed red pepper flakes
- 2 large eggs
- 10–12 fresh basil leaves
- garnish: extra-virgin olive oil

Prep the noodles. Julienne the zucchini with the spiralizer. Place the noodles in a colander and toss them with the salt until the strands are lightly coated. Set the colander in the sink to drain while you prep the other ingredients.

Cook the meat toppings. Heat a large, nonstick skillet over medium-high heat. Crumble the pork and beef into the skillet and cook, breaking up the meat with a wooden spoon. While it cooks, combine the salt, parsley, Italian herbs, pepper, garlic powder, paprika, fennel seeds, and red pepper flakes in a small bowl. When the meat begins to lose its pinkness, add the seasonings and mix to combine. Cut the pepperoni slices in half. When the meat is browned and sizzling, add the pepperoni and stir-fry until slightly crisp. Transfer the meats to a large bowl.

Make the sauce. In the same pan you used for the meat, heat the olive oil over medium-high heat. While it heats, peel and crush the garlic. Add the garlic to the pan, and when it's fragrant, after about 30 seconds, pour in the tomatoes. In a small bowl, mix together the oregano, basil, parsley, salt, garlic powder, onion powder, and red pepper flakes; stir with a fork and add the spices to the pan. Stir to combine, bring the sauce to a boil, and then reduce the heat to low. Beat the eggs in a small bowl, add a spoonful of the tomato sauce to the eggs and stir to combine, then slowly pour the egg mixture into the tomato sauce, stirring constantly to combine. The sauce should thicken slightly and get silky. Keep the heat on a very low simmer.

Cook the noodles. Heat a second large, nonstick skillet over medium-high heat. Rinse the zucchini noodles under running water, drain, and squeeze dry in a clean dish towel. Add the noodles to the heated pan and stir-fry, 2–3 minutes until hot. Add the meat, olives, and jalapeño slices; toss to combine. Use a ladle to add tomato sauce to the noodles, stirring to combine after each addition so it doesn't get soupy. Add the fresh basil and stir.

To serve, divide the noodles among flat bowls, then sprinkle each with crushed red pepper flakes and a drizzle of olive oil.

COOKUP TIPS

Spiralize and sweat the zucchini noodles. Precook the ground meat with the spices and pepperoni. Make the sauce. Store everything separately in airtight containers in the fridge. When it's time to eat, heat a large, nonstick skillet over medium-high heat, and stir fry the whole shebang.

LEMON-GARLIC CHICKEN THIGHS WITH FENNEL

what's up, doc?!

Most of my favorite grassy aromatics—fennel, anise, caraway, chervil, and cumin—are all related. They're members of the carrot family and share a flavor compound called anethol which is 13 times sweeter than sugar. That's why fennel is often paired with lemon and almond for balance. As Niki Segnit wrote in her rousing book *The Flavor Thesaurus*, fennel is "the reason the chicken crossed the road." This simple sauté is casual, comforting bistro food, easily brought to life in one pan and guaranteed to smooth the rough edges off a long day.

Make the almond dust. Warm the ghee in a nonstick skillet over medium-high heat for 2 minutes. Add the almond flour and salt. Cook, stirring occasionally with a silicone spatula, until the flour is toasty brown, about 2 minutes. Transfer the almond dust to a plate to cool. (As it cools, the fat will solidify and make "crumbs," so don't worry if it's just brown dust when you take it out of the pan. Press the dust together into a pile and let it do its thing.)

Cook the chicken. Slice the chicken thighs into ¼-inch-wide strips and toss them with salt and pepper. Warm 1 teaspoon olive oil in a large, nonstick skillet over medium-high heat, 2 minutes. Add the chicken and toss to coat it in the oil, then spread it in a single layer and let it cook undisturbed for 3 minutes. Flip the chicken with a spatula, separating the pieces, and cook an additional 3 minutes. Continue to flip and cook the chicken until it's browned and sizzling on most sides, 5–6 minutes more. Meanwhile…

Prep the fennel. While the chicken browns, remove the leafy fronds and mince some of them to make 2–3 tablespoons; set aside. Remove the root ends of the fennel and thinly slice the bulbs into crosswise strips.

Bring it home. When the chicken is browned, use a slotted spoon to transfer it to a plate. There should be some fat from the chicken in the skillet. If not, add 1 tablespoon olive oil and warm it over medium-high heat for 2–3 minutes. Add the fennel, toss to coat it in the fat, then cover the pan and reduce the heat to medium; cook for 2 minutes. While the fennel cooks, peel and crush the garlic. Remove the lid from the skillet and stir-fry the fennel until it begins to soften and show a few brown spots. Push the fennel to the side of the pan, add 1 teaspoon olive oil, then drop the garlic and pepper flakes into the oil. Stir to combine with the fennel, then add the chicken and accumulated juices to the pan. Stir to combine and cook for 1–2 minutes longer, until it's all caramelized. Remove the skillet from heat, stir in the reserved fennel fronds, and squeeze the juice from the lemon over top.

To serve, divide the sauté among individual plates and sprinkle with the almond dust.

Serves 2–4
Total time:
  35–40 minutes
Tools: nothing
  special

ALMOND DUST:
3 tablespoons almond
  flour
2 teaspoons ghee
pinch salt

CHICKEN & FENNEL:
  1½ pounds
    boneless,
    skinless
    chicken thighs
  1 teaspoon salt
  ½ teaspoon ground
    black pepper
  2–4 teaspoons
    extra-virgin
    olive oil, if
    needed
  2 large fennel
    bulbs
  2 cloves garlic
  ¼ teaspoon
    crushed red
    pepper flakes
  ½ lemon

CHICKEN PESTO MEATBALLS WITH ZUCCHINI NOODLES

taste the awesome '80s

I can't deny it, and I can't hide it: I'm a child of the 1980s. I love Duran Duran. "Lucky Star" Madonna is the best Madonna. And in my favorite movie of all time—*When Harry Met Sally*—one of the characters proclaims, "Pesto is the quiche of the '80s." I started making homemade pesto in college; the difference now is that I omit the cheese, and I've added parsley to make it a little sweeter. These meatballs are fragrant with the quick pesto and simmer gently in a dead-simple tomato sauce, no safety dance required.

Serves 2–4
Total time: 45 minutes
Hands-off time: 10 minutes
Tools: spiralizer, colander, food
    processor, 1-tablespoon scoop

ZUCCHINI NOODLES:
  2–2½ pounds zucchini
  1 tablespoon salt

MEATBALLS:
  ½ cup (packed) fresh basil leaves
  ¼ cup fresh parsley leaves
  ¼ cup walnuts
  1 clove garlic
  1 tablespoon extra-virgin olive
    oil
  1 teaspoon salt
  ¼ teaspoon ground black pepper
  pinch crushed red pepper flakes
  1½ pounds ground chicken

SAUCE:
  1 teaspoon extra-virgin olive oil
  1–2 cloves garlic
  1 (14.5-ounce) can crushed tomatoes
  ½ teaspoon salt
  ¼ teaspoon ground black pepper
  10 large fresh basil leaves

Prep the noodles. Julienne the zucchini with the spiralizer. Place the noodles in a colander and toss them with the salt until the strands are lightly coated. Set the colander in the sink to drain while you prep the other ingredients.

Make the pesto. Place the basil, parsley, walnuts, garlic, olive oil, salt, pepper, and red pepper flakes in the bowl of a food processor and purée until it forms a uniform paste, scraping the sides of the bowl as needed.

Roll the meatballs. Place the ground chicken in a large bowl and add the pesto. Mix until all the ingredients are evenly distributed. Run a dinner plate under cold water, shake off excess water, and set it aside. Moisten your hands with cold water, measure a rounded tablespoon of the chicken, roll it into a ball, and place it on the wet plate; repeat with the remaining chicken.

Start the sauce. Warm the oil in a large, nonstick skillet over low heat for 2 minutes. While it heats, peel and crush the garlic, then add it to the skillet and cook until fragrant, about 30 seconds. Add the crushed tomatoes, salt, and pepper; stir to combine and bring to a simmer. Mince the basil leaves and set aside.

Add the meatballs. Gently place the meatballs in the tomato sauce. It's OK if they touch each other and aren't completely submerged. Partially cover the pan and simmer the meatballs for 10 minutes.

Check the meatballs. When the sauce and meatballs have simmered for 10 minutes, remove the lid, stir to roll the meatballs in the sauce, and simmer, uncovered, while you finish the zucchini noodles.

Cook the noodles. Rinse the zucchini noodles under running water, drain well, and squeeze them in a clean dish towel to remove excess water. Heat another large, nonstick skillet over high heat for 2–3 minutes, then add the prepared zucchini noodles. Sauté the noodles in the dry pan until just tender, 2–3 minutes.

Finish the sauce. Remove the pan from the heat, add the fresh basil leaves, and stir.

To serve, pile meatballs and sauce on top of zucchini noodles in individual bowls. Bonus points for you if you drizzle a little extra-virgin olive oil over the whole thing.

COOKUP TIPS

Spiralize and sweat the zucchini, cook the sauce and meatballs, and store both in separate airtight containers in the fridge. When you're ready to eat, gently reheat the meatballs and sauté the zucchini pasta.

CURRY CHICKEN-SALAD SALAD

so nice, say it twice

In the years since I started eating paleo, I've learned that paleo-friendly food that's worth eating can be found in some surprising places. Everyone told us when we moved to Vermont, "Go to the café at King Arthur Flour!" I was skeptical; What could I possibly eat at a shrine to bread and cookies? The answer was a bright, fresh, protein-packed salad with plenty of spice and contrasting textures. This recipe is a love note to keeping an open mind.

Cook the chicken. Smash and peel the garlic cloves and place them in a large saucepan. Add the chicken, water, bay leaf, salt, and peppercorns. Cover and simmer on low, 15–20 minutes. Turn off the heat and let the chicken sit in the hot water while you prep the salad.

Make the mayo. Place all the mayo ingredients in a pint-size Mason jar. Insert the stick blender and whirl until it's emulsified.

Make the dressing. Peel and crush the garlic cloves and place in a small, microwave safe bowl. Add the ghee, curry powder, cumin, coriander, salt, and ginger; microwave on 80 percent power until the oil is hot, about 20 seconds. In a medium bowl, gently whisk together ⅓ cup of the homemade mayo, the juice of the ½ lime, and the curry oil until smooth.

Prep the fruit and nuts. Place the almonds and coconut in a dry, nonstick skillet and toast them over medium-high heat until golden, 3–4 minutes; transfer to a large mixing bowl. Peel and dice the apple, chop the cilantro, slice the celery and scallions; add them all to the mixing bowl. Add the raisins and toss with two wooden spoons to mix.

Finish the chicken. Remove the chicken from the hot water and place it in a shallow bowl in the freezer until it's cool enough to handle, about 5 minutes. Cut the chicken into ½-inch cubes and add them to the bowl with the nuts and raisins. Add the dressing and toss to combine.

Make the salad bed. Wash the carrots and use a vegetable peeler to cut them into ribbons; place in a large mixing bowl. Tear the lettuce into bite-sized pieces and add it to the bowl, along with the spinach. Add the juice of the ½ lime, olive oil, salt, and pepper; toss well.

To serve, place salad greens on serving plates and top with chicken salad.

YOU KNOW HOW YOU COULD DO THAT?

Serve vinegary cornichons on the side. Replace the raisins with grapes, pineapple chunks, or diced mango.

COOKUP TIPS

Cook the chicken, make the dressing, toast the nuts and coconut, and cut up the raw veggies; store everything in separate airtight containers in the fridge. When it's time to eat, toss the chicken with the curry dressing and prepare the salad bed.

Serves 2–4
Total time: 40–45 minutes
Tools: pint-size Mason jar, stick blender

CHICKEN:
- 3 cloves garlic
- 4 boneless, skinless chicken breasts (4–6 ounces each)
- 2 cups water
- 1 bay leaf
- 1 tablespoon salt
- 1 teaspoon whole black peppercorns

MAYO:
- 1 large egg
- 2 tablespoons lemon juice
- 1¼ cups light-tasting olive or avocado oil
- ½ teaspoon mustard powder
- ½ teaspoon salt

DRESSING:
- 2 cloves garlic
- 1 tablespoon ghee or coconut oil
- 2 teaspoons curry powder
- ½ teaspoon ground cumin
- ½ teaspoon ground coriander
- ¼ teaspoon salt
- ¼ teaspoon powdered ginger
- ½ lime

FRUIT & NUTS:
- ¼ cup sliced almonds
- ¼ cup unsweetened coconut flakes
- 1 Granny Smith apple
- ½ cup fresh cilantro leaves
- 2 stalks celery
- ⅓ cup golden raisins

SALAD BED:
- 2 large carrots
- 1 head Boston or butter lettuce
- 1 (5-ounce) package baby spinach
- ½ lime
- 1 tablespoon extra-virgin olive oil
- ¼ teaspoon salt
- ⅛ teaspoon ground black pepper

MANGO CHICKEN WITH CAULIFLOWER RICE

from the land of a million pagodas

The country of Burma, now known as Myanmar, was cut off from the rest of the world for almost 50 years under the rule of a military dictatorship. Since 2012, the borders have opened up and the country has welcomed tourists. This is good news for adventurous eaters—the cuisine of Mayanmar is a fusion of Thai, Chinese, and Indian influences. This recipe is based on a mind-blowing stir-fry I ate at a Burmese restaurant in San Francisco. It was delicate and powerful at the same time, like reclining against a backdrop of satin cushions in a fragrant salon to recoup your energy.

Make the rice. Break the cauliflower into florets, removing the stems. Place the florets in the food processor bowl and pulse until the cauliflower looks like rice, about 10 pulses. Place the coconut oil in a medium saucepan and heat over medium-high heat for 2 minutes. Add the cauliflower and salt, toss with a rubber spatula until the rice is coated with the oil, then cover the pot and reduce the heat to low. Meanwhile...

Prep the chicken. Pound the chicken to ½-inch thickness between two pieces of plastic wrap with the smooth side of the meat hammer, then cut it crosswise into ½-inch-wide strips. Place the chicken in a bowl and toss with the salt, pepper, and arrowroot powder.

Prep the veggies. Cut the onion and bell pepper into thin slices. Peel the mangoes and cut them into ½-inch chunks; if you do this over a bowl, you can use the mango juice in the sauce. Slice the jalapeño into rings.

Make the sauce. Place all the sauce ingredients in a pint-size Mason jar and shake it like you mean it.

Cook the chicken. Warm the coconut oil in a large, nonstick skillet over medium-high heat, 2–3 minutes. Add the chicken and toss to coat it in the oil, then let it cook undisturbed for 2–3 minutes. While it cooks, wash the bowl you used for the chicken; you're going to need it again. Flip the chicken and stir-fry until it's golden and almost cooked through, about 5–6 minutes. Transfer the chicken to the bowl.

Stir-fry! Place the onion, bell pepper, jalapeño, and mango in the skillet and stir-fry until the veggies are crisp-tender, 2–3 minutes. Return the chicken to the skillet and stir to combine. Add the sauce and stir-fry until thickened and bubbly, 1–2 minutes. Remove the lid from the cauliflower rice and mix in the cilantro leaves.

To serve, divide the cauliflower rice among individual serving plates and top with the stir-fry.

Serves 2–4
Total time: 40–45 minutes
Tools: food processor, meat hammer

RICE:
- 1 large head cauliflower
- 1 tablespoon coconut oil
- 1 teaspoon salt
- ¼ cup cilantro leaves

STIR-FRY:
- 4 boneless, skinless chicken breasts (4–6 ounces each)
- 1 teaspoon salt
- ¼ teaspoon ground black pepper
- 2 teaspoons arrowroot powder
- ½ medium yellow onion
- 1 red bell pepper
- 2 ripe mangoes
- 1 medium jalapeño pepper
- 1 tablespoon coconut oil

SAUCE:
- 3 tablespoons mango juice, orange juice, or water
- 1 tablespoon tomato paste
- 2 tablespoons coconut aminos
- 1 tablespoon chili sauce (sambal oelek or sriracha)
- 1 teaspoon honey (omit for Whole30)
- ½ teaspoon cider vinegar
- ¼ teaspoon salt

YOU KNOW HOW YOU COULD DO THAT?

To make this Whole30 compliant, substitute 1 teaspoon hot sauce and 2 cloves minced garlic for the chili sauce.

COOKUP TIPS

Rice the cauliflower, pound and cut up the raw chicken, and make the sauce; store everything in separate airtight containers in the fridge. When it's time to eat, cut the veggies and follow the stir-fry directions.

FRIED CHICKEN MEATBALLS WITH COLLARD GREENS

finger-lickin' good!

I don't feel like I need to do a hard sell on a recipe called "Fried Chicken Meatballs," but since this space needs to be filled with words, here goes: These are super easy to make. They taste like fried chicken without the annoying deep frying and pesky bones getting in the way. They're scrumptious straight out of the oven, but are also awesome at room temperature for picnics, and they freeze/reheat like champs.

Serves 2–4
Total time: 30–35 minutes
Tools: 1-tablespoon scoop, rimmed baking sheet

MEATBALLS:

- 1½ pounds ground chicken
- 1 teaspoon salt
- ½ teaspoon ground black pepper
- 2 tablespoons extra-virgin olive oil

COATING:

- 3 tablespoons tapioca starch
- ½ teaspoon salt
- ½ teaspoon smoked paprika
- ¼ teaspoon ground black pepper
- ¼ teaspoon rubbed sage
- ¼ teaspoon coarse (granulated) onion powder
- ¼ teaspoon coarse (granulated) garlic powder
- pinch dried marjoram
- pinch ground cayenne pepper
- pinch ground cloves

GREENS:

- 1 bunch collard greens or kale (about 1 pound)
- ½ cup water
- 2 teaspoons extra-virgin olive oil
- 1 clove garlic
- ¼ teaspoon salt
- pinch ground black pepper

Preheat the oven to 425F. Line a rimmed baking sheet with parchment paper.

Season the chicken. Place the ground chicken, salt, and pepper in a large mixing bowl; mix well.

Make the coating. In a shallow bowl, use a fork to combine the tapioca starch, salt, smoked paprika, black pepper, sage, onion powder, garlic powder, marjoram, cayenne pepper, and cloves.

Make the balls. Moisten your hands with cold water, then measure rounded tablespoons of ground chicken and roll the chicken into balls. Roll each ball in the seasoned tapioca starch. Set the chicken balls aside on the baking sheet until you're ready to fry them.

Fry the balls. Place 1 tablespoon oil in a large, nonstick skillet over high heat, 2–3 minutes. Place half of the meatballs in a single layer in the pan, leaving some wiggle room around them. Cook until they're browned on all sides, 4–5 minutes total. Transfer the balls to the baking sheet. Add 1–2 teaspoons oil to the pan and brown the remaining meatballs and transfer them to

the baking sheet. Place the baking sheet in the oven and set a timer for 10 minutes.

Prep the greens. Wash the leaves and remove the tough ribs. Stack the leaves and cut them crosswise into ½-inch strips. Reheat the skillet over medium-high heat. Toss the still-wet greens into the pan, add the water, cover with a lid, and steam for 5 minutes or so, until almost all the water is evaporated. Remove the lid and toss the greens with two wooden spoons until they are very dark green and dry. This takes about 2–3 minutes. Meanwhile, peel and crush the garlic.

Season the greens. Push the greens to the side of the pan, add the oil, and drop the minced garlic into the oil. Cook until fragrant, about 30 seconds. Toss everything together and allow the greens to cook for another 5 minutes. Add the salt and pepper, taste, and adjust the seasonings. Turn off the heat and cover to keep warm until the meatballs are finished.

To serve, divide the greens among dinner plates and top with meatballs.

YOU KNOW HOW YOU COULD DO THAT?

Replace the ground chicken with ground turkey, pork, or beef.

COOKUP TIPS

Season the ground chicken and form the meatballs. Prep the fried chicken coating. Wash and cut the collard greens. Store everything separately in airtight containers in the fridge, then follow the directions for cooking the meatballs and greens.

Pesto, p. 168

Citrus-Mango Relish, p. 168

Chicken Paillard

Tomato, Bacon
& Avocado Relish,
p. 169

Onion-Pepita
Relish,
p. 169

Cucumber-
Pineapple Salsa
p. 168

Mushroom
& Pancetta Jam,
p. 169

Greek Olive
Tapenade,
p. 168

How to: Chicken Paillard

1. POUND

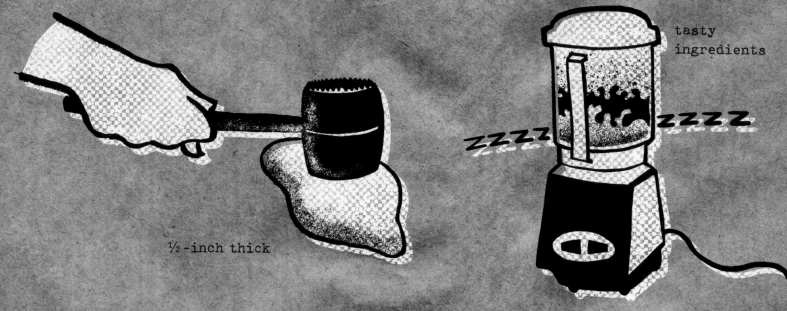

½-inch thick

2. TOPPINGS

tasty ingredients

ZZZZ ZZZZ

3. GREENS

green goodness

4. EAT

CHICKEN PAILLARD

sounds like "pie-yard"

Poor boneless, skinless chicken breasts! They're so mocked and maligned. But it's hard to love them: Their low-fat status can make them flavorless, and they can too easily be cooked into dried-out oblivion.

But let me tell you a story about chicken in Paris.

Once upon a time, Dave and I took a holiday to the City of Lights. One day, we lost track of time wandering around in the Louvre. We walked 10 miles that day, around the Tuileries Garden, through the galleries of the museum, and over bridges back to our hotel. We staggered into the café on the corner and collapsed into our chairs. It was 10:00 p.m. and we had yet to eat dinner. I chose "chicken breast with salad" from the menu because it seemed easy and unconfusing. What arrived was a beautiful sight to behold: a thin, sizzling chicken cutlet topped with arugula, coarse salt, and pepper, and nuzzled up next to a few golden potatoes. It was the cure for a long day, full brain, and sore feet.

So, my friends! Don't be put off by the idea of boneless, skinless chicken breast or by the potentially snooty-sounding French name. A paillard is nothing more complicated than a piece of meat that's been pounded to an even thickness so the resulting cutlet cooks quickly and retains plenty of moisture.

These recipes riff off that Paris dinner, placing the paillard on a bed of greens and topping it with all manner of fresh sauces and relishes made from fruits and vegetables. It's almost like a sandwich where the bread is made from salads. I don't think there's a French name for that.

HERE'S HOW IT WORKS:

1. Pound and cook the chicken.
2. Prep the toppings.
3. Prep the bed of greens.
4. Devour.

All recipes serve 2–4
Total Time: 25–35 minutes, depending on chopping speed
Tools: meat hammer, rimmed baking sheet

1 POUND AND COOK THE CHICKEN

    4 boneless, skinless chicken
        breasts (about 4–6 ounces each)
    1 teaspoon salt
    ½ teaspoon ground black pepper
    1–4 teaspoons ghee or extra-virgin
        olive oil

Preheat the oven to 250F.

One at a time, place each chicken breast between two pieces of plastic wrap and pound it with the smooth side of a meat hammer (or a can, rolling pin, or the bottom of a saucepan). The goal is to make a cutlet of even thickness, somewhere between ¼ and ½ inch thick. (Visit www.meljoulwan.com/wellfedweeknights for a short how-to video.)

Heat 1 teaspoon of the ghee in a large, nonstick skillet over medium-high heat for 1 minute. While the ghee warms, season the chicken on both sides with the salt and pepper. Cook the cutlets one at a time (or two at a time, if they fit in the pan with some wiggle room around them), about 2 minutes per side. Transfer the browned chicken to a baking sheet and place it in the oven to keep warm while you prep the toppings.

2 PREP THE TOPPINGS

See the recipes that follow for ingredients and instructions.

3 PREP THE BED OF GREENS

    a few handfuls arugula, baby
        spinach, or spring mix
    salt and pepper
    extra-virgin olive oil
    your favorite vinegar

Place the greens in a large mixing bowl and add a few shakes of salt and pepper; toss with two wooden spoons. Add equal amounts of oil and vinegar—1 tablespoon each is a good place to start—then toss until the leaves are coated.

4 DEVOUR

To serve, divide the salad greens among individual serving plates. Add a chicken cutlet to each plate and spoon the topping over the chicken.

CHICKEN CAESAR SALAD

don't skip the anchovies

The Caesar salad was invented during the 1920s at Caesar's Palace, just across the border in Tijuana, Mexico. There's some argument about its true creator, but there's no denying the luscious combination of salty anchovy, pungent garlic, tangy lemon, and smooth olive oil—plus crunchy croutons. The Caesar was so popular after World War II, it was immortalized in an episode of the TV show *Bewitched* and a Lucille Ball-Desi Arnaz movie. In 1956, the chefs of the International Society of Epicures in Paris named the Caesar Salad "the greatest recipe to originate from the Americas in 50 years."

Serves 2–4
Total time: 30–35 minutes
Tools: meat hammer, pint-size Mason jar, stick blender

Prep the chicken. Cut the chicken breasts in half crosswise, place each between two pieces of plastic wrap, and pound with a meat hammer to ½-inch thickness. Sprinkle both sides with the salt and pepper. Heat the oil in a large, nonstick skillet over medium-high heat for 2 minutes, then add the chicken and cook 4–5 minutes per side. While the chicken browns…

Make the dressing. Smash and peel the garlic clove and place it in a pint-size Mason jar. Drain the anchovies and add them to the jar along with the egg yolks, 2 tablespoons of the oil, the lemon juice, Dijon mustard, and pepper. Blend with a stick blender until puréed. With the blender running inside the jar, add the remaining ½ cup oil and purée until smooth and thick.

Cover the chicken and prep the greens. When the chicken is browned on both sides, cover the pan with a lid and reduce the heat to low. Wash the romaine and cut it into bite-sized pieces, then place it in a very large mixing bowl.

Make the topping. Heat the ghee in a nonstick skillet over medium-high heat for 2 minutes. Add the almond flour, parsley, garlic powder, and salt. Cook, stirring occasionally, until it's toasty brown, about 2 minutes. Transfer the topping to a plate to cool.

To serve, add a few spoonfuls of dressing to the romaine and toss well until the leaves are coated. Divide the leaves among individual serving plates, then slice the chicken into strips across the grain and add them to each bed of greens. Sprinkle with the crispy topping and additional black pepper.

COOKUP TIPS
Cook the chicken, cut the lettuce, and make the dressing; store everything in separate airtight containers in the fridge. Assemble just before eating.

CHICKEN:
- 4 boneless, skinless chicken breasts (4–6 ounces each)
- 1 teaspoon salt
- ½ teaspoon ground black pepper
- 2 teaspoons extra-virgin olive oil

SALAD & DRESSING:
- 1 clove garlic
- 1 (2-ounce) can anchovy fillets (packed in olive oil)
- 2 large egg yolks
- 2 tablespoons plus ½ cup light-tasting olive or avocado oil
- 3 tablespoons lemon juice
- ½ teaspoon Dijon mustard
- ¼ teaspoon ground black pepper
- 1 large head romaine lettuce

CRISPY TOPPING:
- 2 teaspoons ghee
- 3 tablespoons almond flour
- 1 teaspoon dried parsley leaves
- ⅛ teaspoon coarse (granulated) garlic powder
- pinch salt

STICKY ORANGE SUNFLOWER CHICKEN WITH SESAME BROCCOLI

ooey-gooey good!

This recipe came to be one night while I bemoaned the fact that I couldn't pick up the phone and order sticky chicken wings for delivery. You know what? This recipe comes together faster than waiting for take-out, and it tastes way better than anything that comes out of a cardboard carton.

Serves 2-4
Total Time: 40-45 minutes
Hands-off time: 15 minutes
Tools: grater, pint-size Mason jar, stick blender, 2-quart baking dish

Preheat the oven to 425F.

Make the sauce. Zest the orange and set the zest aside. Use a sharp knife to peel the orange, removing all of the white pith, then separate the sections and place in a pint-size Mason jar. Smash and peel the garlic and add to the jar, along with the rest of the sauce ingredients; whirl the ingredients with a stick blender until smooth. Set it aside.

Toast the sesame seeds. Heat a large, nonstick skillet over medium-high heat, 2 minutes. Add the sesame seeds and stir-fry until toasted, about 3-5 minutes. Transfer to a plate to cool.

Prep the chicken. Combine the ginger, garlic powder, salt, coriander, and pepper in a large bowl and mix with a fork. Add the chicken thighs to the bowl and toss to coat the pieces in the spices. Add the oil to the pan you used for the sesame seeds and reheat the pan over medium-high heat, 2 minutes. Add the chicken in a single layer and brown it, undisturbed, 3-4 minutes. Flip the chicken and brown the other side for 1 minute, then transfer to a 2-quart baking dish.

Thicken the sauce. Pour the sticky sauce into the pan you used for the chicken and heat it, scraping up any brown bits in the pan, until it's thickened a little, 1-2 minutes. Pour the sauce over the chicken and place the baking dish in the oven. Roast the chicken for 15-20 minutes, until the sauce is caramelized. While the chicken cooks, slice the scallions for the garnish and set aside, then cook the broccoli.

Cook the broccoli. Place the water in the skillet you used for the chicken and bring it to a boil. Add the broccoli, cover, and steam it until tender, about 5 minutes. Remove the lid and allow any remaining water to evaporate. Turn off the heat, drizzle the sesame oil over broccoli, toss to coat.

To serve, plate the broccoli and chicken, then top with extra sauce and garnishes.

STICKY SAUCE:
- 1 medium navel orange
- 2 cloves garlic
- ¼ cup coconut aminos
- ¼ cup sunflower seed butter
- 1 tablespoon tomato paste
- 1 tablespoon unseasoned rice vinegar
- 1 tablespoon fish sauce
- 1 teaspoon hot sauce
- 2 tablespoons arrowroot powder

CHICKEN:
- 1 teaspoon powdered ginger
- 1 teaspoon coarse (granulated) garlic powder
- 1 teaspoon salt
- ½ teaspoon ground coriander
- ½ teaspoon ground black pepper
- 8 boneless, skinless chicken thighs (1½ pounds)
- 1 teaspoon extra-virgin olive oil

SESAME BROCCOLI:
- 1 pound broccoli florets
- ½ cup water
- 2 teaspoons toasted sesame oil
- garnish: sesame seeds, scallions

YOU KNOW HOW YOU COULD DO THAT?

Replace the chicken thighs with chicken breast or pork chops. Use almond or cashew butter instead of sunflower seed butter.

COOKUP TIPS

Prepare the sauce and store it in the jar in the fridge. Brown the chicken and steam the broccoli; store both in separate airtight containers in the fridge. When it's time to eat, simmer the sauce and pour over the chicken in a baking dish. While the chicken cooks, stir-fry the broccoli in a nonstick skillet with the sesame oil until hot.

DATE-NUT KALE SALAD

kale really needs to relax

Have you ever massaged your kale? I didn't understand why kale salads were so popular until I learned the massaging trick. Now it all makes sense. Bitter and tough but loaded with vitamins, minerals, and fiber, kale has a well-deserved reputation as a *numero uno* leafy green. When you break down its defenses with a little salt and a lot of tough love, it surrenders, becoming less bitter, more flavorful, and able to stand up to dressings for days. This salad has a sweet-and-sour balance—thanks to the lemon, maple, and dates—with a nutty crunch of slivered almonds that complements the acerbic kale leaves.

Serves 2–4
Total time: 35–40 minutes
Hands-off time: 15 minutes
Tools: meat hammer

SALAD:
- 2 bunches kale (about 2 pounds)
- 1 lemon
- 1 clove garlic
- 2 teaspoons maple syrup (omit for Whole30)
- 1 teaspoon salt
- ½ teaspoon crushed red pepper flakes
- 2 tablespoons extra-virgin olive oil
- 8 medjool dates
- ¼ cup sliced almonds

CHICKEN:
- 4 boneless, skinless chicken breast halves (about 4–6 ounces each)
- 1 teaspoon salt
- ½ teaspoon ground black pepper
- 1 teaspoon extra-virgin olive oil
- ½ cup water

Massage the kale. Remove the tough ribs from the leaves and chop the kale into slivers or bite-sized pieces. Place the leaves in a very large bowl and add a pinch of salt. Toss the leaves to distribute the salt and start massaging. Grab handfuls of kale, rubbing them against each other and squeezing. It's similar to kneading dough, and the harder you are on the kale, the more tender it will be later. The best way to know if you've massaged it enough is to take a little bite: if it's still leathery or bitter, it needs more of a rubdown.

Make the dressing. Squeeze the juice from the lemon into a small bowl. Peel and crush the garlic clove and add it to the lemon juice, then whisk in the maple syrup, salt, and red pepper flakes. While you continue to whisk, drizzle in the olive oil. Pour the dressing over the kale and mix with your hands to coat the leaves. Transfer the bowl to the fridge to marinate while you cook the chicken.

Cook the chicken. Pound the chicken to ½-inch thickness between two pieces of plastic wrap with the smooth side of the meat hammer, then season with the salt and pepper. Warm the oil in a large, nonstick skillet over medium-high heat, 2 minutes. Add the chicken and cook undisturbed until brown on the first side, about 5 minutes. Flip the chicken over, add ½ cup water, and reduce the heat to medium low. Cover the pan and continue to cook until the inside of the chicken is no longer pink, about 5 minutes. Transfer the cooked chicken to a plate to cool a bit.

Finish the salad. Wipe out the skillet with a paper towel and reheat it over medium-high heat. Add the almonds and toast until golden, about 2 minutes. Keep an eye on them; they can burn quickly! Set aside to cool. Pit and chop the dates. Add the almonds and dates to the kale and toss to combine. Shred the chicken with two forks.

To serve, divide the kale among individual serving plates and top with chicken.

YOU KNOW HOW YOU COULD DO THAT?

Replace dates with raisins or dried apricots; replace almonds with chopped pecans or cashews; replace maple syrup with honey; replace lemon juice with orange juice. So, putting that all together, here's another delicious flavor combo: apricots, pecans, honey, and orange juice. Or dates, cashews, honey, and lemon. You're welcome.

COOKUP TIPS

Cook the chicken and make the kale salad in advance; the kale will maintain a pleasing texture for 2–3 days in an airtight container in the fridge.

ITALIAN CHICKEN PATTIES WITH GARLIC CHARD

an all-American Italian favorite

Parmigiana is a classic Italian eggplant dish. It's simple, lightly-breaded, and literally means "in the style of Parma." Chicken Parm is an American invention—a cutlet with thick breading, deep fried and tucked under a blanket of cheese. This recipe is not *autentico* Italian, nor is it truly American. It's a juicy chicken patty with a light tapioca coating that's quickly browned on the stovetop and then lovingly cloaked in basil-infused marinara sauce. *Mange!*

Make the sauce. Warm the olive oil in a medium saucepan over medium-high heat for 2 minutes. While the oil heats, peel and crush the garlic and add it to the pan. When the garlic is fragrant, about 30 seconds, add the tomato paste, cocoa, and Italian herb blend. Cook for 2 minutes, then add the vinegar, tomato sauce, and salt. Bring to a boil, reduce heat to low, and simmer uncovered. Mince the basil leaves and set aside.

Make the garlic oil for the chard. Heat a nonstick skillet over low heat and add the oil. Smash and peel the garlic, add the cloves to the pan, and let them cook in the oil while you make the chicken patties.

Prep the chicken seasonings. Place the chicken, salt, and pepper in a large mixing bowl; mix well. In a shallow bowl, use a fork to blend together the tapioca starch, Italian herb blend, and garlic powder.

Shape and cook the patties. Form the chicken into 4 equal-sized patties, then gently roll each in the tapioca coating.

Place the oil in another large, nonstick skillet and warm it over medium-high heat, about 2 minutes. Place the patties in the pan, leaving some wiggle room around them. Cook undisturbed until the patties are browned on one side, 2–3 minutes, then flip and cook on the other side, 3–4 minutes. Add an additional teaspoon of oil to the pan, if necessary.

Finish the chard. When the chicken patties are browned, increase the heat under the garlic oil to medium high. Wash and coarsely chop the chard. Add the leaves to the pan and toss to coat it with the oil. When it's wilted to your liking, remove the pan from the heat and season it with salt and pepper.

To serve, divide the chard among individual serving plates, top with a chicken patty and some of the sauce, then garnish with minced basil.

YOU KNOW HOW YOU COULD DO THAT?

Replace the ground chicken with ground pork. Also, if you're not doing a Whole30, you can save some time by using Muir Glen Organic Pasta Sauce in place of homemade.

COOKUP TIPS

Make the marinara sauce and store in an airtight jar in the fridge. When it's time to eat, gently reheat the sauce while you make the chard and chicken patties.

Serves 2–4
Total time: 30–35 minutes
Tools: nothing special

MARINARA SAUCE:
1 tablespoon extra-virgin olive oil
1 clove garlic
1 tablespoon tomato paste
½ teaspoon unsweetened cocoa powder
½ teaspoon dried Italian herb blend
1 teaspoon balsamic vinegar
1 (14-ounce) can tomato sauce
¼ teaspoon salt

GARLIC CHARD:
1 tablespoon extra-virgin olive oil
3 cloves garlic
1 pound Swiss chard
¼ teaspoon salt
pinch ground black pepper

CHICKEN PATTIES:
1½ pounds ground chicken
1 teaspoon salt
½ teaspoon ground black pepper
3 tablespoons tapioca starch
1 tablespoon dried Italian herb blend
¼ teaspoon coarse (granulated) garlic powder
1 tablespoon extra-virgin olive oil
garnish: a handful fresh basil leaves

BAKED CHICKEN & RICE WITH KICKIN' CRANBERRY SAUCE

cranberries with an opinion

This is a deceptively decadent meal. Unassuming chicken thighs turn crisp in the oven, and all their chickeny flavor is concentrated in the cauliflower rice for the ultimate pilaf. Just when it's all feeling maybe a bit too indulgent and cozy, the cranberry sauce busts onto the scene with a kick of orange and a jab of jalapeño. This is a roast chicken dinner with plenty of attitude.

Serves 2–4
Total time: 45 minutes
Hands-off time: 30 minutes
Tools: 2 rimmed baking sheets, food processor

CRANBERRY SAUCE:
 4 medjool dates
 1 large navel orange
 12 ounces fresh cranberries
 1 tablespoon extra-virgin olive oil
 ½ teaspoon salt
 4 whole cloves
 2 sticks cinnamon
 1 small jalapeño

RICE:
 1 large head cauliflower
 1 tablespoon extra-virgin olive oil
 ¾ teaspoon salt

CHICKEN:
 1 teaspoon salt
 ½ teaspoon ground black pepper
 ¼ teaspoon coarse (granulated) garlic powder
 ¼ teaspoon paprika
 1½ pounds boneless, skinless chicken thighs

Prep. Preheat the oven to 425F. Line two large, rimmed baking sheets with aluminum foil. Remove the pits from the dates and place the dates in a small bowl. Cover them with hot water to soak while you prep the other ingredients.

Rice the cauliflower. Break the cauliflower into florets, removing the stems. Place the florets in the food processor bowl and pulse until the cauliflower looks like rice, about 10 pulses. You may need to do this in batches. In a large bowl, mix the riced cauliflower with the olive oil and salt. Spread it evenly on one of the prepared baking sheets.

Season the chicken: Combine the salt, pepper, garlic powder, and paprika in a small bowl, then rub it onto the chicken pieces. Place the chicken in a single layer directly on top of the cauliflower rice.

Make the cranberry sauce. Using a vegetable peeler, remove the peel from the orange, taking off as little of the white pith as possible. Save the orange for later and julienne the peel. Remove the dates from the water, place them in the bowl of the food processor, and purée into a smooth paste. Transfer the puréed dates to a large mixing bowl and add the orange peel, cranberries, oil, salt, cloves, and cinnamon sticks. Thinly slice the jalapeño and add it to the bowl. Toss all the ingredients with two wooden spoons and transfer the mixture to the second baking sheet.

Roast everything. Place both pans in the oven and roast until the cranberries begin to burst and release their juices, 10–15 minutes. Remove the cranberry sheet from the oven and allow it to cool a bit. Roast the chicken for an additional 10–15 minutes, until the rice begins to brown and the chicken is sizzling and cooked through. (Poke a piece of chicken with a fork; the juices should run clear. If they're pink, keep roasting.)

Finish the cranberry sauce. Squeeze the juice from the orange into a small bowl. Transfer the roasted cranberries to a medium bowl, remove the cinnamon sticks, and stir in 2–3 tablespoons of the reserved orange juice.

To serve, divide the rice among individual plates, top with chicken, and add cranberry sauce on the side.

YOU KNOW HOW YOU COULD DO THAT?

Replace the chicken thighs with boneless pork chops. If you're feeling fancy, you can add ¼ cup pine nuts or sliced almonds (and/or ¼ cup raisins) to the raw cauliflower rice to make a jeweled pilaf.

COOKUP TIPS

Rice the cauliflower and soak and purée the dates; store both in separate airtight containers in the fridge. When it's time to eat, proceed with the roasting instructions.

GREEN GODDESS SALAD

Ah, the 1920s. Flappers, bob haircuts, and restaurants that created recipes in tribute to famous people! Green goddess dressing was invented by Philip Roemer, the chef of San Francisco's Palace Hotel, to honor thespian George Arliss. The actor starred in a play called *The Green Goddess*, an adventure story about a plane crash in the Asian kingdom of Rukh. There's a Rajah and British soldiers and the titular Green Goddess, who may have caused the crash as retribution for British shenanigans in India... and what that all has to do with garlic, chives, parsley, and tarragon, I don't know. But I give a standing ovation to Chef Roemer and bow with respect to the Green Goddess, because her namesake dressing is fittingly opulent.

CHICKEN:
- 4 boneless, skinless chicken breasts (4–6 ounces each)
- 1 lemon
- 2 cloves garlic
- 2 cups water
- 1 tablespoon salt

DRESSING:
- 1 clove garlic
- 1 large egg yolk
- 2 tablespoons plus ½ cup light-tasting olive or avocado oil
- 2 tablespoons lemon juice
- 2 anchovy fillets or 2 teaspoons anchovy paste
- ¼ cup (packed) fresh parsley leaves
- 2 tablespoons dried chives
- 1 tablespoon dried tarragon leaves

SALAD:
- 2 heads butter lettuce
- 4 scallions
- 1 large avocado
- 1 large seedless cucumber

Cook the chicken. Pound the chicken to ½-inch thickness between two sheets of plastic wrap. Cut the lemon into slices; smash and peel the garlic. In a large saucepan, combine the chicken, water, salt, lemon, and garlic. Bring to a boil, then cover and simmer on low, 15–20 minutes. Turn off the heat and let the chicken continue to cook while you make the salad.

Make the dressing. Smash and peel the garlic clove and place it in a pint-size Mason jar. Add the egg yolk, 2 tablespoons of the olive oil, the lemon juice, and anchovies to the jar. Whirl with the stick blender until puréed. With the blender running inside the jar, add the remaining ½ cup oil and blend until thickened. Mince the parsley and stir it into the dressing, along with the chives and tarragon. Place in the fridge to chill.

To serve, tear the butter lettuce into bite-sized pieces and arrange on individual serving plates. Thinly slice the scallions, avocado, and cucumber; divide among the plates. Remove the chicken from the pan and pat it dry. Cut the chicken crosswise into slices and arrange the slices on top of the salads. Dollop with dressing and serve.

Serves 2–4
Total time: 30–35 minutes
Tools: meat hammer, pint-size Mason jar, stick blender

YOU KNOW HOW YOU COULD DO THAT?

You can replace the chicken with poached shrimp, and if you did the Mini Cookup (p. 39), sliced hard-boiled eggs and cold slow-cooker potatoes are ace additions.

COOKUP TIPS

Cook the chicken and make the dressing in advance; store both in separate airtight containers in the fridge. When it's time to eat, cut the veggies and assemble.

POACHED CHICKEN SMORGASBORD

simple elegance, simply delicious

This is one of my favorite recipes in the book. The elements are homey and probably in your pantry right now. Casual and easy, like an indoor picnic, it's a perfect meal for when you don't feel like cooking or when you need to feed a crowd—after a bracing hike, before a Friday night game, at a lazy Sunday brunch. It's very easy to increase quantities without increasing the work, and it requires no fussy attention from you. But this dish has everything: a little something sweet, something salty, something creamy, and pecans. Pecans make anything great.

CHICKEN:
- 4 boneless, skinless chicken breasts (4–6 ounces each)
- 2 cups water
- 1 tablespoon salt
- 1 lemon
- 2 cloves garlic

CHAMPAGNE VINAIGRETTE:
- 1 clove garlic
- 1 large egg yolk
- 2 tablespoons plus ½ cup light-tasting olive or avocado oil
- 2 tablespoons champagne vinegar
- 1 tablespoon lemon juice
- 1 teaspoon Dijon mustard
- 1 teaspoon dried chives
- ¼ teaspoon dried tarragon leaves
- ¼ teaspoon salt
- ⅛ teaspoon ground black pepper

VEGGIES, FRUIT & NUTS:
- 1 large seedless cucumber
- 1 (15-ounce) can whole beets
- 1 large apple
- a handful dried apricots
- ¼ cup pecan halves
- cornichons

Cook the chicken. Pound the chicken to ½-inch thickness between two sheets of plastic wrap with the smooth side of the meat hammer. Place the chicken in a large saucepan with the water and salt. Cut the lemon into slices, smash and peel the garlic, and add both to the pot. Bring to a boil, then cover and simmer on low, 15–20 minutes. When the time is up, turn off the heat and let the chicken sit covered while you prep the rest of the ingredients.

Make the dressing. Smash and peel the garlic clove and place it in a pint-size Mason jar. Add the egg yolk, 2 tablespoons of the olive oil, the vinegar, lemon juice, mustard, chives, tarragon, salt, and pepper to the jar. Whirl with the stick blender until puréed. With the blender running inside the jar, add the remaining ½ cup oil and blend until smooth.

Prep the vegetables. Cut the cucumber on the diagonal into thin slices. Quarter the beets and cut the apple into wedges.

Finish the chicken. Remove the chicken from the pan and pat it dry. Cut the chicken crosswise into slices.

To serve, arrange all the ingredients on a platter or cutting board—with the dressing on the side—and let everyone build their own perfect plate.

Serves 2–4
Total time:
  30–35 minutes
Tools: meat hammer, pint-size Mason jar, stick blender

YOU KNOW HOW YOU COULD DO THAT?

If you made hard-boiled eggs during a Mini Cookup (page 39), a few sliced eggs are a great addition. In summer, you could add sun-ripened tomatoes to your spread, and in autumn, add cold, boiled new potatoes.

COOKUP TIPS

This is perfect Cookup food. Cook the chicken and make the dressing; store both in separate airtight containers in the fridge. When you're ready to eat, all that's left is to cut the raw veggies and apple.

TAHINI & APRICOT CHOPPED SALAD

Serves 2–4
Total time: 30–35 minutes
Tools: meat hammer, pint-size Mason jar, stick blender, food processor/mandoline

Have you ever had apricot leather? Not the thin, just-tastes-sweet fruit rollup kind. What I'm talking about is the chewy kind that almost bites back. It comes from Syria, wrapped in crinkly cellophane with an illustration of plump apricots on the filigreed label. Inside, the sheet of apricot paste is thick, sweet, tangy, and slightly slippery from the thin coating of olive oil that prevents it from sticking to its fabulous, translucent-orange self. It's one of my favorite tastes on the planet, and this recipe is an elaborate excuse to eat dried apricots. Crunchy, chewy, sweet, nutty, and light, this salad is as rewarding as tearing into a package of apricot paste.

SALAD:
- 2 tablespoons pine nuts
- ½ small red onion
- ¼ small head red cabbage
- ½ medium head green cabbage
- 1 large carrot
- 10 dried apricots
- ¼ cup fresh parsley leaves

CHICKEN:
- 1 teaspoon extra-virgin olive oil
- 4 boneless, skinless chicken breasts (4–6 ounces each)
- ¾ teaspoon salt
- ¼ teaspoon ground black pepper
- ¼ teaspoon ground cumin
- ⅓ cup water

DRESSING:
- 2 cloves garlic
- ½ lemon
- ⅓ cup tahini
- ⅓ cup water
- ½ teaspoon ground cumin
- pinch salt
- pinch ground black pepper

Toast the pine nuts. Warm a large, nonstick skillet over medium-high heat, 1 minute. Add the pine nuts and cook, stirring occasionally, until golden, about 5 minutes. Transfer them to a plate to cool.

Start the chicken. Warm the olive oil in the same skillet you used for the pine nuts over medium-high heat, 2 minutes. Pound the chicken to ½-inch thickness between two pieces of plastic wrap with the smooth side of the meat hammer, then season it with the salt, pepper, and cumin. Place the chicken in the skillet and cook undisturbed until browned on the bottom, about 5 minutes. While the chicken browns, make the dressing.

Make the dressing. Smash and peel the garlic and place it in a pint-size Mason jar. Squeeze the juice from the ½ lemon into the jar, then add the tahini, water, cumin, salt, and pepper; whirl with a stick blender until smooth.

Finish the chicken. Flip the chicken over, cook 2 more minutes, then add the water and reduce the heat to medium-low. Cover the skillet and continue to cook until the chicken is no longer pink inside, 5–10 minutes.

Prep the slaw. Use a mandoline or food processor fitted with the slicing blade to thinly slice the red onion, cabbages, and carrot. With a sharp knife, cut the apricots into slivers and coarsely chop the parsley. Place all the slaw ingredients in a large mixing bowl.

Bring it together. When the chicken is cooked, cut it crosswise into thin slices and add it to the bowl with the slaw. Toss to mix, then add half the dressing to the bowl. Toss to coat the salad with dressing, adding more in small amounts until you're happy with it. Taste and add salt and pepper as needed.

To serve, place the salad on individual serving plates and sprinkle with the pine nuts.

COOKUP TIPS

Toast the pine nuts, cook the chicken, make the dressing, and prep the slaw ingredients in advance; store everything in separate airtight containers in the fridge. Toss it all together just before eating.

COBB SALAD

EAT COBB*

Midnight, Hollywood, 1937. Robert Cobb, owner of the legendary Brown Derby, was peckish. So he and his pal Sid Grauman (of Chinese Theatre fame) grabbed leftovers from the restaurant's fridge: salad greens, avocado, cheese, chicken breast, a hard-boiled egg, bacon. Grauman had recently been to the dentist and wasn't chewing well, so they chopped everything into bite-sized pieces before tossing the salad with a vinaigrette. Unceremoniously and unintentionally, the Cobb salad was born.

Serves 2-4
Tools: meat hammer, pint-size
    Mason jar
Total Time: 35-40 minutes

PROTEIN:
    4 strips nitrate-free bacon
    1 teaspoon dried chives
    1 teaspoon salt
    ½ teaspoon dried tarragon
    ¼ teaspoon ground black pepper
    ⅛ teaspoon coarse (granulated)
        garlic powder
    4 boneless, skinless chicken
        breasts (4-6 ounces each)
    ⅓ cup water
    4 large eggs

DRESSING:
    ¼ cup red wine vinegar
    1 tablespoon Dijon mustard
    1 teaspoon dried chives
    ½ teaspoon dried thyme leaves
    ¼ teaspoon salt
    ⅛ teaspoon ground black pepper
    ½ cup extra-virgin olive oil

SALAD:
    1 head iceberg or leaf lettuce
    ½ medium red onion
    a handful black olives
    1 medium tomato
    1 avocado

Prep the egg pot. Place 4 cups water in a medium saucepan, cover the pan, and bring the water to a rolling boil.

Prep the proteins. Cut the bacon crosswise into ¼-inch-wide pieces. Place the chopped bacon in a large, cold nonstick skillet, turn the heat to medium-high, and fry the bacon until it's crisp, about 3-4 minutes. While it cooks, combine the chives, salt, tarragon, pepper, and garlic powder in a small bowl. Place the chicken between two pieces of plastic wrap and using the smooth side of the meat hammer, pound the chicken to ½-inch thickness.

Cook the chicken. Remove the pan from the heat and transfer the bacon with a slotted spoon to a paper towel-lined plate. Remove all but 1-2 teaspoons of the fat from the pan. Reheat the pan over medium-high heat. While it heats, sprinkle the spice blend on both sides of the chicken. Cook the chicken, undisturbed, 5 minutes. Flip the chicken and cook, 2 minutes. Add the water to the pan, cover with a lid, reduce the heat to medium, and cook undisturbed while you make the rest of the salad.

Boil the eggs. When the water boils, use a spoon to lower the eggs one at a time into the boiling water. Cover the pan, reduce the heat to low, and simmer for 10 minutes. SET A TIMER!

Make the dressing. In a pint-size Mason jar, combine the vinegar, mustard, chives, thyme, salt, and pepper; shake it like you mean it. Add the oil and shake the jar again with vigor.

Prep the vegetables. Thinly slice the lettuce and onion. Halve the olives. Dice the tomato and avocado.

Chill the eggs and check the chicken. Fill a large bowl with lots of ice and cold water. When the timer rings, remove the eggs from the pot with a spoon and lower them into the ice bath. Let them chill out for 5 minutes. Poke a chicken breast with a fork, if the juices run clear, it's cooked, and you can turn off the heat. If the juices are pink, let it continue to cook while you prep the salad.

Make the salad. Peel and slice the eggs. Divide the veggies among individual plates. Slice the chicken crosswise. Top the greens with chicken and egg, then drizzle with the dressing.

YOU KNOW HOW YOU COULD DO THAT?

Swap your greens: Try watercress, romaine lettuce, spring mix, or endive. Enjoying sunny skies like in L.A.? Toss the chicken breasts on the grill instead of cooking them on the stovetop.

COOKUP TIPS

Prep all the components and store them in separate airtight containers in the fridge, then toss together just before eating.

* EAT COBB: Egg, Avocado, Tomato, Chicken, Onion, Bacon, Black Olives

ZUCCHINI PASTA WITH CHICKEN & PISTACHIOS

totally twirlable

This recipe is an homage to the pasta recipes that show up on food magazine covers every spring. You know the ones: They feature a bowl of pasta flecked with herbs and golden chicken—and smiling, painfully chic people gathered around a picnic table on a hillside, all bathed in dappled sunlight. It makes you want to immediately pack a bag and buy a ridiculously expensive last-minute ticket to Tuscany. I'm here to remind you of a few key points: (a) Plan your trips more deliberately than that; (b) You are equally as stunning as *those people*; and (c) This recipe is a mini vacation anytime you need it.

Serves 2–4
Total time: 35–40 minutes
Tools: spiralizer, meat hammer, colander

NOODLES:
- 2–2½ pounds zucchini
- 1 tablespoon salt
- 1 tablespoon extra-virgin olive oil
- 2 cloves garlic
- ¼ teaspoon ground cumin
- ¼ teaspoon ground black pepper

CHICKEN:
- 4 boneless, skinless chicken breasts (4–6 ounces each)
- 1 tablespoon extra-virgin olive oil or ghee
- 1 teaspoon salt
- ½ teaspoon ground black pepper

AROMATICS:
- 2 scallions
- 7–10 fresh mint leaves
- ¼ cup shelled pistachios
- 1 tablespoon lemon juice

Prep the noodles. Julienne the zucchini with the spiralizer. Place the noodles in a colander and toss them with the salt until the strands are lightly coated. Set the colander in the sink to drain while you prep the other ingredients.

Cook the chicken. Pound the chicken to ½-inch thickness between two pieces of plastic wrap with the smooth side of the meat hammer, then slice it crosswise into strips. Warm the olive oil in a large, nonstick skillet over medium-high heat, 2–3 minutes. Add the chicken, sprinkle it with the salt and pepper, then toss to coat it in the oil. Spread the chicken in a single layer and let it cook undisturbed, 2–3 minutes. Flip with a spatula, separating the pieces and cook for an additional 2–3 minutes on the other side. Continue to flip and cook the chicken until it's browned and sizzling on most sides, about 2 minutes more. Transfer the chicken to a plate and cover it loosely with aluminum foil.

Prep the aromatics. Thinly slice the scallions, mince the mint leaves, and coarsely chop the pistachios. Add everything to a bowl with the lemon juice, mix with a fork, and place nearby because the next part goes quickly.

Finish the noodles. Place the olive oil in a small bowl. Peel and crush the garlic, then add it to the bowl with the oil. Add the cumin and pepper to the bowl, mix with a fork, and set it nearby. Rinse the zucchini noodles under running water, drain them well, and squeeze them in a clean dish towel to remove excess water. Return the skillet you used for the chicken to the stove and reheat it over medium-high heat, 2–3 minutes. Place the prepared zucchini noodles in the dry pan and sauté them until just tender, 2–3 minutes. Push the noodles to the side of the pan, and reduce the heat to medium low. Add the garlic oil to the pan and cook for 20 seconds, stirring constantly. Push the zucchini noodles into the oil and stir gently until they're coated. Turn off the heat and add the chicken to the noodles, along with the mint-pistachio mixture. Toss to combine.

To serve, divide the pasta among individual bowls and arm everyone with a big spoon to twirl the strands.

COOKUP TIPS

Spiralize and sweat the zucchini, and cook the chicken in advance; store both in separate airtight containers in the fridge. When it's time to eat, prep the aromatics, stir-fry the zucchini noodles, and bring it all together.

CHINESE CHICKEN SALAD

sunshine in a bowl

Chinese Chicken Salad reminds me of a lunch I shared with my husband Dave in California. You know how sometimes ordinary days turn out to be just perfect? This was one of those days. We were visiting Los Angeles, and we went to an upscale outdoor shopping mall, as you do. We found our way to a rooftop food court and ordered ginormous salads. And there we sat—in dazzling sunshine, looking cool in our sunglasses, languidly eating the freshest, crunchiest vegetables and watching the impossibly pretty people. The whole experience was like a full-release exhale. I hope this salad gives you a little taste of that on your ordinary days.

Toast the almonds. Heat a large, non-stick skillet over medium-high heat for 2 minutes. Add the sliced almonds and stir-fry until golden, about 2 minutes. Transfer to a plate to cool.

Cook the chicken. Pound the chicken to ½-inch thickness between two pieces of plastic wrap with the smooth side of the meat hammer, then season with the salt and pepper. Place the oil in the skillet you used for the almonds and warm it over medium-high heat, 2 minutes. Add the chicken and cook it undisturbed until the bottoms have browned, 4–5 minutes. Flip the chicken over, add the water to the skillet, and reduce the heat to medium-low. Cover the skillet and continue to cook until the inside of the chicken is no longer pink, about 5 minutes. Transfer the chicken to a plate and place it in the fridge to cool while you prep the rest of the ingredients.

Make the dressing. Smash and peel the garlic clove, peel and chop the ginger, and place both in a pint-size Mason jar. Add the rest of the dressing ingredients to the jar and whirl with a stick blender until smooth.

Prep the vegetables. Peel and grate the carrot. Thinly slice the cabbage, crosswise. Slice the pepper into thin strips. Cut the scallions in half lengthwise, then into 2-inch-long batons. Coarsely chop the cilantro. Place all the vegetables in a large mixing bowl. Shred the chicken and add it to the bowl. Pour in the dressing and toss to coat.

To serve, divide the salad among individual serving plates and sprinkle with sliced almonds.

COOKUP TIPS

Toast the almonds, cook the chicken, make the dressing, and prep the vegetables in advance; store everything in separate airtight containers in the fridge. Toss together just before eating.

Serves 2–4
Total time: 30–35 minutes
Tools: meat hammer, pint-size Mason jar, stick blender, grater

CHICKEN:
- ¼ cup sliced almonds
- 4 boneless, skinless chicken breast halves (about 4–6 ounces each)
- 1 teaspoon salt
- ½ teaspoon ground black pepper
- 1 teaspoon extra-virgin olive oil
- ⅓ cup water

DRESSING:
- 1 clove garlic
- 1-inch piece fresh ginger
- ⅓ cup unseasoned rice vinegar
- 2 tablespoons coconut aminos
- 1 tablespoon sunflower seed butter
- 2 teaspoons light-tasting olive or avocado oil
- 1 teaspoon toasted sesame oil
- ¼ teaspoon hot sauce

SALAD:
- 1 large carrot
- ½ medium head Napa cabbage (about 1½ pounds)
- 1 large red bell pepper
- 6 scallions
- ¼ cup cilantro leaves

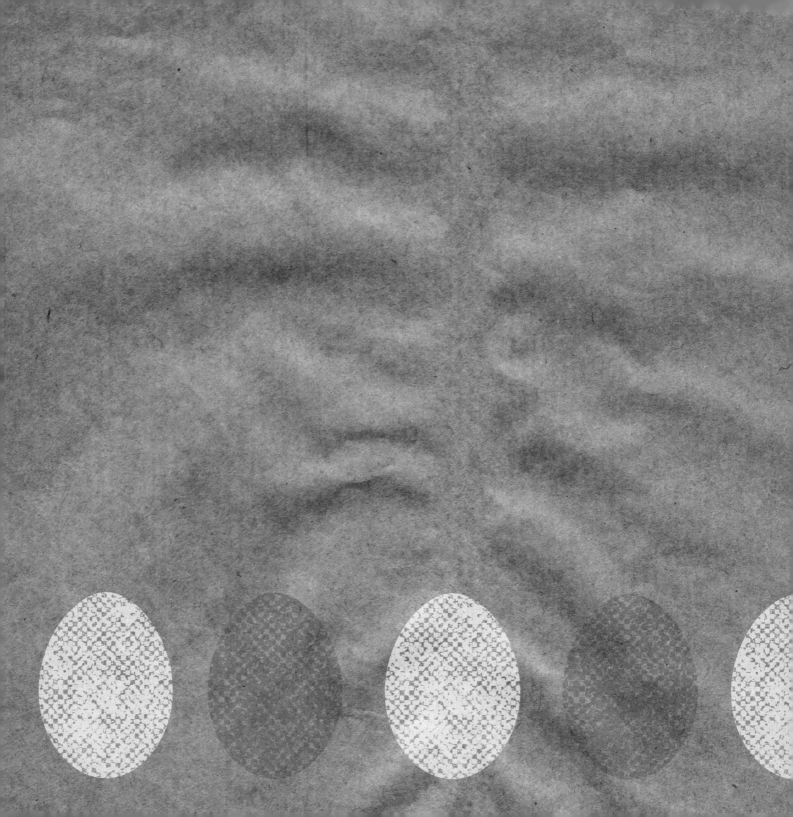

BLT EGG SALAD

an epic diner mash-up

The classic bacon-lettuce-and-tomato sandwich was first mentioned in a cookbook in 1903, and its popularity grew after World War II when supermarkets sold the ingredients year-round. Egg salad has been on menus since the invention of mayonnaise in 1756 and when it became standard on lunch counter menus in the early 1900s, it was served on a bed of lettuce, not as a sandwich. In this recipe, we ditch the bread of the BLT and marry its crisp bacon, cool lettuce, and juicy tomatoes with the creamy, rich texture of egg salad for the ultimate no-bread-needed diner plate.

Prep the egg pot. Place 4 cups water in a medium saucepan, cover, and bring the water to a rolling boil. While it does its thing, cook the bacon.

Fry the bacon. Cut the bacon cross-wise into ¼ inch pieces. Place the chopped bacon in a large, cold skillet, turn the heat to medium-high, and fry the bacon until it's crisp, 3–4 minutes. Remove the pan from the heat and use a slotted spoon to transfer the bacon to a paper towel-lined plate.

Boil the eggs. When the water boils, use a ladle or spoon to lower the eggs one at a time into the boiling water. Cover, reduce the heat to low, and simmer for 10 minutes. SET A TIMER!

Prep the veggies. Dice the sun-dried tomatoes and thinly slice the scallions; transfer both in a mixing bowl. Place the spring mix in another large mixing bowl; set aside. Cut the carrot, bell pepper, and cucumber into sticks and set aside.

Make the mayo. Place all of the mayo ingredients in a pint-size Mason jar and whirl with a stick blender for about 30 seconds. Voila! Mayo is done. Set it aside.

Chill the eggs: Fill a large bowl with plenty of ice and cold water. When the eggs are ready, remove them from the pot with a slotted spoon and lower them into the ice bath. Let them chill for 5 minutes.

Make the egg salad. Peel and chop the eggs and place them in the mixing bowl with the scallions and sundried tomatoes. Add the bacon and ¼ cup mayo. Mix to combine, and add more mayo, 1 tablespoon at a time, until you reach your desired consistency.

Make the bed: Toss the spring mix with the vinegar, oil, salt, and pepper.

To serve, place the greens on individual dinner plates and top with a mound of egg salad and veggie sticks.

COOKUP TIPS

Boil the eggs. Cook the bacon. Cut the veggies. Make the mayo. Store everything separately in airtight containers in the fridge, then dress the greens and mix the egg salad just before serving.

Serves 2–4
Total time: 30–35 minutes
Hands-off time: 10 minutes
Tools: pint-size Mason jar, stick
  blender

EGG SALAD:
  4 cups water
  12 large eggs
  6 strips nitrate-free bacon
  6 sun-dried tomato halves
  3 scallions

MAYO:
  1 large egg
  2 tablespoons lemon juice
  ½ teaspoon mustard powder
  ½ teaspoon salt
  1¼ cups light-tasting olive oil
    or avocado oil

VEGGIES:
  lots of spring mix
  2–4 carrots
  2 green or red bell peppers
  1 seedless cucumber
  1 tablespoon cider vinegar
  2 teaspoons extra-virgin olive oil
  ¼ teaspoon salt
  ⅛ teaspoon ground black pepper

FRETTA

Let's get something straight right off the bat: This recipe is neither a true frittata, nor an omelet—and it's more than merely scrambled eggs. It's a fretta, the monster breakfast (or wholly pleasing dinner) served in greasy-spoon diners all over central New York. It's loosely based on an Italian frittata and usually incorporates pizza toppings: pepperoni, mushrooms, peppers, and onions. It's kind of like junk food made acceptable with the addition of protein-packed eggs.

shout out to the All Night Egg Plant diner

Prep. Warm 2 teaspoons oil in a large, nonstick skillet over medium-high heat for 2 minutes. While the oil heats, slice the mushrooms, dice the onion and bell pepper, and seed and mince the jalapeño; set aside.

Cook the mushrooms. Add the mushrooms to the hot skillet with a pinch of salt, and stir to evenly coat with oil. You'll hear them sizzle! Continue cooking for 1–2 minutes, stirring frequently, until they release their moisture. Continue cooking over medium-high heat, stirring occasionally, until all the moisture has evaporated and the mushrooms begin to turn brown, 5–8 more minutes. Transfer the mushrooms to a plate.

Sauté the meats and veggies. Add another 2 teaspoons of oil to the skillet and warm it over medium-high heat, 2 minutes. While the oil heats, cut the ham, pepperoni, and salami into large dice; set aside. Add the onion, pepper, and jalapeño to the pan and cook until just crisp-tender, 1–2 minutes. Add the meats and cook them until they begin to brown and crisp, 4–5 minutes.

Add the eggs. In a small bowl, whisk the eggs with the salt and pepper and pour them into the skillet. Allow the eggs to set a bit, then gently stir to create large curds. Cook to your desired doneness. Turn off the heat and mince the parsley.

To serve, divide the eggs among individual serving plates and sprinkle with parsley. Devour immediately.

YOU KNOW HOW YOU COULD DO THAT?

Got slow cooker potatoes (p. 43)? Add cubes to the pan while you brown the meats.

COOKUP TIPS

Cut the veggies and meats in advance and store them in separate airtight containers in the fridge.

Serves 2–4
Total time: 25–30 minutes
Tools: nothing special

- 1–2 tablespoons extra-virgin olive oil
- 4 ounces white mushrooms
- ½ medium sweet onion
- ½ green or red bell pepper
- 1 small jalapeño
- 4 ounces nitrate-free ham steak
- 2 ounces Applegate Farms Uncured Pork Pepperoni
- 2 ounces Applegate Farms Natural Genoa Salami
- 8 large eggs
- ½ teaspoon salt
- ¼ teaspoon ground black pepper
- garnish: fresh parsley leaves

COMFORT RICE AND COMFORT NOODLES

the best solo dinner

Back in the day, a bowl of spaghetti with olive oil and breadcrumbs was one of my go-to meals when I was on my own for dinner. It could be thrown together quickly, and it was soothing and nonconfrontational. I don't miss the pasta, but I wanted to recreate that experience: a warm, comforting bowl of food that can be twirled to make big, soft, round bites... the kind of food you eat while wearing pajamas, unplugged from the rest of the world. Trust me: These do not taste like bowls of vegetables. The garlic and olive oil transform these dishes so they taste like neither vegetables nor eggs, but some miraculous, snuggly merging of the two.

COMFORT RICE

Serves 1
Total time: 20-25 minutes
Tools: food processor

RICE:
- ½ medium head cauliflower
- 2 teaspoons extra-virgin olive oil
- ½ teaspoon salt

COMFORT:
- ½ teaspoon coconut oil or ghee
- 1 tablespoon almond flour or almond meal
- pinch salt, plus more as needed
- 1 clove garlic
- ¼ cup fresh parsley leaves
- 3-4 large eggs
- 1 teaspoon dried chives
- 1 tablespoon extra-virgin olive oil

Prep the rice. Break the cauliflower into florets, removing the stems. Place the florets in the food processor bowl and pulse until the cauliflower looks like rice, about 10 pulses; set aside.

Make the crumbs. Warm the coconut oil in a large, nonstick skillet over medium-high heat, 2 minutes. Add the almond flour and salt; stir to coat it in the fat. Cook, stirring occasionally, until toasty brown, about 1 minute. Transfer to a plate to cool. As it cools, the coconut oil will solidify and make "crumbs," so don't worry if it's just brown dust when you take it out of the pan. Push the dust together into a pile and let it do its thing.

Cook the cauliflower. Reheat the skillet over high heat. Add the oil, cauliflower, and salt. Toss to coat the cauliflower with the oil. Cover the skillet, reduce the heat to low, and cook until the cauliflower is tender, about 5 minutes.

Prep the eggs. Peel and crush the garlic and mince the parsley; place both in a small bowl. Crack the eggs into another small bowl and add the chives, along with a few shakes of salt and pepper. Beat with a fork until just combined; set aside.

Put it together. Push the cauliflower rice to one side of the skillet and add the olive oil and garlic-parsley mixture. When the garlic is fragrant, about 20 seconds, pour the eggs into the pan. Toss the rice with the egg until it's coated, then let it cook undisturbed, 30 seconds or so. Then alternate stirring and resting, until the egg is set and clinging to the rice. Taste and season with more salt and pepper to your liking.

To serve, transfer the rice to a deep bowl and sprinkle with the almond flour crumbs. Eat with a spoon.

COMFORT NOODLES

Serves 1
Total time: 20-25 minutes
Tools: spiralizer, colander

NOODLES:
- 1 large zucchini (about ½ pound)
- ¾ teaspoon salt

COMFORT:
- ½ teaspoon coconut oil or ghee
- 1 tablespoon almond flour or almond meal
- pinch salt, plus more as needed
- 1 clove garlic
- ¼ cup fresh parsley leaves
- 3-4 large eggs
- 1 teaspoon dried chives
- ⅛ teaspoon ground black pepper
- 1 tablespoon extra-virgin olive oil

Prep the noodles. Julienne the zucchini with the spiralizer. Place the noodles in a colander and toss them with the salt until the strands are lightly coated. Set the colander in the sink to drain while you prep the other ingredients.

Make the crumbs. Warm the coconut oil in a large, nonstick skillet over medium-high heat, 2 minutes. Add the almond flour and salt; stir to coat it in the fat. Cook, stirring occasionally, until toasty brown, about 1 minute. Transfer to a plate to cool. As it cools, the coconut oil will solidify and make "crumbs," so don't worry if it's just brown dust when you take it out of the pan. Push the dust together into a pile and it will all work out.

Prep the eggs. Peel and crush the garlic and mince the parsley; place both in a small bowl. Crack the eggs into another small bowl and add the chives, along with a few shakes of salt and pepper. Beat with a fork until just combined; set aside.

Cook the noodles. Rinse the zucchini noodles under running water, then squeeze them dry in a clean dish towel. Reheat the skillet over high heat, 1 minute. Add the zucchini noodles and cook until just tender, 2–3 minutes. Push the noodles to the side of the pan and reduce to medium-low heat. Add the olive oil and garlic-parsley mixture. When the garlic is fragrant, about 20 seconds, pour the eggs into the pan. Toss the zucchini noodles with the egg until the strands are coated, then let it cook, undisturbed, 30 seconds or so. Then alternate stirring and resting until the egg is set and clinging to the noodles. Taste and season with more salt and pepper to your liking.

To serve, transfer the noodles to a deep bowl and sprinkle with the almond flour crumbs. Slurping and ridiculously big bites are heartily encouraged.

COOKUP TIPS
Spiralize and sweat the zucchini—or rice the cauliflower in the food processor—and store in an airtight container in the fridge. When it's time to eat, make the crumbs and cook the noodles or rice with the eggs.

50 COMFORTING THINGS

IN NO PARTICULAR ORDER...

1. the cool side of the pillow
2. the movie you've seen so many times you know the dialogue by heart
3. changing into your pjs
4. your favorite snuggly blanket
5. a steaming cup of tea on a cold day
6. the smell of cinnamon and vanilla
7. a fresh snowfall waiting for you to make footprints
8. a brand new box of crayons
9. deep, rhythmic breathing with your eyes closed
10. a just-opened jar of Sunbutter
11. having someone play with your hair
12. the weight in your lap of a warm, purring cat
13. savasana, a.k.a. lying flat on the floor on your back
14. the song you sang in the car with your best friend as teenagers
15. jumping into a cold pool on a hot day
16. the sound of rain when you're napping
17. a sip of icy cold water after a hard workout
18. a baked potato with just the right amount of salt
19. the scent of a loved one on a piece of clothing
20. waking up without the alarm
21. a full-contact hug that goes on as long as you want it to
22. the adoring gaze of your dog
23. walking barefoot on soft grass
24. taking a shower after playing outside
25. massaging lotion into your hands
26. cat head-butts
27. t-shirts with no tags at the back of the neck
28. a good cry
29. a walk on the beach
30. stargazing on a blanket in the backyard
31. the scent of a fireplace on the winter air
32. a long soak in a warm bath
33. a steaming mug of bone broth
34. crossing the last item off a to-do list
35. a refrigerator full of paleo food
36. waking up to the smell of coffee brewing
37. falling asleep in the backseat to the murmur of people talking in the front seat
38. driving your car with the windows down and the radio up
39. reading a children's story out loud (I recommend *Alexander and the Terrible, Horrible, No Good, Very Bad Day* or *Hug Machine*.)
40. spending all day in squishy clothes with your favorite book (I recommend *Jane Eyre* or *The Night Circus*.)
41. flossing and brushing your teeth before bed
42. when someone scratches the itch you can't reach
43. the re-run of that one TV show you love
44. the crunch of leaves under your feet in autumn
45. lighting a candle with a match
46. the feel of sunshine on your back
47. when your hiccups stop
48. getting the shower water temperature just right
49. taking a nap with somebody else (or a kitten/bunny/dog)
50. a spontaneous dance break in the kitchen

REYKJAVIK SALMON & SOFT-BOILED EGG SALAD

Verði þér að góðu (bon appetit)

When Dave and I visited Reykjavik, Iceland, our hotel served up an epic buffet every morning in the breakfast room. I loved it so much, I documented it in my journal, listing every item on the buffet with asterisks next to the ones I ate. It was my first time trying pickled herring, and the smoked salmon was unlike any I'd eaten before. It was beyond tender; nouns like "silk" and "velvet" come close. This recipe is the result of the stunningly fresh and flavorful local ingredients I piled on my plate each morning. It's salty, crispy, creamy, cool—and whenever I eat it, it reminds me of our Icelandic adventures.

Serves 2–4
Total time: 25–30 minutes
Tools: pint-size Mason jar, stick blender

SALAD:
  8 large eggs
  12 ounces smoked salmon
  2 medium cucumbers
  dill pickles (spears or chips)
  a few sprigs fresh dill
  1 lemon

MAYO:
  1 large egg
  2 tablespoons lemon juice
  ½ teaspoon mustard powder
  ½ teaspoon salt
  1¼ cups light-tasting olive or avocado oil

Prep the egg pot. Place 4 cups water in a medium saucepan, cover the pan, and bring the water to a rolling boil over high heat. Don't watch the pot; it will never boil that way. Instead, make the mayo.

Make the mayo. Place all the mayo ingredients in a pint-size Mason jar and whirl with a stick blender for about 30 seconds. Done! Set it aside.

Cook the eggs. When the water is boiling, use a spoon to lower the eggs one at a time into the boiling water. Cover the pan, reduce the heat to low, and simmer the eggs for 9 minutes. NINE MINUTES EXACTLY! This produces whites that are firm and yolks that are just-gelled. Nine minutes, friends; this is the magic number. SET A TIMER!

Prep the salad. Slice the salmon, cucumbers, and pickles. Mince the dill. Cut the lemon into wedges. Arrange the salmon and veggies on a serving platter or individual plates. Then prepare an ice bath for the eggs: Fill a large bowl with plenty of ice and cold water.

Chill the eggs. When the eggs are finish cooking, remove them from the pot with a slotted spoon and lower them into the ice bath. Let them chill out for 5 minutes, then peel and cut them in half.

To serve, add the eggs to the salmon salad, top the whole bounty with a dollop of mayo, then sprinkle with minced dill and a squeeze of lemon juice.

COOKUP TIPS

Cook the eggs and make the mayo in advance; store both in separate airtight containers in the fridge. When it's time to eat, all you need to do is chop and assemble.

SHAKSHUKA WITH GARLICKY WILTED SPINACH

Shakshuka is huevos rancheros by way of the Sahara desert. It's a stovetop casserole composed of cloud-like eggs that are lovingly simmered in a silken, spiced tomato sauce. The dish is an everyday breakfast or dinner in North African countries like Morocco, Egypt, and Tunisia—and it's wildly popular in Israel, too, the result of Jewish immigration in the 1950s. In cafés, it's often served in sizzling, individual-sized cast-iron skillets. Once you've tried shakshuka, you'll find yourself daydreaming about when you'll eat it again.

Serves 2-4
Total time: 35-40 minutes
Tools: nothing special

GARLICKY WILTED SPINACH:

- 1 tablespoon extra-virgin olive oil
- 3 cloves garlic
- 2 (5-ounce) packages baby spinach
- ¼ teaspoon salt
- pinch ground black pepper

SHAKSHUKA:

- 4 teaspoons extra-virgin olive oil
- 1 medium sweet onion
- 1 large red bell pepper
- 3 cloves garlic
- 2 teaspoons ground cumin
- 2 teaspoons paprika
- 1½ teaspoons salt
- ½ teaspoon Aleppo pepper
- ½ teaspoon ground black pepper
- ¼ cup tomato paste
- 1 (28-ounce) can fire-roasted crushed tomatoes
- 8-12 large eggs
- ½ cup fresh parsley or cilantro

Start the spinach. Place the oil in a large, nonstick skillet and warm it over low heat. Smash and peel the garlic, add it to the pan, and let it mellow out in the oil while you make the shakshuka.

Start the shakshuka. Warm the oil in another large, nonstick skillet over medium-high heat, 2-3 minutes. While the oil heats, halve the onion and bell pepper, then cut them into thin strips. Cook the vegetables gently until very soft, about 7 minutes. While the veggies cook, peel and mince the garlic; place it in a small bowl and add the cumin, paprika, salt, Aleppo pepper, and black pepper. Add the spices to the pan and cook until fragrant, 30 seconds. Add the tomato paste to the pan and cook for 1 minute. Pour in the crushed tomatoes and simmer until thickened, about 5 minutes.

Cook the eggs. Make indentations in the sauce with the back of a spoon and gently crack the eggs into the wells. Season the eggs with a few shakes of salt and pepper. Cover the skillet with a lid and cook until the eggs are just set, 7 to 10 minutes. (You may want to spoon some of the tomato sauce over the whites to help them cook; be gentle and don't agitate the yolk.) While the eggs cook, mince the parsley.

Finish the spinach. Increase the heat under the garlic oil to medium high. Add the spinach and toss to coat it with the oil. When the spinach is almost all wilted, turn off the heat and season with the salt and pepper.

To serve, divide the spinach among individual serving plates, then top it with eggs, generous spoonfuls of sauce, and a dusting of minced parsley.

YOU KNOW HOW YOU COULD DO THAT?

Make a meat sauce: When you start the shakshuka, brown 1 pound ground lamb or beef before sautéing the onion and pepper, then proceed with the rest of the recipe—or make these ingredient substitutions to change the country of origin:

Tex-Mex: Omit the paprika and add 1 tablespoon chili powder. Garnish with minced cilantro and a squeeze of lime juice.

Italian: Omit the cumin and paprika. Add 1 tablespoon dried Italian herb blend. Garnish with minced basil leaves.

COOKUP TIPS

Prep the sauce and store it in an airtight container in the fridge. When it's time to eat, start the spinach, reheat the sauce, and pick up at "Cook the eggs."

SEXY SCRAMBLED EGGS

If the Fretta (page 201) is an overt, enthusiastic, affectionate hug, this recipe is a subtle, seductive glance across the room. It's scrambled eggs, all grown up and comfortable with who they are. In my imagination, this is the effortlessly tempting meal that Bogie whipped up for Lauren Bacall, circa 1945, while she lounged around wearing his silk pajamas. But you don't need candlelight and witty repartee to enjoy this scramble, and I won't judge if you end up eating it while watching Netflix in your jammies.

Prep the mushrooms. Place a large, nonstick skillet over medium-high heat. While it warms, place the balsamic vinegar, oil, Italian herb blend, salt, pepper, and garlic powder in a large bowl and whisk until combined. Remove the stems from the mushroom caps and add the caps to the bowl. Roll them around in the marinade until coated. Place the mushrooms smooth-side down in the skillet and cook, uncovered. They'll release their moisture and begin to caramelize. After about 5 minutes, flip the caps and cook them another 1–2 minutes, until they're browned and tender. (If you have very large mushroom caps, cover the pan with a lid for the last 2 minutes of cooking.) Transfer the mushrooms to a plate and cover them with foil to keep them warm.

Cook the eggs. Reheat the same skillet you used for the mushrooms and warm it over medium-high heat, 2 minutes. While it heats, cut the salami into thin strips.

Add the salami to the pan and cook until crispy and browned, about 2 minutes. Reduce the heat to medium, crack the eggs into the same mixing bowl you used for the mushrooms, and add the chives, salt, and pepper; whisk until just combined. Pour the eggs into the pan. Stir gently and almost continuously to make soft curds. Take a moment to mince the basil. When the eggs are cooked to your liking, remove them from the heat.

To serve, place mushroom caps on individual serving plates. Add a handful of spinach leaves to each cap, then top with eggs and a sprinkle of basil.

YOU KNOW HOW YOU COULD DO THAT?
Replace the salami with pepperoni or pancetta. For Whole30, you can replace the deli meats with prosciutto.

Serves 2
Total time: 15–20 minutes
Tools: nothing special

MUSHROOMS:
2 tablespoons balsamic vinegar
1 tablespoon extra-virgin olive oil
½ teaspoon dried Italian herb blend
¼ teaspoon salt
¼ teaspoon ground black pepper
¼ teaspoon coarse (granulated) garlic powder
4 portobello mushroom caps

EGGS:
4 ounces Applegate Farms Natural Genoa Salami
8 large eggs
1 tablespoon dried chives
½ teaspoon salt
¼ teaspoon ground black pepper
a few handfuls baby spinach

garnish: a handful fresh basil

TEX-MEX SKILLET

un poco caliente y picante

My first-bite recipe testers are trusted friends and family members who join me for family dinners where new dishes are tasted, chewed, and evaluated. This recipe was a big hit with my taste testers because it's the food equivalent of a Labrador retriever—easygoing, reliable, and comforting. Bonus: It requires the bare minimum of cooking skills, so cooking it is relaxing, too.

4 teaspoons extra-virgin olive oil
½ medium yellow onion
¾ pound yellow summer squash
1 medium red bell pepper
1 ½ pound ground beef
1 teaspoon salt
½ teaspoon ground black pepper
4 large eggs
1 cup salsa
a handful fresh cilantro
3–4 scallions

Cook the veggies. Warm 2 teaspoons olive oil in a large, nonstick skillet over medium-high heat, 2 minutes. While the oil heats, dice the onion. Add the onion to the skillet with a pinch of salt and cook, stirring occasionally, until soft, about 5 minutes. While the onion cooks, cut the squash into thin half-moons and the bell pepper into strips. Add the squash and pepper to the pan and stir-fry until crisp-tender, 5–7 minutes; transfer the veggies to a large bowl.

Cook the meat. Crumble the beef into the skillet and cook, breaking up the meat with a wooden spoon, until it is just pink, then sprinkle with the salt and pepper. When the meat is browned, add it to the bowl with the veggies.

Cook the eggs. Add the remaining 2 teaspoons olive oil to the pan and warm it over medium-high heat. In a small bowl, whisk the eggs with a pinch of salt and pepper. Pour the eggs into the skillet, stirring and cooking until they're almost set. Return the meat and vegetables to the pan, pour in the salsa, and mix everything together into one beautiful mess. Remove the skillet from the heat, then mince the cilantro and slice the scallions.

To serve, divide the sauté among individual serving dishes and sprinkle with cilantro and scallions.

YOU KNOW HOW YOU COULD DO THAT?

Replace the ground beef with ground turkey. You can significantly change the flavor by swapping salsa flavors; try green, red, varieties of heat, or chipotle.

Serves 2–4
Total time:
   25–30 minutes
Tools: nothing
   special

ENGLISH BREAKFAST

brinner makes you a winner

A proper British fry-up is a hearty way to start—or end—the day. This version of the traditional breakfast classic takes brinner to a new, healthier level, and it couldn't be simpler. Pop everything—eggs, sausages, bacon, tomatoes, and mushrooms—into the oven and let it do its thing. Now you can enjoy a nice cuppa and spend a few minutes visiting with Sherlock Holmes.

4 plum tomatoes
8 white mushrooms
1-2 tablespoons extra-virgin olive oil
2-4 links nitrate-free sausage
4 slices nitrate-free bacon
1-2 tablespoons extra-virgin olive oil
salt and ground black pepper
8 large eggs
garnish: fresh parsley leaves or fresh
    chives (or both!)

Preheat the oven to 450F. Line two large, rimmed baking sheets with aluminum foil.

Prep the veggies and meat. Cut each tomato lengthwise into 3–4 slices; cut the mushrooms into ¼-inch-thick slices. Cut the sausage into pieces. Arrange the tomatoes, mushrooms, bacon, and sausage on the baking sheets, alternating rows of meat and vegetables. Brush the tomatoes and mushrooms lightly with olive oil, then sprinkle them with salt and pepper. Place the baking sheet in the oven; it doesn't matter if the oven temperature hasn't yet reached 450F. Set a timer for 20 minutes.

Prep the eggs. While the veggies and meats roast, brush the insides of 8 cups of a muffin tin with olive oil, then crack an egg into each cup. When the meats and veggies have roasted for 20 minutes, place the eggs in the oven and set the timer again: 8 minutes for soft, runny yolks; 9–10 minutes for gelled yolks; 11–12 minutes for hard yolks. Remove the eggs when they're cooked to your liking, and if the bacon isn't quite crisp enough yet, set a timer for 5 more minutes. Mince the parsley and/or chives.

To serve, scoop the eggs out of the muffin cups with a spoon and place on individual serving plates with tomatoes, mushrooms, sausage, and bacon. Sprinkle with the minced herbs.

YOU KNOW HOW YOU COULD DO THAT?

If you have slow cooker potatoes (p. 43) handy, add ¼-inch slices to the baking sheets with the other veggies; brush with oil. You could also replace the sausage or bacon with nitrate-free ham steak.

Serves 2–4
Total time:
    40–45 minutes
Hands-free time:
    30 minutes
Tools: 2 rimmed
    baking sheets,
    muffin tin

CHINESE PANCAKE

say "yes" to secret sauce

There is nothing authentically Chinese about this recipe. In fact, I'm not even sure why I decided to call it a Chinese pancake, except that it just felt right. This dish is a collision of the concepts of "omelet" and "pancake." It's sort of like egg foo yong, but with the zucchini noodles as a key ingredient, it becomes its own kind of thing. Loaded with umami, this sorta-pancake is simultaneously supple and solid. Don't skip the super secret sauce!

Prep the noodles. Julienne the zucchini with a spiralizer. Place the noodles in a colander and toss generously with salt until the strands are lightly coated. Set in the sink to drain while you prep the other ingredients.

Make the pancake batter. Crack the eggs into a medium bowl, and add the coconut aminos, Chinese five-spice powder, sesame oil, salt, and cayenne pepper; whisk until combined and set aside. Thinly slice the scallions and set them aside.

Make the sauce. Smash and peel the garlic clove and place it in a pint-size Mason jar. Add the egg yolk, 2 tablespoons of the olive oil, the rice vinegar, lemon juice, coconut aminos, salt, sesame oil, and red pepper flakes to the jar and whirl with a stick blender until smooth. With the blender running inside the jar, add the remaining ½ cup oil and purée until thickened.

Finish the noodles. Rinse the zucchini noodles under running water, drain well, and squeeze them dry in a clean dish towel. Heat a large, nonstick skillet over medium-high heat, 2 minutes. Add the zucchini noodles and stir-fry for 1–2 minutes until

wilted and dry. Add the shrimp and sliced scallions; toss to combine.

Cook the pancake. Pour 2 teaspoons oil into the edge of the pan so it runs under the zucchini. Then pour the egg batter into the pan and swirl the skillet so the eggs run into and under the zucchini. Pat it smooth, cover the pan with a lid, and cook, undisturbed, for 6 minutes, then reduce the heat to low and cook until the eggs are set, about 5 minutes more. Flip the pancake out of the pan and onto a cutting board. Let it cool for a minute or two before cutting.

To serve, cut the pancake into wedges, drizzle it with sauce, and sprinkle with scallions and cilantro.

YOU KNOW HOW YOU COULD DO THAT?
Replace the shrimp with cooked ground pork or chicken.

COOKUP TIPS
Spiralize the zucchini and store in an airtight container in the fridge. Make the Spicy Secret Sauce and store it in the Mason jar in the fridge. When it's time to eat, finish the noodles and make the pancake.

Serves 2–4
Total time: 35–40 minutes
Tools: spiralizer, colander, pint-size Mason jar, stick blender

NOODLES:
1 pound zucchini
1 teaspoon salt

PANCAKE:
8 large eggs
2 teaspoons coconut aminos
1 teaspoon Chinese five-spice powder
1 teaspoon toasted sesame oil
½ teaspoon salt
¼ teaspoon cayenne pepper
8 ounces cooked salad shrimp
4 scallions
4 teaspoons extra-virgin olive oil
garnish: green scallion tops, cilantro leaves

SPICY SECRET SAUCE:
1 clove garlic
1 large egg yolk
2 tablespoons plus ½ cup light-tasting olive or avocado oil
1 tablespoon unseasoned rice vinegar
1 tablespoon lemon juice
2 teaspoons coconut aminos
½ teaspoon toasted sesame oil
¼ teaspoon salt
⅛ teaspoon crushed red pepper flakes

SHRIMP PATTIES WITH SESAME SNOW PEAS

like appetizers for dinner

When I was a kid, there was nothing I wanted more at the Chinese restaurant than the pupu platter. First, there was the name. Hilarious! Second, there was the tiny hibachi grill in the center of the platter. Third: shrimp toast. Oh, shrimp toast! It was greasy, crispy, salty, and squishy. It was also the ultimate American-Chinese appetizer of the 1960s, when white bread collided with chestnuts to create delights of questionable Polynesian origin at tiki parties all over suburbia. This recipe combines shrimp, herbs, and water chestnuts to recreate the briny appeal without the problematic toast.

SHRIMP PATTIES:
- 1½ pounds raw shrimp
- 1 (8-ounce) can water chestnuts
- 1 teaspoon water
- ½ teaspoon cream of tartar
- ¼ teaspoon baking soda
- 1 clove garlic
- 1 tablespoon fresh cilantro leaves
- 1 tablespoon dried chives
- ½ teaspoon salt
- 3–4 teaspoons coconut oil

SNOW PEAS:
- ¼ cup water
- 1 pound snow peas
- 2 teaspoons ghee
- 1 teaspoon sesame seeds

DIPPING SAUCE:
- 1 clove garlic
- 1 scallion
- 1-inch piece fresh ginger
- ¼ cup unseasoned rice vinegar
- ¼ cup coconut aminos
- ½ teaspoon toasted sesame oil
- ¼ teaspoon crushed red pepper flakes

Serves 2–4
Total time: 35–40 minutes
Tools: grater, pint-size Mason jar

Prep the shrimp patty ingredients. Peel and devein the shrimp. Drain the liquid from the water chestnuts. Combine the water, cream of tartar, and baking soda in a small bowl. Smash and peel the garlic clove.

Make the shrimp paste. In the bowl of a food processor, combine the peeled shrimp, water chestnuts, baking soda paste, garlic, cilantro, chives, and salt. Pulse until the mixture forms a smooth paste, then place the food processor bowl in the fridge while you cook the snow peas.

Cook the snow peas. Place the water in a large, nonstick skillet and bring it to a boil. Wash the snow peas and add them to the pan. Toss with two wooden spoons until the peas are dark green and the water has evaporated. Add the ghee and sesame seeds; stir-fry 1 minute and transfer them to a bowl. Lightly cover the bowl with aluminum foil to retain the heat.

Make the sauce. Peel and crush the garlic. Thinly slice the scallion. Peel and grate the ginger. Place the aromatics in a pint-size Mason jar along with the vinegar, coconut aminos, sesame oil, and red pepper flakes. Shake to combine.

Cook the patties. In the same skillet you used for the snow peas, warm 2 teaspoons of the coconut oil over medium-high heat. Wet your hands and measure ¼ cup shrimp paste, then shape it into a small patty. Place it in the pan and repeat; you should be able to get 4–5 shrimp cakes in the pan. Cook on one side until golden, about 2–3 minutes, then flip and brown the other side, another 1–2 minutes. Remove the patties to a plate as they brown and repeat with the remaining shrimp paste.

To serve, divide the patties and snow peas among individual serving plates along with ramekins of dipping sauce.

YOU KNOW HOW YOU COULD DO THAT?
Leftovers soup: Place shrimp patties in a bowl with zucchini noodles (Mini Cookup, p. 39) and your favorite flavor of bone broth. You could also add (or substitute) shrimp patties in the Banh Mi Bowl (p. 137).

COOKUP TIPS
Make the shrimp paste, steam the snow peas, and prep the dipping sauce in advance, then store everything in separate airtight containers in the fridge. Just before eating, stir-fry the snow peas, then shape and cook the patties.

ZUCCHINI PASTA WITH WHITE CLAM SAUCE

*"You can never lose your family."**

Clam sauce always, always reminds me of a special movie night I shared with my mom. It was just the two of us on a wintry night. We tossed a giant antipasto salad (something similar to Italian Hoagie Salad, page 133 and cooked linguine and clam sauce together. (My mom is a pro at clam sauce; hers always has the perfect amount of garlic! Of course it does; she's Sicilian.) Then we settled under a blanket in the den, *The Godfather* on the TV, plates nestled in our laps. I'm not saying that's the only way to enjoy pasta with clam sauce—I'm just saying it's the best way.

Start the sauce. Warm the olive oil in a medium saucepan over medium heat. Smash and peel the garlic cloves and add them to the oil.

Make the pasta. Julienne the zucchini with the spiralizer. Place the noodles in a colander and toss them with the salt until the strands are lightly coated. Set the colander in the sink to drain while you prep the other ingredients.

Make the sauce: To the pot with the garlic oil, add the clams, about half their juice, and the champagne vinegar. Increase the heat to medium high and simmer gently for 10–15 minutes. While the sauce simmers, mince the parsley and toast the pine nuts.

Toast the pine nuts. Warm a nonstick skillet over medium-high heat, about 2 minutes. Add the pine nuts and toast until golden, stirring frequently, about 3 minutes. Transfer them to a plate to cool.

Cook the noodles. Reheat the skillet you used for the pine nuts over medium-high heat. Rinse the zucchini noodles under running water, drain well, and squeeze them dry in a clean dish towel. Add them to the heated pan and stir-fry 2–3 minutes until hot.

The big finish. Taste the clam sauce and add salt, if necessary. Pour the clam sauce over the noodles, add the parsley, and toss to combine.

To serve, divide the noodles and clam sauce among individual serving bowls, top with 1 teaspoon ghee, then sprinkle with crushed red pepper flakes, ground black pepper, and toasted pine nuts.

YOU KNOW HOW YOU COULD DO THAT?

Make red clam sauce: Drain the clams before adding them to the garlic oil and add 1 (14.5-ounce) can fire-roasted, diced tomatoes to the pan; proceed.

COOKUP TIPS

Spiralize and sweat the zucchini and cook the clam sauce in advance; store both separately in airtight containers in the fridge. When it's time to eat, stir-fry the noodles and follow the directions for the big finish.

Serves 2–4
Total time: 25–30 minutes
Tools: spiralizer, colander

CLAM SAUCE:
- ⅓ cup extra-virgin olive oil
- 4 cloves garlic
- 4 (10-ounce) cans whole baby clams
- 1 tablespoon champagne vinegar or lemon juice
- ½ cup fresh parsley
- ¼ cup pine nuts
- 4 teaspoons ghee

NOODLES:
- 2–2 ½ pounds zucchini
- 1 tablespoon salt

garnish: crushed red pepper flakes, black pepper

* The Godfather

TROPICAL COLESLAW

(a piña colada you eat)

Coconut and pineapple are a natural combination: If they grow together, they go together. The pineapple simultaneously cuts through and emphasizes the creamy, nutty flavor and fatty mouthfeel of the coconut. Add shrimp (or other crustaceans), and you've got a tropical trifecta that instantly transports your taste buds to a delightfully trashy swim-up bar with balmy breezes, sand between your toes, and a chill soundtrack.

SLAW:
- ¼ cup unsweetened coconut flakes
- 1 cup canned pineapple chunks, packed in juice
- ½ small red onion
- ½ large head green cabbage
- ¼ medium head red cabbage
- ½ large red bell pepper
- ¼ cup fresh cilantro
- 1½ pounds cooked shrimp (any size)
- ¼ cup macadamia nuts

DRESSING:
- 1 large egg yolk
- 2 tablespoons plus ½ cup light-tasting olive or avocado oil
- 1 tablespoon lime juice
- 1 tablespoon champagne vinegar
- 1 teaspoon fish sauce
- ¼ teaspoon salt
- ⅛ teaspoon ground black pepper

Toast the coconut. Warm a large, nonstick skillet over medium-high heat, 2 minutes. Add the coconut and cook, stirring occasionally, until it's golden, 3–5 minutes.

Make the slaw. Drain the pineapple and reserve 2 tablespoons of the juice. Cut the pineapple chunks in half and place them in a large mixing bowl with the reserved pineapple juice. Grate the onion and add it to the bowl. Using a mandoline or the slicing blade of a food processor, slice the cabbages and bell pepper; add them to the bowl. Mince the cilantro and add it to the bowl. Place the shrimp in the bowl and toss all the ingredients. Coarsely chop the macadamia nuts and set aside.

Make the dressing. Place all the ingredients in a pint-size Mason jar and whirl with the stick blender until emulsified.

Put it all together. Pour about half the dressing into the bowl with the salad, add the coconut flakes, and toss the salad with two wooden spoons until evenly coated. Take a bite and let your taste buds tell you if it needs more salt, pepper, or dressing. To serve, divide the salad among individual serving dishes and sprinkle with macadamia nuts.

YOU KNOW HOW YOU COULD DO THAT?
Replace the shrimp with cooked crab or lobster or cooked and shredded chicken or pork. You could also substitute cubes of mango for the pineapple.

COOKUP TIPS
Make the dressing and prep the slaw ingredients in advance, then store them in separate airtight containers in the fridge. Toss everything together just before eating.

Serves 2–4
Total time: 30–35 minutes
Tools: grater, food processor/mandoline, pint-size Mason jar, stick blender

Curry

Asian Cashew

Tropical

Firecracker

Vietnamese

Italian

Tuna Salad
Platters
p. 230

Lemon-Herb

Harvest

How to: Tuna Salad Platters

1. MAYO

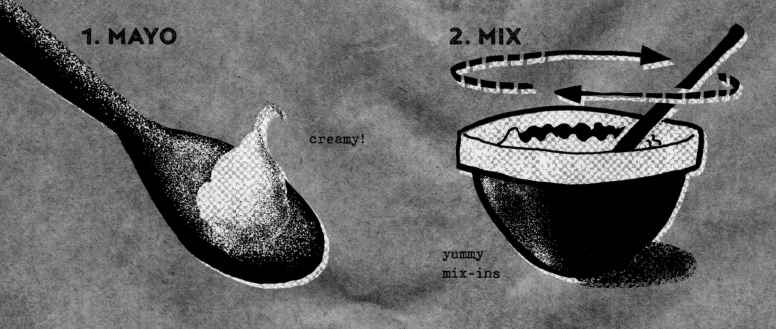

creamy!

2. MIX

yummy
mix-ins

3&4. CUT

cut crudité

pick out
go-alongs!

5. EAT

fit
for
a salty
sea captai

TUNA SALAD PLATTERS

from plain-old to party platter

Getting the most enjoyment from a meal is often about the mental game. Case in point: If I say I'm eating "tuna" for dinner, it doesn't generate any excitement for me. At all. Instead, if I think of it as a "tuna salad platter" and surround the tuna with some of my favorite nibbles, it's like I'm dining in a totally kickass café where they only serve food I like.

All recipes serve 1–2*
Total Time: 25–30 minutes, depending on chopping speed
Tools: pint-size Mason jar, stick blender

*Note: These recipes are designed for 1–2 people. If you're feeding a whole crew, you'll need to double up and crack open a lot of cans.

Between us friends, I eat these kinds of platters any time of day—including breakfast—because I like to secretly pretend it's a cocktail party (although at my cocktail parties, we drink tea instead of booze).

Daydreaming and role playing aside, there are a few other reasons to love these platters. There's no cooking required—just chopping and mixing—and these recipes come together fast, so they can save the day when you're so hungry, you're *hangry* or dangerously close to making a take-out call. The recipes are easy to double, so you can eat some now and save some for later, and if you have lots of flavorful go-along options in your pantry, everyone can customize their own plates… which provides plenty of goodwill for delightful conversation. Boom! Your weeknight dinner is now a swanky soiree.

HERE'S HOW IT WORKS:

1. Make the mayo.
2. Mix the tuna salad.
3. Cut the crudité.
4. Select your go-alongs.
5. Assemble and enjoy.

1 MAKE THE MAYO

1 large egg
2 tablespoons lemon juice
½ teaspoon mustard powder
½ teaspoon salt
1¼ cups light-tasting olive or avocado oil

Place the egg, lemon juice, mustard, and salt in a pint-size Mason jar; whirl with a stick blender until smooth. With the blender running inside the jar, slowly pour in the oil and blend until thickened.

2 MIX THE TUNA SALAD

For all recipes, drain the tuna, transfer it to a medium mixing bowl, and use a fork to flake the fish. Add the other ingredients and mix well. See the recipes that follow for specific ingredients and preparation.

3 CUT THE CRUDITÉ

1 large carrot
2 large stalks celery
1 large seedless cucumber
1 large bell pepper, any color

Wash veggies and cut into eye-pleasing shapes.

4 SELECT YOUR GO-ALONGS

Add color, texture, and flavor contrasts to your plate with a few of these salad bar favorites:

* avocado
* artichoke hearts
* hearts of palm
* pickles
* olives
* pepperoncini
* roasted red peppers
* hard-boiled eggs
* nuts
* berries
* sliced apples or pears
* grapes
* orange/grapefruit segments

5 ASSEMBLE AND ENJOY

Arrange the tuna salad on a pretty plate with crudité and your favorite go-alongs.

HARVEST TUNA SALAD

2 (5-ounce) cans tuna, packed in olive oil or water
¼ cup dried cranberries or cherries
¼ cup pecans, chopped
2 stalks celery, thinly sliced
4 scallions, thinly sliced
1 teaspoon Dijon mustard
2–3 tablespoons mayo

CURRY TUNA SALAD

2 (5-ounce) cans tuna, packed in olive oil or water
1 apple, diced
¼ cup raisins
¼ cup sliced almonds
2 stalks celery, thinly sliced
4 scallions, thinly sliced
1 teaspoon curry powder
½ teaspoon lime juice
2–3 tablespoons mayo

TROPICAL TUNA SALAD

2 (5-ounce) cans tuna, packed in olive oil or water
¼ cup toasted coconut flakes*
¼ cup sliced almonds
4 scallions, thinly sliced
1 teaspoon lime juice
½ teaspoon powdered ginger
¼ teaspoon ground allspice
2–3 tablespoons mayo
*Toast coconut in a dry, nonstick skillet over medium heat, 3–5 minutes.

LEMON-HERB TUNA SALAD

2 (5-ounce) cans tuna, packed in olive oil or water
4 scallions, thinly sliced
1 teaspoon Dijon mustard
1 teaspoon lemon juice
1 tablespoon dried chives
½ teaspoon coarse (granulated) onion powder
½ teaspoon dried tarragon leaves
2–3 tablespoons mayo

ITALIAN TUNA SALAD

2 (5-ounce) cans tuna, packed in olive oil or water
a few sundried tomatoes, chopped
a handful basil leaves, minced
¼ cup black olives, chopped
4 scallions, thinly sliced
½ teaspoon balsamic vinegar
2–3 tablespoons mayo

ASIAN CASHEW TUNA SALAD

2 (5-ounce) cans tuna, packed in olive oil or water
¼ cup roasted cashews, chopped
4 scallions, thinly sliced
2 stalks celery, thinly sliced
½ teaspoon crushed red pepper flakes
½ teaspoon powdered ginger
⅛ teaspoon Chinese five-spice powder
1 teaspoon coconut aminos
2–3 tablespoons mayo

VIETNAMESE TUNA SALAD

2 (5-ounce) cans tuna, packed in olive oil or water
½ large seedless cucumber, minced
½ large carrot, grated
a handful basil leaves, minced
a handful cilantro leaves, minced
4 scallions, thinly sliced
1 teaspoon fish sauce
1 teaspoon lime juice
2–3 tablespoons mayo

FIRECRACKER TUNA SALAD

2 (5-ounce) cans tuna, packed in olive oil or water
½ to 1 jalapeño pepper, minced
4 scallions, thinly sliced
¾ teaspoon Aleppo pepper or crushed red pepper flakes
¼ teaspoon mustard powder
pinch cayenne pepper
½ teaspoon red wine vinegar
2–3 tablespoons mayo

YOU KNOW HOW YOU COULD DO THAT?

These recipes assume 2 cans of tuna, but you could substitute 1 (14.75-ounce) can salmon or 2 (3.75-ounce) cans boneless, skinless sardines.

COOKUP TIPS

Make the mayo in advance, then when you're hungry, all that's required is chopping and mixing. You can also cut your crudité and mix the tuna salad— minus the mayo—in advance. Store everything in separate airtight containers in the fridge—the tuna and veggies will taste fresh for 2–3 days. When you're ready to eat, mix in the mayo and dig in!

BUYING TUNA

Become a label detectuve! Some tuna packed in spring water contains sneaky soy and gluten. You want a brand that's simply tuna, olive oil or water, and salt. To be good to the environment while you're good to your body, look for tuna that's caught my troll or pole-and-line—and if you're pregnant or planning to become pregnant, limit yourself to 12 ounces a week of light tuna or 6 ounces of albacore (white).

Harvest Tuna Salad
p. 230

SHRIMP REMOULADE

a New Orleans classic

Remoulade is a French condiment that begins as aioli or mayo and is gussied up with capers, shallots, chopped pickles, herbs, and acid to become a sort of tartar sauce with aspirations. In Cajun country, the addition of paprika and hot sauce gives it a bang, and the resulting sauce is tart, spicy, and undeniably creamy. It's traditionally served with seafood, and in this recipe, it dresses up cool shrimp, hard-boiled eggs, and greens for a salad platter that's worthy of a celebratory dinner.

Prep the pans. For the eggs: Place the water in a medium saucepan, cover, and bring to a rolling boil. For the shrimp: Place the water in a medium saucepan or skillet over high heat. Smash and peel the garlic clove, cut the lemon into wedges, and add them to the pot, along with the salt; bring to a boil.

Cook the shrimp. When the shrimp water boils, add the shrimp to the pan, stir, and bring it back to a boil, then immediately turn off the heat and cover the pan. Let the shrimp sit undisturbed in the hot water while the eggs cook.

Cook the eggs. When the egg water reaches a boil, use a spoon to lower the eggs one at a time into the boiling water. Cover the pan, reduce the heat to simmer, and cook for 11 minutes. SET A TIMER!

Prep the salad. Thinly slice the lettuce, cucumber, bell pepper, and onion. Arrange the veggies on individual dinner plates.

Chill the shrimp and eggs. Place about a dozen ice cubes in a large bowl and add cold water. When the eggs are finished cooking, use a slotted spoon to remove them from the hot water and place

them in the ice water to cool. Use the slotted spoon to remove the shrimp from the pan and add them to the bowl with the eggs. Allow both to cool for 10 minutes.

Make the remoulade. Smash and peel the garlic clove and place it in a pint-size Mason jar. Add the egg yolk, 2 tablespoons of the olive oil, the lemon juice, vinegar, mustard, hot sauce, coconut aminos, paprika, salt, and cayenne to the jar. Whirl with the stick blender until puréed. With the blender running inside the jar, add the remaining ½ cup oil and blend until smooth. Mince the scallion and parsley, add them to the jar, and stir with a fork to combine.

To serve, remove the eggs and shrimp from the bowl with a slotted spoon. Peel both, cut the eggs, and add both to the salad plates. Drizzle with the remoulade sauce and sprinkle with parsley leaves.

COOKUP TIPS

The eggs and remoulade can be made up to 5 days in advance, and the cooked shrimp can be refrigerated overnight. When it's time to eat, assemble the platters and *laissez les bon temps rouler*.

Serves 2–4
Total time: 30–35 minutes
Tools: pint-size Mason jar, stick blender

BOILED EGGS:
  4 cups water
  8 large eggs

SHRIMP:
  2 cups water
  1 clove garlic
  1 lemon
  1 tablespoon salt
  1½ pounds large, easy-peel raw shrimp

SALAD:
  2–3 romaine lettuce hearts
  1 large seedless cucumber
  1 large green bell pepper
  ½ medium red onion
  a handful parsely leaves

REMOULADE:
  1 clove garlic
  1 large egg yolk
  2 tablespoons plus ½ cup light-tasting olive or avocado oil
  2 tablespoons lemon juice
  1 tablespoon cider vinegar
  1 teaspoon Dijon mustard
  1 teaspoon hot sauce
  1 teaspoon coconut aminos
  2 teaspoons paprika
  ¼ teaspoon salt
  ⅛ teaspoon cayenne pepper
  1 scallion
  ¼ cup fresh parsley leaves

DECONSTRUCTED SUSHI BOWL

sushi you eat with a fork

Sometimes, a "project" recipe can be fun. You know the kind I mean, right? You research the recipe, buy special ingredients, and set aside a weekend afternoon to roll up your sleeves and spend the day playing in the kitchen. But then, most days, you just want to eat. Rightly or wrongly, I think of sushi rolls as a project: There's all that fine chopping and rolling and... well, I guess I'm lazy when I'm hungry. This recipe delivers the contrasting flavors and textures of a fresh maki roll in a friendly bowl.

Cook the rice. Break the cauliflower into florets, removing the stems. Place the florets in the bowl of a food processor and pulse until the cauliflower looks like rice, about 10 pulses. Warm the oil in a large, nonstick skillet over medium-high, 2 minutes. Add the cauliflower and salt; toss with a rubber spatula to coat the rice in oil, then cover the pan and turn the heat to low. Set a timer for 15 minutes.

Crisp the nori. Place the olive oil in another nonstick skillet and warm it over medium-high heat, 2 minutes. While the oil heats, stack the nori sheets and cut them into quarters. Roll each pile of quarter-sheets into a thin cylinder, then cut it into very thin strips. Add them to the pan, toss to coat with the oil, and stir-fry until very dark green and crisp, about 2 minutes. Transfer to a plate and sprinkle with a little salt.

Make the wasabi. Mix the wasabi powder with water according to the package directions and set aside.

Prep the shrimp bowl ingredients. Slice the dark green part of the scallions into 2-inch-long batons. Peel and dice the mango. Cut the red pepper into thin strips. Dice the avocado. Cut the shrimp into bite-sized pieces, if necessary.

To serve, give each of your dining companions a bowl of rice and encourage them to add wasabi paste, coconut aminos, and rice vinegar, according to their whims. Then invite them to top their rice with shrimp, scallions, mango, bell pepper, and avocado. Sprinkle each bowl with crispy nori strips and sesame seeds.

YOU KNOW HOW YOU COULD DO THAT?

Beat an egg or two, cook like a thin omelet, then cut it into strips and add to the bowl. Or replace the shrimp, mango, and bell pepper with smoked salmon, cucumber slices, and julienned jicama.

COOKUP TIPS

Rice and cook the cauliflower and store it in an airtight container in the fridge. When it's time to eat, prep the other ingredients while you reheat the rice. Visit www.meljoulwan.com/wellfedweeknights for a quick video with tips on cutting nori sheet.

Serves 2–4
Total time: 35–40 minutes
Tools: food processor

CAULIFLOWER RICE:
  1 large head cauliflower
  1 tablespoon extra-virgin olive oil
  ¾ teaspoon salt

CRISPY NORI:
  1 teaspoon extra-virgin olive oil
  4 sheets nori

RICE GARNISH:
  wasabi powder
  coconut aminos
  unseasoned rice vinegar
  toasted sesame seeds

SHRIMP BOWL:
  4 scallions
  1 ripe mango
  1 medium red bell pepper
  1 avocado
  1½ pounds cooked shrimp

THAI YUMMY SALAD

that's not an opinion, it's the name

Serves 2–4
Total time: 30–35 minutes
Tools: pint-size Mason jar

Dave and I don't eat in restaurants very often, but about every other week, he insists on treating me to a dinner I don't have to cook. I usually pick Thai food because I cannot get enough of the Yummy Salad at a nearby restaurant. This recipe is my less-sugary, peanut-free, more veggie-loaded version of that irresistible dish. The magic in this dish is its balance of the five major tastes: sweet, sour, salty, bitter, and hot. Nothing makes sweet taste sweeter than a salty-sour background. There's cabbage and spinach (bitter); carrot, cucumber, red bell pepper, and pineapple (sweet); scallions and chives (hot); citrus juice (sour); and fish sauce (mmmm... salty).

SHRIMP:
- 1½ pounds raw shrimp (any size)
- 3 cups water
- 1 tablespoon salt

DRESSING:
- 2 red or green Thai chiles or jalapeños
- 3 cloves garlic
- 1 navel orange
- 1 lime
- 2 tablespoons fish sauce
- 1 tablespoon light-tasting olive or avocado oil
- 1 tablespoon coconut sugar or honey (omit for Whole30)

SALAD:
- ½ large head green cabbage
- 3 scallions
- ½ large red bell pepper
- ½ large seedless cucumber
- ½ cup fresh basil leaves
- ½ cup fresh mint leaves
- a few handfuls baby spinach
- ½ cup canned pineapple chunks, packed in juice
- ¼ cup dry-roasted pepitas

Prep the shrimp pot. Place the water and salt in a large skillet or medium sauce-pan and bring it to a boil over high heat. While you wait for the water to boil, make the dressing.

Make the dressing. Smash the chiles with the side of a knife, then smash and peel the garlic cloves; place both in a pint-size Mason jar. Squeeze the juice from the orange and the lime into the jar, then add the fish sauce, oil, and sugar. Screw the lid on tightly, shake it with enthusiasm, then let it sit at room temperature while you make the rest of the salad.

Cook the shrimp. Add the shrimp to the boiling water and stir. Cover and remove the pan from the heat. Let the shrimp cook while you make the salad. Do not lift the lid! Let them rest in their sensory deprivation tank.

Prep the salad. Thinly slice the cabbage. Cut scallions and red pepper into match-sticks. Slice the cucumber into thin half-moons. Roughly chop the herbs. Drain the pineapple over a bowl to catch the juice. Place all the ingredients except the pepitas in a large mixing bowl and toss to combine.

Put it all together. Drain the shrimp, rinse under cold running water, and peel. Remove the garlic cloves and jalapeño chunks from the dressing. Place the shrimp in a medium bowl and toss it with a little of the dressing, then drizzle the rest of the dressing over the salad. Toss for 2 minutes. (Sing a verse of your favorite song to kill the time.)

To serve, divide the salad among individual plates, top with shrimp, and then sprinkle with pepitas.

YOU KNOW HOW YOU COULD DO THAT?
Replace the shrimp with cooked or canned salmon or sliced, cooked chicken or pork. You can swap vegetables in and out of this salad, just try to keep at least one sweet and one bitter. No fish sauce? Replace it with 2 tablespoons coconut aminos mashed with 1–2 anchovy fillets.

COOKUP TIPS
Cook the shrimp, cut the raw vegetables, and make the dressing; store everything in separate airtight containers in the fridge. When it's time to eat, assemble, toss, and serve.

COCKTAIL ALERT!
Save the pineapple juice when you drain the can of pineapple! Divide the leftover juice among cocktail glasses over ice, top with sparkling water, then garnish with a wedge of lime and a mint leaf.

BASIL-COCONUT CURRY

super smooth & pleasantly aromatic

Curry is the result of culinary cross-pollination, so there's no single, definitive type of this smooth amalgam of spices and creamy sauce. From Nepal to Sri Lanka, Indonesia to Thailand, and Myanmar to Japan, curries are part of the local cuisine. This recipe is a mash-up of traditions. It features a spice blend inspired by Indian curries, combined with the coconut milk, basil leaves, and lime usually associated with Thai dishes. The result is a spicy sauce that's rich, not too hot, and easy to adapt to your personal tastes.

Prep the spice blend. Heat the coconut oil in a large, nonstick saucepan over medium heat, about 2 minutes. While the oil heats, peel and grate the ginger, then peel and crush the garlic. Add them to the pan and cook, 1 minute. Mix the coriander, cinnamon, cardamom, pepper, salt, chili powder, turmeric, and cloves in a small bowl; add to the pan and cook, 30 seconds.

Make the curry. Pour the coconut milk and fish sauce into the pan and stir well to combine; bring to a simmer. Prep the vegetables and add them to the pan in this order: Wash and trim the green beans, seed the jalapeño and slice it into rings, cut the cucumber into ¼-inch-thick half moons, slice the red pepper into ½-inch strips. When all the veggies have been added to the pan, stir and reduce the heat to medium-low. Cover the pan and cook until the vegetables are almost tender, 10–12 minutes. Add the shrimp and basil leaves (save a few for garnish!), cover, and cook until the shrimp are pink and opaque, 3–5 minutes. Cut the lime into wedges.

To serve, spoon the curry into bowls and sprinkle with more basil and a squeeze of lime juice.

YOU KNOW HOW YOU COULD DO THAT?

Replace the shrimp with chunks of salmon or white fish, or with thinly-sliced chicken breast, pork loin, or beef sirloin. You could also swap strips of Japanese eggplant for the cucumber, or use cilantro instead of basil.

COOKUP TIPS

Make the spice blend. Cut the veggies and store them in separate airtight containers in the fridge. Just before eating, prepare the ginger and garlic, then follow the rest of the instructions. If you prep cauliflower rice or sweet potatoes during a Mini Cookup (p. 39) you can use them as a bed for the curry.

Serves 2–4
Total time: 35–40 minutes
Tools: grater, nothing special

SPICE BLEND:
  1 tablespoon coconut oil
  1-inch piece fresh ginger
  3 cloves garlic
  1 teaspoon ground coriander
  1 teaspoon ground cinnamon
  1 teaspoon ground cardamom
  1 teaspoon ground black pepper
  ¾ teaspoon salt
  ½ teaspoon chili powder
  ½ teaspoon turmeric
  ½ teaspoon ground cloves

CURRY:
  1 (14.5 ounce) can unsweetened coconut milk
  1 tablespoon fish sauce
  8 ounces green beans
  1 jalapeño pepper
  1 seedless cucumber
  1 red bell pepper
  1½ pounds raw shrimp
  a few handfuls fresh basil leaves
  1 lime

SESAME-ALMOND COD WITH CAULIFLOWER RICE

deep dive into flavor

Cod lives and grows in the deep, dark, cold Arctic Ocean, and this somewhat forbidding environment helps make it a nutrition powerhouse. It's an excellent source of Omega-3 fatty acids, B12, and B6. But let's be honest: Getting excited *emotionally* about a cod fillet is a pretty difficult task. Oh, cod! It's a little dull—until it's bundled under a rugged blanket of tahini and almonds. Now that same cod is both good for you and Good.

Serves 2-4
Total time: 40-45 minutes
Hands-off time: 15 minutes
Tools: food processor, rimmed baking
  sheet

CAULIFLOWER RICE:
  1 large head cauliflower
  1 tablespoon extra-virgin olive
    oil
  ¾ teaspoon salt

FISH AND SAUCE:
  2 cloves garlic
  ¼ cup unsalted, roasted almonds
  6 tablespoons tahini
  ¼ cup lemon juice
  1½ pounds cod fillets
  ½ teaspoon salt
  ¼ teaspoon ground black pepper
  ¼ cup fresh parsley
  1 lemon

Preheat the oven to 450F.

Rice the cauliflower. Break the cauliflower into florets, removing the stems. Place the florets in the food processor bowl and pulse until the cauliflower looks like rice, about 10 pulses. You may need to do this in batches. In a large bowl, mix the riced cauliflower with the olive oil and salt. Spread it evenly on the baking sheet.

Make the sauce. Smash and peel the garlic; place it in the bowl of a food processor with the almonds. Pulse a few times, then add the tahini and lemon juice; purée until smooth. You want a texture like thick cake frosting (mmm... savory cake frosting), so add water 1 tablespoon at a time, if necessary, to get the right thickness.

Prep the fish. Place the fish directly on top of the cauliflower rice and sprinkle the fillets with the salt and pepper. Use a butter knife to spread the tahini mixture evenly over the fish.

Bake everything. Place the baking sheet in the oven and roast the rice and fish for 10–15 minutes, until the nut crust is lightly browned and the fish is opaque. While the food is in the oven, mince the parsley and cut the lemon into wedges.

To serve, divide the cauliflower rice among individual serving plates, top each with fish, then squeeze fresh lemon juice over the fillets and sprinkle with minced parsley.

YOU KNOW HOW YOU COULD DO THAT?
Replace the cod with snapper, haddock, or flounder.

COOKUP TIPS
Rice the cauliflower and make the tahini-almond purée in advance; store both in separate airtight containers in the fridge. When it's time to eat, warm the tahini-almond paste in the microwave so it's spreadable, spread the cauliflower rice on a baking sheet and follow the instructions from "Prep the fish."

MEDITERRANEAN TUNA CAKES WITH ROASTED VEGETABLES

like a madcap aventure in Italy

One of the reasons I'm so delighted by seasonings is that they can take you somewhere else in the world. So when I mix up a batch of tuna with lemon zest, black olives, mint, and parsley, I'm no longer in my kitchen. For just a little while, I'm Sofia Loren in Naples, breaking hearts and, perhaps, conspiring on a daring heist of some sort, definitely wearing enormous black sunglasses and probably clad in very impractical—but quite fetching—high heels while riding a pink Vespa. Probably.

Serves 2-4
Total Time: 45 minutes
Hands-off Time: 15 minutes
Tools: grater, pint-size Mason jar, stick blender, 2 rimmed baking sheets

TUNA CAKES:
1 large white potato (about ¾ pound)
3 (5-ounce) cans tuna (packed in water or olive oil)
½ cup fresh parsley leaves
¼ cup fresh mint leaves
¼ cup pitted black olives
2 scallions
1 lemon
2 large eggs
½ cup almond flour
1 teaspoon salt
¼ teaspoon ground black pepper
¼ teaspoon baking soda
1-2 tablespoons extra-virgin olive oil

ROASTED VEGETABLES:
1½ pounds green beans
1 red bell pepper
1 tablespoon extra-virgin olive oil
½ teaspoon salt
¼ teaspoon ground black pepper

ROASTED RED PEPPER SAUCE:
1 clove garlic
2 tablespoons lemon juice
2 tablespoons plus ½ cup light-tasting olive or avocado oil
1 roasted red bell pepper
½ teaspoon salt
½ teaspoon paprika
¼ teaspoon ground black pepper
¼ teaspoon cayenne pepper
1 tablespoon fresh parsley leaves
1 large egg yolk

Preheat the oven to 425F. Line two rimmed baking sheets with parchment paper.

Cook the potato. Wash the potato, poke it a few times with a fork, and wrap the damp potato in a paper towel. Microwave on high for 7–8 minutes or until it's very soft. When the time is up, cut the potato in half and let it cool a bit.

Prep the veggies. Wash and trim the green beans. Thinly slice the bell pepper. Place the veggies in a large bowl and toss them with the olive oil, salt, and pepper. Spread them in a single layer on one of the prepared baking sheets.

Mix the tuna cakes. Drain the liquid from the tuna and crumble the fish into a large bowl. Mince the parsley and mint leaves, halve the olives, slice the scallions, and zest the lemon; add all of this to the bowl. Add the eggs, almond flour, salt, pepper, and baking soda. Peel the potato and crumble the flesh into the bowl. Mix all the ingredients with a wooden spoon (or get rustic and use your hands!) until combined.

Shape the tuna cakes. Grab the second baking sheet and brush the parchment paper with some of the olive oil, then, using a ⅓ measuring cup, scoop equal-size patties of the tuna onto the parchment. The patties should be about 2½ inches wide and about 1 inch thick; brush their tops with olive oil. Bake both the veggies and the tuna cakes for 20–25 minutes, until the veggies are tender and the cakes are browned.

Make the sauce. While the tuna cakes and veggies bake, smash and peel the garlic and drop it into a pint-size Mason jar. Add the lemon juice, 2 tablespoons

of the oil, the roasted pepper, salt, paprika, black pepper, cayenne pepper, and parsley to the jar. Purée the ingredients with a stick blender, then add the egg yolk and purée again. With the blender running inside the jar, gradually add the remaining ½ cup oil until the sauce is combined and thickened. Refrigerate the sauce until it's time to eat.

To serve, place tuna cakes and roasted veggies on dinner plates, then drizzle with red pepper sauce

YOU KNOW HOW YOU COULD DO THAT?

Swap ingredients to change up the flavor! (Replace Red Pepper Sauce with a dollop of plain homemade mayo (p. 39).

MIDDLE EASTERN TUNA CAKES

Add the following:

- 1 teaspoon lemon juice
- ¼ teaspoon za'atar spice blend
- ¼ teaspoon crushed red pepper flakes or Aleppo pepper
- ¼ teaspoon ground cumin

FIRECRACKER TUNA CAKES

Omit the mint, olives, and lemon zest. Add the following:

- ½ to 1 large jalapeño pepper, finely minced
- ½ teaspoon crushed red pepper flakes
- ½ teaspoon red wine vinegar
- ¼ teaspoon mustard powder
- pinch ground cayenne pepper

FIESTA TUNA CAKES

Omit the parsley, mint, olives, and lemon zest. Add the following:

- ½ cup fire-roasted, diced tomatoes
- ¼ cup pickled jalapeño rings, chopped
- ¼ cup fresh cilantro leaves, minced
- 1 teaspoon chili powder
- ½ teaspoon ground cumin
- 2 tablespoons lime juice

WALDORF TUNA CAKES

Omit the mint and olives. Add the following:

- 1 small apple, diced
- ¼ cup pecan halves
- ½ teaspoon mustard powder

TEX-MEX TUNA CAKES

Omit the parsley, mint, olives, and lemon zest. Add the following:

- ¼ cup fresh cilantro leaves, minced
- ½ ripe avocado, diced
- 1 small tomato, diced
- ¼ teaspoon chili powder
- ⅛ teaspoon ground cumin

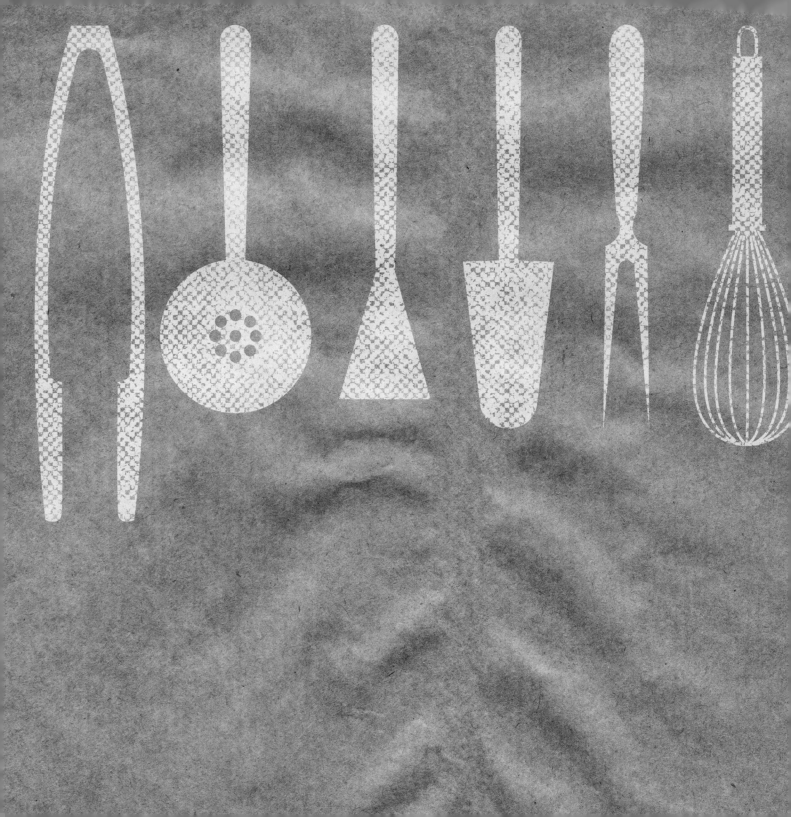

RESOURCES

RESOURCES

I like what I like, and once I've found something I love, I don't usually experiment too much. That's why this isn't a lengthy, list of all the paleo resources out there. It's my personal list of bests; I use all of these myself, and I think they're top notch. You'll also find these links at www.meljoulwan.com/wellfedweeknights

MELISSA JOULWAN'S WELL FED

www.meljoulwan.com
I update my site several times each week with new recipes, daring tales of my workouts, kitchen adventures (and disasters), useful bits of information to help you find motivation and inspiration in all areas of your life, and sometimes truly awesome pictures of my cat, Smudge.

MY AMAZON STORE

www.meljoulwan.com/store/
I'm a big fan of Amazon, because they have so many of the things I love. This store is my curated collection of "Good Stuff You Can Buy From Amazon," including essential kitchen tools that I use every day, the paleo books I read, "take me away" fiction, and other things that catch my fancy.

GRASS-FED/PASTURED MEAT

All of these sites offer delicious, nutrient-packed meat, a wide variety of other healthy products, and reasonable prices (with deals for ordering in larger quantities). They are all staffed by real people, who seem to genuinely care about their products and the people who eat them.

Lava Lake Lamb

www.lavalakelamb.com
The tastiest, sweetest pastured, grass-fed lamb and grass-fed beef. Top-notch environmental practices. Lively blog with plenty of paleo-friendly recipes.

Rocky Mountain Organic Meats

www.rockymtncuts.com
Extremely flavorful organic, grass-fed beef. The best ground beef I've ever eaten.

Tendergrass Farms

www.tendergrass.com
The best place for pastured bacon and lard. Very friendly people behind the company and excellent customer service.

U.S. Wellness Meats

www.grasslandbeef.com
Wide variety of products like grass-fed dairy, wild-caught seafood, snacks, and pet food, in addition to grass-fed beef, lamb, poultry, bison, pork, and rabbit. Plus, sugar-free bacon!

SPICES

These are my trusted suppliers for the spicy substances that turn ingredients into meals. They're owned by real people, not giant corporations, and their spices are fresh, vibrant, and reasonably priced.

Penzeys Spices

www.penzeys.com

Primal Palate Organic Spices

www.primalpalate.com/organic-spices

Spicely

www.spicely.com

OTHER PALEO FOOD

Barefoot Provisions

www.barefootprovisions.com
Purveyors of awesome paleo products, including pastured beef tallow, pork lard, and cage-free duck fat, as well as nuts, nut butters, paleo snacks, and more.

Primal Kitchen

www.primalkitchen.com
Launched by Mark Sisson, an expert on primal living. Products include reasonably-priced avocado oil, mayo, salad dressings, protein bars, and more.

Thrive Market

thrivemarket.com
A membership-based online store for paleo-friendly products at 25–50% off retail; vast selection, fast delivery.

INTERNATIONAL CONVERSIONS

Hello, international friends! These charts should include everything you need to convert my American amounts for your metric kitchen gadgets. When in doubt, you can always turn to Google. Just enter something like this into the Google search field: "2 pounds in kilograms." Google will serve up the answer faster than you can say "Mmmmm.... duck fat!"

WEIGHT

1 ounce	28 g.
1½ ounces	42.5 g.
2 ounces	57 g.
3 ounces	85 g.
4 ounces (¼ pound)	113 g.
5 ounces	142 g.
6 ounces	170 g.
7 ounces	197 g.
8 ounces (½ pound)	227 g.
16 ounces (1 pound)	454 g.
32 ounces (2 pounds)	907 g.
35¼ ounces (2.2 pounds)	1 g.

OVEN TEMPERATURES

Fahrenheit	Celsius	British Gas
200	95	0
225	110	¼
250	120	½
275	135	1
300	150	2
325	165	3
350	175	4
375	190	5
400	200	6
425	220	7
450	230	8
475	245	9
500	260	10

CONVERSION FORMULAS

Convert	Multiply
ounces to grams	ounces by 28.35
pounds to kilograms	pounds by .454
teaspoons to milliliters	teaspoons by 4.93
tablespoons to milliliters	tablespoons by 14.79
fluid ounces to milliliters	fluid ounces by 29.57
cups to milliliters	cups by 236.59
cups to liters	cups by .236
inches to centimeters	inches by 2.54

VOLUME

¼ teaspoon	1 ml.
½ teaspoon	2.5 ml.
¾ teaspoon	4 ml.
1 teaspoon	5 ml.
1¼ teaspoons	6 ml.
1½ teaspoons (½ tablespoon)	7.5 ml.
2 teaspoons	10 ml.
½ tablespoon	7.5 ml.
1 tablespoon (½ fluid ounce)	15 ml.
2 tablespoons (1 fluid ounce)	30 ml.
¼ cup	60 ml.
⅓ cup	80 ml.
½ cup (4 fluid ounces)	120 ml.
⅔ cup	160 ml.
¾ cup	180 ml.
1 cup (8 fluid ounces)	240 ml.
1¼ cups	300 ml.
1½ cups	360 ml.
1⅔ cups	400 ml.
2 cups (1 pint)	460 ml.
3 cups	700 ml.
4 cups (1 quart)	0.95 l. (950 ml.)
4 quarts (1 gallon)	3.8 l.

LENGTH

⅛ inch	3 mm.
¼ inch	6 mm.
½ inch	1¼ cm.
1 inch	2½ cm.
2 inches	5 cm.
3 inches	7½ cm.
4 inches	10 cm.
5 inches	13 cm.
6 inches	15 cm.
12 inches (1 foot)	30 cm.

MEET THE WELL FED WEEKNIGHTS TEAM

MELISSA JOULWAN
Author

Melissa Joulwan is the author of the best-selling *Well Fed* cookbook series, *Living Paleo For Dummies*, and *Rollergirl: Totally True Tales From The Track*. She also blogs at www.MelJoulwan. com where she writes about her triumphs and failures in the gym, in the kitchen, and in life.

After a lifetime of yo-yo dieting and food as the enemy, Melissa found the paleo diet in 2009 and has been happily, healthily following it ever since. That year, she also underwent a thyroidectomy. In the aftermath of the surgery and recovery, she became particularly interested in how diet affects hormones, body composition, mood, and motivation. These days, Melissa's workouts are just as likely to include yoga and meditation as lifting heavy things and trying to stay ahead of the stopwatch.

Her favorite things include the novel *Jane Eyre*, the music of Duran Duran from any era of the band, leopard print everything, and stompy black boots. In 2017, she's planning to sell all of her stuff and move to Prague with only a suitcase, her laptop, her husband Dave, and her cat Smudge.

Melissa's favorite *Well Fed Weeknights* recipes are Spicy Nigerian Beef Street Fries and Tiki Hot Dogs. But she eats Blueberry Pie Salad the most often.

DAVID HUMPHREYS
Photographer & Illustrator

David holds a Master's degree in cartooning from the Center for Cartoon Studies in White River Junction, Vermont. His photographs and illustrations have appeared in the best-selling *Well Fed* cookbooks, as well as the *New York Times* best-seller *It Starts with Food*.

David believes that the combination of images and words in comics makes them a far better tool for communicating potentially difficult subjects—including emotion—than words or images can do on their own. He feels equally strongly that that good food is one of the fundamentals of feeling awesome. He's currently working on a book that tells the story of good nutrition through powerful comics.

His favorite *Well Fed Weeknights* recipes are English Breakfast and Ground Beef & Gravy.

SMUDGE
Mascot

Smudge was foisted upon the authors in 2009 by a white witch. Small and unassuming, she seemed to be a benevolent cat, so she was allowed to stay. By 2011, she was appointed CEO of Smudge Publishing, LLC—she is better than some and worse than others (although she displays an unerring apathy to food photography and copyediting). She is best known for sneak attacks from the stairway railing, the patented "Barrel Roll of Joy," and her soft belly, widely recognized as the mushiest spot on Earth.

Her favorite *Well Fed Weeknights* recipe is Tuna Salad Platters.

CAMERON SIEWART
Content Strategy

Cameron Siewert lives a double life: the first as owner of content strategy education and consulting shop Contenterie, and the second as a writer of essays and fiction. She originally hails from a small town in the Texas Panhandle but currently splits her time between Austin (in her waking life) and a compound of adobe casitas in the Sangre de Cristo mountains (in her dream life).

Food is hands-down her most enduring love. Her best meal ever was whole grilled sea bream at the home of a local winemaker and guesthouse proprietor on the island of Hvar, Croatia.

Her favorite *Well Fed Weeknights* recipes are Vietnamese Lamb and Shakshuka (a variation of which was her favorite hangover food in a past life, i.e., her early twenties).

PEGGY PAUL CASELLA
Copy Editor

Peggy is a cookbook editor and writer, urban gardening/local food enthusiast, and the creator of ThursdayNight Pizza.com, a food blog centered on making weekly pizzas from scratch. In her editing/writing life, she wrangles hundreds—sometimes thousands—of recipes each month from chefs, writers, and publishers all over the country; she also coaches authors through the cookbook publishing process.

As a freelance writer, Peggy contributes to a variety of publications and web sites, including a regular column on seasonal produce for *GRID Magazine*, a Philadelphia publication focused on green living. She also authors a bi-weekly newsletter for Fair Food, a non-profit dedicated to promoting sustainable agriculture in the Greater Philadelphia region. When she's not working, Peggy can be found renovating her hundred-year-old rowhome, digging in the garden, or wandering outside in the sunshine.

Her favorite *Well Fed Weeknights* recipe is Reykjavik Salmon & Soft-Boiled Egg Salad.

WALKER PALECEK
Copy Editor

A word nerd, new mom, and athlete in Austin, Texas, Walker is a former gymnast who makes pull ups and handstands look as easy as walking. She's been a contributor to the Reebok CrossFit Games web site and *WOD Talk Magazine*.

Walker jumped at the chance to take out her red pen again for the latest installment of the *Well Fed* series. Nutritious, "Mel-icious" meals ready in 45 minutes or less were exactly what this she needed. A stick blender and slow cooker potatoes have revolutionized dinner at her house.

Her favorite *Well Fed Weeknights* recipe is Buffalo Chicken (or really anything from Meat & Potatoes!).

MICHEL VRANA
Designer

There's nothing Michel likes more than designing books. He published comics and graphic novels for five years, ran a boutique design studio for ten, and through all of it, always loved book design the most. In 2009, he decided to concentrate on book design, and set up a home studio to do just that.

From time to time he's invited to lecture about book design. The rest of the time you'll find him at home reading manuscripts, sketching, or creating book covers.

His favorite *Well Fed Weeknights* recipe is Burger Deluxe Potato.

SANDI GETBAMRUNGRAT
Photography Assistant

Sandi was born in Bangkok, raised in New York City. A printmaker turned cartoonist, she recently graduated from The Center for Cartoon Studies with an MFA. She loves to eat spicy food and considers herself an adventurous eater.

Growing up eating homemade Thai food, Sandi learned to cook by watching her mother and aunt in the kitchen. Red curry is her go-to dish. She can't get enough of coconut water and fruit pops. She hopes to illustrate her mom's recipes and to turn them into a graphic cookbook one day.

With their impressive ability to help people eat healthier, she strongly believes that Mel and Dave are superheroes. She's a better cater because of them.

Her favorite *Well Fed Weeknights* recipe is the Bánh Mì Bowl.

INDEX

A

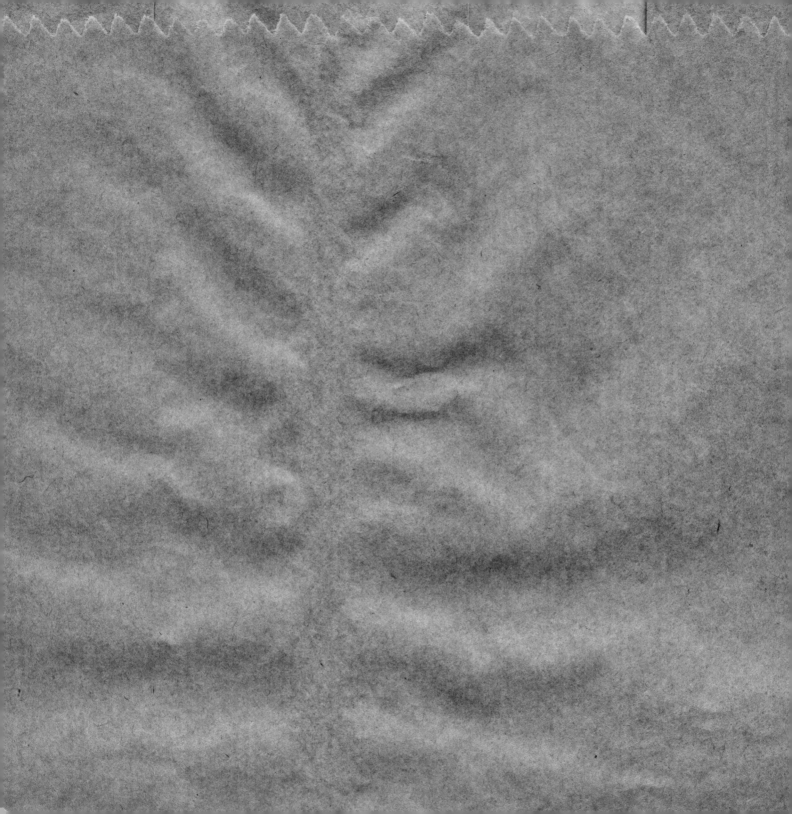